Anonymus

Transactions of the Gaelic Society of Glasgow

Volume I - 1887-91

Anonymus

Transactions of the Gaelic Society of Glasgow
Volume I - 1887-91

ISBN/EAN: 9783743310957

Manufactured in Europe, USA, Canada, Australia, Japa

Cover: Foto ©ninafisch / pixelio.de

Manufactured and distributed by brebook publishing software (www.brebook.com)

Anonymus

Transactions of the Gaelic Society of Glasgow

Comunn Gailig Ghlascho.

Transactions

of the

Gaelic Society of Glasgow.

Vol. I.—1887-91.

"Cha mhisde sgeul math aithris dà uair."

PUBLISHERS—

Archibald Sinclair, 10 Bothwell Street, Glasgow;
J. Grant, 25 George IV Bridge, Edinburgh;
H. Macdonald, Esplanade, Oban.

PREFACE.

THE objects which the Gaelic Society of Glasgow had in view in resolving to publish their transactions were, that a record of the Society's doings should be available to all the members and others who might be interested, and that such literary productions as were at their command, should be put in some permanent form of easy access. For want of similar means of preservation, much valuable matter, read before kindred societies, is continually being lost. Even those who have the privilege of hearing are only a little better off than those who have not that advantage. To listen to an essay or lecture, and the discussion which usually follows, is, without doubt, pleasing and profitable; but it has not the amount of educative influence which the same matter, committed to type, has. But it is when we take into consideration the fact that the former exercises a passing influence on only a few minds, while the latter may act on many minds over a long interval of time, that we see the full excess of value of the one over the other. No doubt many papers read before Highland societies find their way into the magazines and weekly newspapers, and, in that way, do a considerable amount of good—much more, perhaps, than would be generally credited—and, among them, some of those included in this volume can be counted. But even these, after being read once, run the risk of never being seen again, and, what is of more consequence, are not likely to come under the eyes of future generations. In the case of literature given in book form, it is different; it is always accessible.

In the present transitionary state of the Gaelic race, it is of the utmost importance that the future generations should not lose touch with their country's past. This is necessary for the preservation of those best characteristics which have so frequently won admiration from aliens, and which have sustained them as a people through trying social, political and religious difficulties.

In one of the essays embodied in the following pages it is said "We are living in the midst of a Celtic *renaissance*." All who have been following the course of events during the last fifteen years will homologate that statement. Much of this Celtic *renaissance*, as far as the Highlands is concerned, is due to the writings of Highlanders in the South, mostly connected with some society or other. This should be an incentive to all who have the love of the Gaelic race and their land in their hearts to further stimulate the movement by becoming members of Gaelic societies, and contributing to, or helping the circulation of, literature bearing upon Highland life and history and the Gaelic language.

It is an honourable characteristic of the Highlander that he is fond of education; and it is well known that the poor of the Highlands are more ready to make sacrifices in its acquisition than the poor among their wealthier neighbours. But the fact remains that the Highlanders, as a people, are comparatively poor, and, on that account, less able than their neighbours to acquire education and, at the same time, patronise and support their own literature. It is, therefore, all the more incumbent on those who can afford it to make up for their brethren's drawbacks.

The subjects treated of in the following pages cover a wide field embracing History, Manners and Customs, Philology, Folklore, Booklore and general Literature; and, while the ordinary reader cannot fail to be entertained and instructed, the studious may find useful information to aid them in their studies.

Some valuable papers which were not available to the Society for publication in this volume have already appeared, or are to appear, elsewhere.

Outside of its purely literary usefulness the Society has exercised a beneficial influence on matters of importance to the Highland people; and it has the satisfaction of being able to state that the census of the Gaelic speaking population of Scotland, the returns for which will soon be issued, is due to its initiative. A resolution moved on April 29th, 1890, calling upon Parliament to make provision for the enumeration of those who speak Gaelic only and those who speak Gaelic and English, caused the matter to be taken up in the House of Commons, and included in the Census Schedules for 1891. The result is that there will henceforth be *reliable* data for estimating the extent and the growth or decay of the Gaelic Language in Scotland.

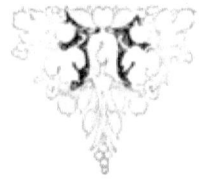

CONSTITUTION AND RULES.

I.—The Society shall be called "THE GAELIC SOCIETY OF GLASGOW."

II.—The objects of the Society shall be:—The cultivation of the Gaelic Language; the cultivation and development of Celtic Philology, Literature, and Music; the elucidation of Celtic antiquities; and the fostering of a Celtic spirit among the Highlanders of Glasgow.

III.—The Society shall be composed of persons of Celtic extraction, or of such as take an interest in its objects. All applicants for admission to membership shall be proposed and seconded at an ordinary meeting, and on payment of their subscription, their names shall be entered on the Membership Roll.

IV.—The Subscriptions of Members to the Funds of the Society shall be:—Life Members, one payment of £2 2s.; Honorary Members, annually, Ladies 3s., Gentlemen 7s. 6d.; Ordinary Members, annually, 3s.

V.—The Business of the Society shall be conducted by a Board of Management, consisting of the President, Vice-Presidents, Secretary, Treasurer, and Directors: five to form a quorum. The members of the Board shall retire annually, but shall be eligible for re-election at the Annual Business Meeting of the Society.

VI.—The Society shall meet in the Religious Institution Rooms, Buchanan Street, or other convenient place, on the last Tuesday of each Month, from October to April: seven to be a Quorum.

VII.—The Annual Business Meeting of the Society shall be held on the last Tuesday of April. No part of the Constitution shall be altered or amended except at this meeting, and then only on the resolution of at least two-thirds of the Members present. But notice of any such alteration or amendment must be in the hands of the Secretary within at least one Month of said Meeting.

OFFICE-BEARERS FOR SESSION, 1887-88.

Patrons.

Prof. J. S. Blackie.
Rev. R. Blair, M.A.
Rev. A. Cameron, LL.D.

W. Jolly, Esq., F.R.S.E.
Sheriff Nicolson, LL.D.
Rev. William Ross.

Hon. President.
Professor D. MACKINNON, M.A.

President.
ALEXANDER MACNEILL, Esq.

Vice-Presidents.
Mr. MAGNUS MACLEAN, M.A.
Mr. HUGH MACLEOD.
Mr. HENRY WHYTE, (*Fionn*).

Treasurer.
Mr. ARCHIBALD MACLEAN, Industrial School, Paisley.

Secretary.
Mr. ALEXANDER MACDONALD, M.A.,
14 Gt. George Street, Hillhead.

Directors.

Mr. John Campbell.
    Thomas Gunn.
    R. C. Macdiarmid.
    John Macfadyen.
    Dugald Macfarlane.
    M. Macfarlane.

Mr. A. W. Macleod.
 ,, Neil Macleod.
Dr. H. Murray.
Mr. Archibald Sinclair.
 ,, Hugh Stewart.
 ,, Duncan Whyte.

OFFICE-BEARERS FOR SESSION, 1888-89.

Patrons.

Prof. J. S. Blackie.
Rev. R. Blair M.A.
J. Boyd, Esq., H.M.I.S.
Rev. A. Cameron, LL.D.
Rev. W. Fraser M.A.
W. Jolly, Esq., F.R.S.E.
J. Mackay, Esq., C.E.
Sheriff Nicolson.

Hon. President.
Professor D. MACKINNON, M.A.

President.
ALEXANDER MACNEILL, Esq.

Vice-Presidents.
Mr. R. C. MACDIARMID.
Mr. ALEXANDER MACDONALD, M.A.
Mr. HENRY WHYTE.
Mr. DUNCAN WHYTE.

Treasurer.
Mr. DUNCAN THOMSON, Banker, Partick.

Secretary.
Mr. MAGNUS MACLEAN, M.A., 21 Hayburn Crescent, Partick.

Directors.

Mr. John Campbell.
Dr. A. Clerk.
Mr. Thomas Gunn.
,, M. Macfarlane.
,, John Mackay.
,, D. Maclachlan, B.L.
,, Archd. Maclean.
Mr. A. W. Macleod.
,, Hugh Macleod.
,, Donald Macphie.
Dr. H. Murray.
Mr. Archibald Sinclair.
,, Hugh Stewart.

OFFICE-BEARERS FOR SESSION, 1889-90.

Patrons.

Prof. J. S. Blackie.
Rev. R. Blair, M.A.
J. Boyd, Esq., H.M.I.S.
Rev. W. Fraser, M.A.
W. Jolly, Esq., F.R.S.E.

J. Mackay, Esq., C.E.
Rev. J. Maclean, D.D.
Sheriff Nicolson, LL.D.
D. Ross, Esq., LL.D.
Rev. William Ross.

Hon. President.
Professor D. MACKINNON, M.A.

President.
ALEXANDER MACNEILL, Esq.

Vice-Presidents.
Dr. A. CLERK. Dr. R. C. MACDIARMID.
Mr. ALEX. MACDONALD, M.A., F.E.I.S.
Mr. DUNCAN WHYTE.
Mr. HENRY WHYTE, (*Fionn*).

Treasurer.
Mr. DUNCAN THOMSON, Writer and Banker, Partick.

Secretary.
Mr. MAGNUS MACLEAN, M.A., F.R.S.E., 21 Hayburn Crescent, Partick.

Directors.

Mr. Thomas Gunn.
  „ Hugh MacColl.
  „ M. Macfarlane.
  „ J. Mackay, (Kingston)
  „ James Mackellar.
  „ Archd. Maclean.
  „ A. W. Macleod.

Mr. Hugh Macleod.
  „ Don. Macphie, F.E.I.S.
Dr. Hugh Murray.
Mr. Colin Macritchie.
  „ Archibald Sinclair.
  „ Duncan Sharp.
  „ Hugh Stewart.

OFFICE-BEARERS FOR SESSION, 1890-91.

Patrons.

Prof. J. S. Blackie.
Rev. R. Blair., M.A.
J. Boyd, Esq., H.M I.S.
W. Jolly, Esq., F.R.S.E.
J. Mackay, Esq., C.E.

Prof. Mackinnon, M.A.
Rev. J. Maclean, D.D.
Sheriff Nicolson, LL.D.
D. Ross, Esq., LL.D.
Rev. William Ross.

Hon. President.

Rev. A. STEWART, LL.D., (Nether Lochaber).

President.

Mr. HENRY WHYTE, (Fionn).

Vice-Presidents.

Dr. A. CLERK.   Mr. HUGH MACCOLL.
Dr. R. C. MACDIARMID.
Mr. ALEX. MACDONALD, M.A., F.E I.S.
Mr. DUNCAN WHYTE.

Treasurer.

Mr. DUGALD MACLACHLAN, B.L.
33 Renfield Street.

Secretary.

Mr. MAGNUS MACLEAN, M.A., F.R.S E.,
21 Hayburn Crescent, Partick.

Directors.

Dr. Iain Clerk.
Mr. Thomas Gunn.
,, M. MacFarlane.
,, J. Mackay (Kingston)
,, James Mackellar.
,, A. W. Macleod.
,, Hugh Macleod.

Mr. Alex. Macneill.
,, Don. Macphie, F.E.I.S.
Dr. Hugh Murray.
Mr. Colin Macritchie.
,, Duncan Reid.
,, Archibald Sinclair.
,, Duncan Sharp.

Mr. Hugh Stewart.

OFFICE-BEARERS FOR SESSION, 1891-92.

Patrons.

Prof. J. S. Blackie.	Prof. Mackinnon, M.A.
Rev. R. Blair, M.A.	Rev. J. Maclean, D.D.
J. Boyd, Esq., H.M.I.S.	Sheriff Nicolson, LL.D.
W. Jolly, Esq., F.R.S.E.	D. Ross, Esq., LL.D.
J. Mackay, Esq., C.E.	Rev. William Ross.

Hon. President.
Rev. A. STEWART, LL.D., (*Nether Lochaber*)

President.
Mr. HENRY WHYTE, (*Fionn*).

Vice-Presidents.
Dr. A. CLERK.   Dr. R. C. MACDIARMID.
Mr. ALEX. MACDONALD, M.A., F.E.I.S.
Rev. EWEN A. RANKIN, B.D.
Mr. DUNCAN WHYTE.

Treasurer.
Mr. JOHN MACKAY, 17 Dundas Street, Kingston.

Secretaries.
Mr. MALCOLM MACFARLANE,
12 High Street, Paisley.
Mr. MAGNUS MACLEAN, M.A., F.R.S.E.
21 Hayburn Crescent, Partick.

Directors.

Mr. Hugh Cameron.	Mr. Alex. Macneill.
Dr. Iain Clerk.	,, Don. Macphie, F.E.I.S
Mr. Hugh Maccoll.	,, Colin Macritchie.
,, James Mackellar.	,, Donald Nicolson.
,, A. R. Mackenzie.	,, Duncan Reid.
,, A. W. Macleod.	,, Archibald Sinclair.
,, Hugh Macleod.	,, Duncan Sharp.

Mr. HUGH STEWART.

CONTENTS.

Introduction.	1
Inaugural Meeting.	3
Gilleasbuig Aotrom, by Mr. Neil Macleod,	8
Donald Macleod, the Skye Bard—his life and songs, by Mr. R. C. Macdiarmid, M.B., C.M.,	18
Uist old Hymns, by Mr. Alexander Carmichael, Corr. M.S.A., Scot.,	34
Sketches of Kintyre, by Mr. Duncan Reid.	47
Oidhche air Chèilidh, by Rev R. Blair, M.A.,	70
The Science of Thought, exemplified in the Gaelic Language, by Mr. Dugald MacFarlane, B.A.,	88
The Feeling for Nature in Gaelic Poetry, by Mr. W. Jolly, F.R.S.E., H.M.I.S.,	108
Historical Notes on Education in the Highlands, by Mr. J. Boyd, H.M.I.S.,	120
Some Ancient Celtic Customs, by Mr. Henry Whyte, (*Fionn*),	127
Notes on Ancient Gaelic Medicine, by Dr. A. Clerk,	156
Life in the Highlands a hundred years ago, by Mr. J. G. Mackay,	171
Some Rare Gaelic Books, by Rev Dr. Masson,	193
Celticism—its influence on English Literature, by Mr. Alex. MacDonald, M.A., F.E.I.S.,	218
The Relation of Celt and Norseman in Saga Times, by Mr. D. Ross, LL.D.,	239
The Celtic Muse in Lowland Garb, by Mr. John Mackay,	247
Ancient Celtic Laws, by Mr. Hugh Macleod,	275

THE GAELIC SOCIETY OF GLASGOW.

INTRODUCTION.

THERE being a felt want among the Highlanders of Glasgow of some wide, energetic, and representative medium to promote the much-neglected claims and interests of Celtic Literature, several gentlemen deeply interested in matters pertaining to the Celt, held some preliminary meetings with a view to found a society. The result of these meetings having proved highly favourable to the project, ultimately on the 26th October, 1887, at a meeting held in the Religious Institution Rooms, 177 Buchanan Street, the Society was formally instituted—and designated "THE GAELIC SOCIETY OF GLASGOW."

The meeting for that date was called by circular which referred as follows to the need for such a Society in Glasgow:—

"1. Glasgow is a recognized centre of culture and "scholarship and contains more Gaelic-speaking people "and educated Highlanders than perhaps any other "town, or even county in the kingdom. From its

"commercial relation with the North and West of
"Scotland it has become essentially the 'Capital of
"the Highlands.'
"2. The Gaelic language at present receives more
"attention and respectful recognition than probably
"it ever got before; and the Celts of Glasgow should
"not be behind their brethren elsewhere in showing
"their patriotism and attachment to their mother
"tongue.
"3. Highland customs, folklore, and traditions of
"great and acknowledged literary value will be for
"ever lost or forgotten unless Highlanders everywhere
"take concerted action for their preservation. The
"expected representative character of the Society
"should afford unusual facilities for the focusing of
"light on many interesting but obscure points in
"connection with these subjects.
"4. It is felt that the best remedy for the orthograph-
"ical discrepancies to be met with in Gaelic books,
"and for the paucity of current Gaelic literature, is
"the creation and stimulation among Highlanders of
"real interest in Gaelic.
"5. The young people who every year come in large
"numbers from the Highlands to Glasgow ought, if
"possible, to have an opportunity of at least learning
"to read and write Gaelic at evening classes, which
"instruction the proposed Society might undertake to
"superintend."

INAUGURAL MEETING.

[29TH NOVEMBER, 1887.]

We take the following report of the Inaugural Meeting from the *Oban Times* :—

Last Tuesday the Inaugural Meeting of the Gaelic Society of Glasgow, was held in the Religious Institution Rooms, Glasgow. There was a large and representative attendance. Mr. Alexander Macneill, President, occupied the chair, and among those present were :—Rev. W. Fraser, M.A., Argyle Free Church ; Mr. W. Jolly, H.M. Inspector of Schools ; Messrs. Magnus Maclean, M.A. ; Alexander Macdonald, M.A., Secretary ; H. Macleod, Writer ; A. W. Macleod ; M. MacFarlane, Paisley ; A. Maclean, Paisley ; Archd. Sinclair, Printer ; H. Whyte (*Fionn*); T. Gunn, C. Macritchie, Duncan Reid, H. Stewart, John Macfadyen, R. C. Macdiarmid, and others.

The Minutes of the previous Meetings having been read and adopted, the President, who was well received, said :—

GENTLEMEN,—From the minutes of former meetings which have been read in your hearing, you are aware of the various steps which have been taken to found " The Gaelic Society of Glasgow," under whose banner we are met this evening These initiatory meetings have been smaller than one could have wished, but they were thoroughly representative, and it is not for us to despise the day of small things, for as the tiny acorn becomes the deep-rooted, wide-spreading, stalwart oak, so we trust this Gaelic Society may yet become one of great power and usefulness, that its influence may be felt among the widely-scattered children of the Gael, and that the Society itself may be *Cruaidh mar am fraoch buan mar an darach*—hard as the heather, lasting as the oak. And now allow me to thank you for the honour you have conferred upon me in making me the first President of this Society. I assure you, gentlemen, that I appreciate the honour you have done me, and feel the responsibility of the office to which you have appointed me, and my utmost desire shall be to discharge the duties that devolve upon me in such a manner as shall best further the aims of the Society, and conduce to its future usefulness. The gentlemen you have selected as office-bearers are such as anyone might feel proud to be associated with, for they are enthusiastic representative Celts, while many of them have distinguished themselves as scholars, and enriched the literature of our country. I feel a peculiar pleasure in having my friend and school-fellow, Professor Mackinnon of the Celtic Chair, as Honorary President. Now, it may be pertinently asked if there is room for such a Society as this in Glasgow, seeing we have already in our city so many Highland district associations, all of them doing excellent work, and giving ample evidence of the necessity of their existence. While this is so, and while I would be the last to undervalue the importance of these associations or belittle the work that they perform, yet I am inclined to think that such a society as we are inaugurating will find ample ground for action, and will not in any way interfere with the labours, or encroach on the domains of any of these existing associations. The membership of these district associations is confined by geographical boundaries or circumscribed by insular limits, whereas the Gaelic Society knows no provincial limitations, but is decidedly cosmopolitan, throwing open its portals as you are aware, with true Highland hospitality to every member of the ever-extending Celtic race at home and abroad. Glasgow is the recognized centre of Celtic enthusiasm and probably contains more Gaelic-speaking Highlanders than any city or county in the kingdom, while a glance at the number of "Macs" in the Glasgow Directory will amply prove the vast number of people of Celtic extraction that are to be found in the City, and to these also our Society is open. Indeed, it appears to me that such a society supplies a felt want, and fills a blank hitherto unoccupied by any of our numerous associations. With such an extensive constituency to appeal to, I cannot see why the Gaelic Society of Glasgow should not enlist a large and representative membership and become a thorough success. But gentlemen, however large the constituency may be, it stands to reason, that unless the objects and aims of our Society are such as commend themselves to the intelligence of this constituency its membership may be limited and unrepresentative. A perusal of the constitution of the Gaelic Society will at once make it evident that its aims and objects are such as should enlist the hearty approval and enthusiastic support of every person who claims to have a single drop of Celtic blood in his veins, or who is in sympathy with the race to which the majority of us are proud to belong. The objects are the cultivation of the Gaelic Language; the cultivation and developement of Celtic Philology, Literature and Music; the elucidation of Celtic Antiquities; and the fostering of a Celtic spirit among the Highlanders of Glasgow.

Now, gentlemen, these objects are so excellent in themselves and so perspicuously stated that I shall not detain you with any comments upon them, further than to add that—strange as it may appear, yet nevertheless true—we have a better field for the accomplishment of these objects in Glasgow, than we would have in any particular part of the Highlands. We have in this city Highlanders from all parts of the Highlands and so we can the more readily examine into any of these peculiarities of dialects which are so interesting, or arrive at the exact meaning of those provincialisms which crop up, and which are often so perplexing to the Celtic student. There is another thing in connection with this Society which affords me great pleasure. It is unsectarian and non-political. Within its precincts the drum ecclesiastic shall not be beaten, nor shall the political flag be unfurled, but the oft-divided Gael shall meet on a common platform, to discuss the genius of his language, to develop its literature and its music, to examine those relics of Celtic Art which prove the inventive genius of the race—in other words to carry out in the best and most comprehensive spirit, the tw well known Ossianic precepts —'*Cuimhnich air na daoine o'n d' thainig thu.*' (Remember the race from which you have sprung) and '*Lean gu dlùth ri cliù do shinnsre.*' (Follow closely the fame of thy forefathers.)

Mr. JOLLY said that he was pleased indeed to see such a large and enthusiastic meeting. He had a great love for the Highland people, and he welcomed such a society as representative of that noble race, and he hoped it would have a prosperous career. There was great need for such a society. He was often pained at the amount of ignorance that prevailed in the Lowlands regarding the present condition and aims of the Highland people, and it would be one duty of this Society to place before their Lowland friends the true history, literature and art of the Celt, as well as explain the present aspirations of the people. The question was frequently asked—Was there a Celtic Literature? He unhesitatingly replied that there was—one of great power and beauty and of great historical importance. Then there was Celtic Art, which had flourished apart with a power and a height of development which was quite astonishing, as proved by Dr. Anderson, of Edinburgh. Such men as Mr. A. Carmichael, had done much to collect folk-lore and art specimens, and he trusted that much of the rich treasures which Mr. Carmichael had collected might be published. He wished the Gaelic Society every success.

[22nd December, 1887.]

At the Meeting of the Society held on this date, Dr. H. Cameron Gillies, London, read a Paper on "Gaelic Grammar."

[31st January, 1888.]

At the Meeting of the Society held on this date, Professor Mackinnon, Edinburgh, the Hon. President of the Society, read a Paper entitled "Jerome Stone, the post-Ossianic Collector." The paper has since been printed in the Transactions of the Gaelic Society of Inverness. Mr. Magnus Maclean, M.A., also read a Paper on "Gaelic in Highland Schools."

[28th February, 1888.]

At the Meeting of the Society held on this date, Mr. Neil MacLeod, Edinburgh, author of '*Clarsach an Doire*,' read a Paper on '*Gilleasbuig Aotrom*.' Mr. Henry Whyte, Vice-President, also read a Paper entitled '*An Gaidheal anns a' bhaile-mhór*.'

Mr. MacLeod's Paper was as follows:—

GILLEASBUIG AOTROM.

Bho chionn trì-fichead no ceithir-fichead bliadhn' air ais, mu 'n robh Taighean bhochd air an togail feadh na Gàidhealtachd, cha robh ceàrn no baile de 'n dùthaich anns nach robh neach éiginn a chòmhnuidh a bha dol fodh 'n ainm "amadan." Bha na h-amadain sin de chaochladh gnè. Cuid dhiubh faoin, neo-chiontach, gun chcilg, mar an leanabh beag. Cuid eile dhiubh borb, seòlta, garg, agus crosta; agus mar a thachair do gach ceàrn eile de 'n dùthaich, bha 'chuid fhéin aig Eilean-a'-cheò dhiubh. Ach am measg amadain an Eilein air fad, dleasaidh "Gilleasbuig Aotrom" an t-ionad is àirde. Bheireadh amadain eile an Eilein an t-àite sin dha, agus theireadh Gilleasbuig fhéin gu 'n robh làn chòir aig air.

Bha déigh mhòr aig Gilleasbuig air a bhi 'n cuideachd nan uailsean, agus déigh mhòr aig na h-uailsean air a bhi 'n comunn Ghilleasbuig. Cha robh cuirm no fleadh, féill no banais, a b' fhiach ainmeachadh, a thachradh eadar dà cheann an Eilein, nach feumadh Gilleasbuig a bhi 'n sin.

Air feasgar latha féille ann am Port-rìgh, bha dinneir mhór aig uailsean an eilein ann an àrd thaigh-òsda 'bhaile. Bha 'n latha fuar, fliuch, agus bha mòran de dhaoine bochd mu 'n dorus nach faigheadh a stigh, ach 'n uair a thàinig Gilleasbuig rinn e rathad dha fhéin, gus an d' ràinig e an seòmar anns an robh na h-uailsean cruinn. Chuir iad uile fàilte chridheil, chàirdeil air Gilleasbuig. "Co ás a thàinig thu mar so, 'Illeasbuig?" arsa Fear a' Choire. "Ma ta, le bhur cead, a dhaoine uailse," arsa Gilleasbuig, "thàinig mi à Ifrinn." "Ubh ubh, 'Illeasbuig," arsa Fear a' Choire, "'s làidir a' chainnt sin. Agus dé mar a tha gnothaichean a' dol air an aghaidh 's an ionad sin?" "Tha" arsa Gilleasbuig, "Fhir a' Choire, gle choltach ris mar a tha gnothaichean a dol air an aghaidh ann an so féin—na daoine saibhir 'g an gabhail a steach, 's na daoine bochda 'g an cumail am muigh."

Thachair Fear a' Choire agus Gilleasbuig ri 'chéile air la àraidh—Gilleasbuig agus cnaimh mór feòla aige 'g a chriomadh, agus e 'n deigh a dheanamh gu math lom. "Cha chreid mi nach 'eil thu sgith de 'n chnaimh sin a nis 'Illeasbuig," arsa Fear a' Choire, "bu chòir dhuit a thoirt do'n chiad chù a thachras riut." "So dhuit e ma ta," arsa Gilleasbuig, "tha mi 'creidsinn nach tachair cù cho mòr riut fhéin rium car latha no dhà."

Mu'n àm 's an robh Gilleasbuig a làthair thainig ministir eadar a bhi Gallda 'us Gàidhealach, ris an abradh iad "Maighstir Sutar," do Sgìr Dhiùranais. 'S e làn sgoilear a bha'n Sutar, foghlumaichte ann an iomadh canain, ach aig nach robh ach fior dhroch Ghàidhlig. Agus na bu mhiosa na sin, tha e coltach gu'n robh Sutar tuilleadh a's déidheil air a bhi 'n comunn Mac-na-braiche; agus ged a bha Gilleasbuig mar a bhà e, bha e faicinn nach robh caithe-beatha Shutair a' co-fhreagradh ris an dreuchd chudthromach a ghabh e os laimh. Ach ciod air bith aobhar bho'n do thachair e, fhuair Gilleasbuig làn cheannas air Sutar. Bha eagal anma aig Sutar roimh Ghilleasbuig. Cha robh ni dh' iarradh e air Sutar nach faigheadh e. Ach feumaidh sinn aideachadh nach robh Gilleasbuig còir ach anabharrach mi-thaingeil ri aghaidh gach caoimhneis agus deadh-ghean a bha Sutar a' nochdadh dha. Chàineadh e Sutar gu 'bhrògan, agus 'n uair a bhiodh e sgith dhe air gach dòigh eile dh' éireadh e air le bàrdachd. Ann an aon de na rannan sin tha Gilleasbuig a' toirt dhuinn cùnntas air ùrnuigh Shutair :—

    "'N uair a theid thu do'n chùbaid
    Ni thu ùrnuigh 'bhios gleusda,

Bidh cuid dhi 'na Gàidhlig,
'Us pàirt dhi 'na Beurla ;
Bidh cuid dhi 'na h-Eabhra,
'Na Fraingeis, 's 'na Greugais,
'S a' chuid nach tuig cach dhi
Bheir e gair air Fear Gheusdo."

Eadar dà uair-dheug agus uair 's a' mhaduinn, air oidhche ghruamach gheamhraidh, agus Sutar gu socair blàth 'na leabaidh, chual' e bualadh trom, làidir aig an dorus. Dh' éirich Sutar, chuir e 'cheann a mach air uinneig an t-seòmair, agus dh' éibh e, "Cò 'bha 'n sud?" Fhreagair Gilleasbuig gu'n robh esan. "Thus," arsa Sutar, "ciod e 'tha dhìth ort mu'n àm so dh' oidhche?" "Ciod e," arsa Gilleasbuig, "a bhiodh a dhìth air neach 's am bith mu'n tràth so dh' oidhche, ach suipeir mhath, agus leabaidh mhath 'na déigh."

Bha fios aig Sutar nach robh math cur an aghaidh 'Illeasbuig, agus ged 'bu leisg b' feudar dha éiridh agus Gilleasbuig a leigeadh a stigh." "An nis," arsa Sutar, (an deigh do Ghilleasbuig a shuipeir a ghabhail,) "theid thu mach agus caidlidh tu gu maduinn air lobhta an stàbuill. Tha leabaidh bhlàth ghlan ann, agus bidh tu gle cheart gu latha." "Ma ta," arsa Gilleasbuig, "cha'n fhaca mise riamh 'n uair a thigeadh caraid a dh' amharc air duin'-uasal, nach rachadh e agus nach sealladh e a sheòmar-leaba dha, agus mar sin thig thus' a mach agus seall dhomhsa an t-àite 's am bheil mi gu laidhe." Cha robh aig Sutar còir ach falbh a mach le Gilleasbuig. Thachair gu'n robh dorus an stàbuill glaisde, ach fhuair na fearaibh fàradh faisg air laimh, agus chaidh sud a shocrachadh ris an uinneig. "Suas,"

arsa Gilleasbuig ri Sutar, "bidh mis' as do dheigh."
Ach 'n uair a fhuair Gilleasbuig Sutar as an t-sealladh
a stigh air an uinneig, thog e am fàradh air a ghualainn agus dh' fhalbh e, agus e aig an àm cheudna ag
ràdh, "'Nis a Shutair, ma tha 'n leabaidh cho math 's a
tha thu a gabhail ort, gabh fhéin do leoir dhi gu latha.
Oidhche mhath leat. Theid mise stigh agus gabhaidh
mi an leabaidh 'tha blàth." Cha robh aig Sutar bochd
ach toiseachadh air éibheach gus an d' thug e mach
daoine a leig a bruid e.

An ath Dhi-dòmhnaich chaidh Gilleasbuig do'n eaglais
a dh' eisdeachd Shutair, agus ma chaidh cha b' ann gu
sìth. Shuidh e shuas an staidhir ri bile na lobhta far
am biodh sàr chothrom aig' air a' chothional fhaicinn
bho bhalla gu balla. Thàinig Sutar, agus thoisich seirbheis an latha mar a b' àbhaist. 'N uair a thug
Gilleasbuig sùil sios air feadh a' chothionail, co gu mishealbhach a thachair a bhi 'n a shuidhe dìreach fodha
ach bodach mòr, cam, crosta, a bha 'n a fhior nàmhaid
do Ghilleasbuig, agus Gilleasbuig 'n a fhior nàmhaid
dhà. 'N uair a chunnaic Gilleasbuig am bodach,
chrath e 'cheann agus rinn e gàire ris féin. 'N uair
a dh' éirich an cothional 'nan seasamh aig a chiad
ùrnuigh, chuir Gilleasbuig a làmh 'na phòca agus thug
e mach ugh mòr tunnaig, agus thòisich e ri bile na
lobhta air cuimse a dheanamh air ceann a' bhodaich.
Mu dheireadh leig Gilleasbuig as an t-ugh, agus bhris
e 'na smùr air sgall a' bhodaich. Ma bhris, "chaidh
an ceòl air feadh na fìdhle," chaidh am bodach gu ùpraid,
's chaidh an cothional gu gàireachdaich. Chunnaic
Sutar nach robh feum an cumail na b' fhaide an latha

sin, agus leig e mu sgaoil iad le coire 'Illeasbuig chòir.
Beagan ùine an deigh sin thachair Sutar agus Gilleasbuig ri chéile ann an coille an Dùin—àite fàsail aonaranach—agus smaointich Gilleasbuig ann féin gu'n robh an cothrom gu math air ni-éigin a chur a Sutar. Thàinig Gilleasbuig air aghaidh agus chuir e an fhailte chridheil chàirdeil sin air Sutar. Ach an deigh dhoibh beagan còmhraidh a bhi aca ri 'cheile—"Feumaidh tu," arsa Gilleasbuig, "airgiod a thoirt dhomh a gheibh bròganan, tha mi gun stiall bhròg agam." "Ma tha," arsa Sutar, "cha toir mise bròg no aodach dhuit. Cha 'n 'eil annad ach droch dhuine." "Am fear mor g'an tog mis," arsa Gilleasbuig, "ma theid do bheò na do mharbh as a' bhad so gus an toir thu dhòmhsa rud a gheibh brògan." Ghabh Sutar bochd an t-eagal, thug e 'mach a leabhar-pòca agus thug e litir do Ghilleasbuig thun a' ghreusaiche air son bhròg. "Ciod e tha 'n so," arsa Gilleasbuig. "Tha," arsa Sutar, "litir a gheibh brògan dhuit." "Cò 'ghabhadh do litir-sa?" arsa Gilleasbuig, "thoir dhòmhs' an t-airgiod agus cuir do litir far nach abair mi." Cha robh ann do Shutar ach an t-aon ni, agus thug e'n t-airgiod do Ghilleasbuig; agus 'n uair a fhuair Gilleasbuig an litir anns an dara laimh, agus an t-airgiod anns an laimh eile—"Seall tu sud a nis," arsa Gilleasbuig, gheibh an litir na brògan agus bidh an t-airgiod agam fhin." Air maduinn àraidh ann am Port-righ, ghabh Gilleasbuig cuairt thun a' chladaich. Chunnaic e bàta ann a' sin a bha air tilleadh bho iasgach. Bha sgioba 'bhàta shuas am baile a' gabhail drama; agus cha 'n fhaca Gilleasbuig còir gniomh a b' iomchuidhe na trosg cho math 's a

chunnaic e 's a' bhàta 'ghoid. Ghabh e suas gu tigh duin' uasail a bh' ann 's a' bhaile leis an trosg. Bhuail Gilleasbuig an clag, agus cò thachair a fhreagairt ach an duin'-uasal fhéin. "An ceannaich sibh trosg math?" arsa Gilleasbuig. "Ceannaichidh," arsa an duine. "agus taing air son fhaotainn. Ciod a' phrìs a tha thu ag iarraidh air?" "Tha," arsa Gilleasbuig, "tasdan. agus gloine uisge-bheatha." "Gheibh thu sin ma ta," arsa 'n duine. 'N uair a fhuair Gilleasbuig pàidheadh an truisg, thubhairt e "'Nis, bho nach 'eil a bheag agam féin r' a dheanamh, theid mi thun an uillt agus glanaidh mi dhuibh e." "Ro math," ars an duine. Ach 's ann a dh' fhalbh Gilleasbuig leis an trosg agus reic e ann an seachd taighean eile e aig a' phrìs cheudna, ach cha d' fhàg e'n trosg aig a h-aon aca; chaidh e air ais leis thun a' bhàta as an do ghoid e e. 'N uair a ràinig e'n cladach bha sgioba 'bhata ag obair air glanadh an éisg. Thilg Gilleasbuig an trosg sios 'n am measg, aig an àm cheudna ag ràdh, "sud agaibh, a ghillean còir, bhur trosg, agus ma phàidheas e sibhse cho math 's a phàidh e mise, 's math am beathach e." Bha e 'na chleachdadh aig Gilleasbuig sgriob a thoirt gu tìr-mór 'n uair a bhuaileadh e 'na cheann. Thachair dha bhi air latha Sàbaid àraidh ann an Gleann-seille, agus co dhiubh 's e spiorad math no droch spiorad a chuir 'na cheann dol do 'n eaglais chaidh e innte. Ghabh e suas feadh na h-eaglais gus an d' ràinig e staidhir na cùbaid. Shuidh e aig bonn na staidhir gu socair stolda 's a bhata fodh uchd. Shaoil leis a' mhinistir chòir gur ann bodhar a bha Gilleasbuig, agus 's ann a ghabh e bàigh mhór ris a' choigreach a shuidh gu dìblidh cho faisg air an éisdeachd. Bha gnothaichean a' dol air aghaidh gu réidh riaghailteach car greiseig, gus an d' thàinig coig no sea de chìobairean le 'n cuid chon a stigh. 'N uair a thachair na coin ri 'chéile thoisich iad air dranndan, agus bha na h-uile coltas air gu'n robh an aimhreit gu bhi air a bonn. Cha d' eisd Gilleasbuig an corr; ghabh e sios 'n am measg le 'bhata, ach an àite sìth a chur orra, 's ann a chuir e h-uile cù 's an eaglais 'an claigiun a chéile. Cha robh am ministir fada caochladh a bheachd air Gilleasbuig. "B' fheàrr leam," arsa am ministir ris an luchd-dreuchd aige, "gu'n cuireadh sibh an duine truagh ud a mach as an eaglais." "Cha ruig iad a leas an dragh a chur orra fhéin," arsa Gilleasbuig. "Tha mise fada gu leòr an so, agus ma 's e ceòl feadaireachd tha 'n pailteas an sud dhe do shearmon—moran 'ga ràdh 's beagan 'g a dheanamh; latha math leat fhir mo chridhe." Ghabh Gilleasbuig a mach, agus chunnaic e each bàn an ceangal ri cairt aig ceann na h-eaglais. Cha 'n fhaca Gilleasbuig gniomh a b' iomchuidhe na 'n ròp a bha 'n crochadh ri clag na h-eaglais a cheangal ri earball an eich bhàin. Chaidh e 'n sin 'na shìneadh ann an raoin arbhair a tha shios fodh 'n eaglais gus am faiceadh e ciod a thachradh. Cha do chuir an t-each bàn car dheth fhad 's a bha e 'faotainn criomadh faisg air, ach 'n uair a theann e ceum no dhà mach, bhuail an clag buille, 's thug an t-each bàn leum as; agus 'n uair a thuig e gur ann ris fhéin a bha 'n gnothach an ceangal, chaidh e gu ùpraid, agus ma chaidh thoisich an clag. Cha robh buille a bhuaileadh e nach toireadh crith air an eaglais. Mu dheireadh thoisich an

cothional air tighinn a mach, agus a h-uile neach a
thigeadh a mach bha e fuireach a muigh, gus mu
dheireadh an robh iad a muigh air fad agus am
ministir air an ceann. Bha Gilleasbuig ag amharc
orra le subhachas, agus e làn riaraichte leis a cho-
dhùnadh gus an d' thug e seirbheis an latha. Bhiodh
Gilleasbuig air a chòmhdach ann an trusgan math mar
'bu tric—ad àrd, deise dhubh, agus léine gheal. Bha
nailsean an eilein 'ga chumail daonnan ann an aodach
math. Bha e mar sin ullamh air daoine do nach
b' aithn' e a mhealladh, agus a thoirt orra chreidsinn
gu 'n robh e rud nach robh e idir. Thàinig e air lath'
àraidh gu tigh ann an oisinn iomalaich de'n dùthaich;
bhuail e aig an dorus, agus dh'éibh e "Cò tha stigh?"
"Cha 'n 'eil moran a stigh," arsa bean an taighe,
"thigibh air bhur 'n aghaidh." "Am bheil duine stigh
ach thu fhéin?" arsa Gilleasbuig. "Tha," ars' ise, "tha
Iain, fear an taighe stigh, ach tha e air an leabaidh."
"Ciod e tha cur air?" arsa Gilleasbuig. "Ma ta," ars'
ise, "cha 'n 'eil mi fhìn robh chinnteach, ach tha e air
a' leabaidh bho chionn choig bliadhna." "Tha e
tuilleadh a's fad' air a' leabaidh," arsa Gilleasbuig, "ach
's e lighiche a tha annam-sa agus cha 'n 'eil fios nach
dean mi feum dhà." "Nach mise tha taingeil," arsa
'bhean bhochd, "bhur leithid a thighinn rathad an
taighe." "Cha d' thàinig a dheireadh ort," arsa Gilleasbuig. "Ciod e 'tha agad anns a' phoit sin air an
teine?" arsa Gilleasbuig. "Tha," ars' ise, "cearc a tha
bruich do Iain." "Cearc!" arsa Gilleasbuig. "Nan
toireadh tu dha cearc anns an t-suidheachadh anns am
bheil e an ceart uair, bhiodh e cho marbh ri sgadan

agad mu'n ruitheadh ceithir-uairean-fichead." "Ach," arsa Gilleasbuig, "thoir thusa dheth a' chearc, agus thoir dhomhs' i agus innsidh mi dhuit a rithist ciod a ni sinn ri Iain." 'S ann mar sin a thachair. Thàinig a' chearc dheth agus dh' ith Gilleasbuig air a shocair fhéin i. "Seall tu 'nis," arsa Gilleasbuig, "mar a ni thu ri Iain. Tha bò agad a mach aig ceann an taighe agus laogh òg aice. Beir air an laogh agus dean feannadh-builg air, agus cuir seiche an laoigh air Iain, agus cuir fodh 'n bhoin e, agus mar a gabh i ris cuir a h-uile cù 's a' bhaile rithe mach air na creagan."

Thog a' bhean bhochd a dà laimh, agus thug i an dorus oirre dh' iarraidh dhaoine: chunnaic i gu'n robh an duine às a chiall. Ach mu'n do thill i, thug an lighiche am monadh air. Ach an ceann latha no dhà thill Gilleasbuig agus callach air de gach seòrsa,—ìm, càise, cearcan agus feòil. Dh' fhàg e sud aig a' chaillich air son Iain, 's cha do chuir an léigh an còrr dragh oirre.

Ach feumaidh sinn ar cead a ghabhail de Ghilleasbuig aig an àm so; agus cha b'e paipeir goirid a chaidh a sgriobhadh ann an cabhaig a bheireadh ceartas do'n eachdraidh aige. Ghabhadh e iomadh paipeir agus feasgar fada gu sin a dheanamh.

Ge b'e ionad anns am bheil a chòmhnuidh tha dòchas agam gu'm bheil e sona. Tha mi creidsinn gu'm bi iomadh latha agus linn mu'm bi gàire subhach, sunndach luchd-aiteachaidh Eilean-a'-cheò air a dhùsgadh le a leithid a rithist.

[27TH MARCH, 1883].

At the Meeting of the Society held on this date,

Rev. G. R. MacPhail, M.A., Dundee, read a Paper on "The place of Gaelic in the study of Philology."

Dr. R. C. MacDiarmid, Whiteinch, also read a Paper on "Donald MacLeod, the Skye Bard—his life and songs."

Dr. MacDiarmid's Paper was as follows :—

DONALD MACLEOD, THE SKYE BARD— HIS LIFE AND SONGS.

One of the aims of this Society is to utilise, as far as possible, the provincial knowledge of Gaelic and kindred subjects possessed by Highlanders resident in this city. Nothing could further this object better than that members who have the honour of writing papers for our meetings should deal, when convenient and desirable, with subjects which, while of general interest, have special reference to their native village or parish. Besides, the essayist, when not a specialist, should select a subject with which he is likely to be most familiar. Guided to some extent by these considerations, I have thought it appropriate to say a little about a man with whose name, and some of whose songs, I have been more or less familiar since my early childhood, and whose merit and standing as a Gaelic poet certainly entitle him to a high place among our bards.

Donald Macleod, or as he is popularly known in Skye, *Dòmhnull nan Oran*, was born in Glendale, Isle of Skye, in the year 1787. His father, Neil Macleod, was a small farmer, and a man of remarkable shrewdness and intelligence. It does not appear, however, that he posed as a bard, but his sagacity and counsel were often the means of amicably settling disputes and petty quarrels among his neighbours. His mother, Janet Macpherson, was a kind-hearted and amiable woman. Donald, being the only son, would have probably received the best available school education, but in those days schools, especially in the Highlands, were few and far between, so young Donald's education was comparatively neglected. Still, when he left school, he could speak and write English fairly well, and in after years he managed to accumulate a vast store of general information. He composed his first song—*Moladh aitreamh Ruairidh*, at the age of fifteen years, the subject being a new house belonging to Roderick Macneil, a successful merchant at Stein, and an intimate friend of the poet's father.

When Macleod was about twenty years of age, the military resources of this country were severely taxed in the endeavour to check the rapacity of Napoleon Bonaparte, and "pressing" or conscription had to be resorted to in the Highlands as well as in other parts of the country. The natural anxiety of the bard's father to prevent his only son from being carried away to the wars, induced him to make every effort to get him into some official situation which would protect him from the obtrusive attentions of the recruiting party; and, through the kindness and influence of Macleod of Macleod, he succeeded in obtaining the appointment of collector of road rates for Skye. This situation gave the young poet unusual facilities for collecting folk-lore and Gaelic poetry. He acquired an intimate acquaintance with the manners, customs, traditions, and insular peculiarities of the Skye people, and it is a matter sincerely to be regretted that a history of Skye, which he contemplated publishing, was never finished.

The biography of a poet, no matter how brief, would scarcely be considered complete unless it contained a romantic tale of the subject's first or early love. Donald Macleod's life furnishes a typical example of the joys and sorrows incidental to the course of true love which, we are assured, never ran smooth. He was scarcely twenty years of age when he fell passionately in love with a Miss Stewart, daughter of Mr. Stewart, farmer, Borrodale, who appears to have been comparatively well-off. Miss Stewart seems to have reciprocated her admirer's attachment, but her parents strongly disapproved of her having anything to do with Macleod, and often resorted to very unpleasant and somewhat energetic means of curtailing or preventing his visits to the farm. The lovers, however, managed to meet occasionally, and would have got on fairly well in the circumstances, were it not for the persistent espionage they had to suffer from Kenneth Stewart, Miss Stewart's cousin, who stayed at Borrodale, and took much pleasure in telling the young lady's mother of her daughter's clandestine meetings with her lover. This led to more parental stringency and watching, and our bard is forced to lament his hard fate in a love song which is decidedly one of his best early efforts. He took a characteristic way of temporarily ridding himself of, and punishing the informer at Borrodale. His official duties as collector of rates gave him opportunities of knowing the movements of the pressing party in the island. One night he came in great haste to Mrs. Stewart, and told her confidentially that the "press gang" were in search of Kenneth Stewart—*Gu'n d' thàinig an crann air Coinneach*. The result of this timely information was that Kenneth fled to the hills and hid himself in a cave for three months, and his abscence from Borrodale, I have no doubt, was duly appreciated and taken advantage of. But death put an end to this very interesting love episode. Miss Stewart died at the early age of twenty-one.

About the age of twenty-three, Macleod published a quarto volume of Gaelic poems—many of the pieces being composed by himself.

Getting tired of the peripatetic business of money-collecting, he obtained the post of fisherman for Macleod of Macleod—a situation he held for some years. For a man of his restless energy and Bohemian tendencies this work must have been somewhat monotonous; and it is not surprising, therefore, that he should soon have made up his mind to fish on his own account. Induced by a desire to better his position and see more of the world, he emigrated to America, where he stayed for upwards of fifteen years He tried his luck at several occupations while residing in that country—one of these being that of a checker in a flour mill. Here he checked the grain coming in and the flour going out. But the prosaic and unremunerative character of his experience and work across the Atlantic, strengthened, no doubt, by a hankering for the old country, made him leave America and come back to his native land. On his return, he set up in Glendale as a general merchant, and very shortly afterwards married. His wife's age when the knot was tied was only nineteen years, while his own was sixty—a fact which shows that "the ancient spirit was not dead," and that his poetic partiality for a bonny face was stronger than mere mercenary motives. This marriage proved a happy and prolific one, for we find that they had a family of ten—four sons and six daughters. Of these, three sons and four daughters are still living. Two of the sons—Neil and John—have given excellent proof of their having inherited the poetic genius of their father, and at present Neil Macleod is probably the best known and most popular Gaelic poet living. His book, *Clàrsach an Doire*, has been so well received, that, I believe, the first edition is already exhausted. John has not published a book although he has composed a large number of Gaelic songs—many of them not inferior to those of his father or brother in originality of conception, vigour, and strength of expression.

Donald Macleod died in 1873 at the ripe old age of eighty-six years, and was buried in *Cill Chomhain*, Glendale, not far from the spot where he was born, and amidst the scenes he loved so well, and which formed the theme of several of his songs. Neither the hoarse roar or gentle murmur of the *Allt Mòr*, which passes close to his resting-place, nor the diapason of the ever-changing, ever-lasting waves of *Polldill nan creag òrda's na tràigh mine*, will ever again disturb his peaceful slumber or awaken the poetic echoes of his imagination. His funeral was largely attended by his friends and admirers in Duirinish.

I have a faint recollection of his appearance. He was rather below the middle height, or, at least, appeared to me to be so, owing to his advanced age and his being much bent. When travelling, he always dressed scrupulously, and wore a tall hat. He was well-known all over Skye, not only for his poetry, but also for his ready wit and conversational powers. He was a beautiful and an eloquent Gaelic speaker and had a wonderful command of the characteristic idioms and ample vocabulary of that language. He possessed a remarkably retentive memory and could repeat long poems, whether composed by himself or by others, without the least hesitation or loss for a word. He very seldom sang his own verses. He used to recite them in a slow, deliberate, and impressive manner, yet he had a most accurate ear for musical sounds, and such was his extreme fastidiousness regarding the smoothness of his lines and correctness of his rhythm, that Mackenzie, in his "Beauties of Gaelic Poetry," remarks that it often led him into the error of writing bad grammar and words of no meaning. No doubt such errors are somewhat conspicuous in his old book; but it is only fair to state that that book was edited by a gentleman in whose Gaelic scholarship Macleod had great confidence. He is not, therefore, altogether responsible for the many errors in grammar, spelling, accentuation, and punctuation, which are so glaring in this old collection. With careful editing, these faults would not have been more obtrusive than similar ones in some of our best Gaelic books.

No one need pose as a Gaelic bard in the Highlands unless he is always able to demonstrate that he is a wit and a punster as well as a rhymster. He must excel in *gearradh cainnte*. Donald Macleod's power of repartee, which, however, he never paraded, was remarkable, but his quiet, caustic replies and humorous remarks were never offensive; except, perhaps, when he particularly wished them to be so.

One or two examples of his ready wit may be given. He once happened to be at Portree on a market night. The inns were crowded with visitors, and all the sitting rooms in one of them had to be converted into bedrooms. One of the latest arrivals at this inn was Donald Macleod, and one of the guests, wishing to have some fun at the bard's expense, thus accosted him:—"*Ma ta, a dhuine chòir 's iomadh cù a rinn cobhart riut bho'n thuit an oidhche.*" "*Tha mi 'creidsinn gur iomadh,*" arsa Dòmhnull, "*ach tha mi 'faicinn gu'm bheil a h-aon dhiubh nach do sguir fhathast.*" ["Well, my good man, many a dog must have barked at you since nightfall." "I believe that is so," replied Donald, "but I see that one of them which has not yet stopped."]

On another occasion Mr. Hector Maclean, a leading Free Church elder in Duirinish, called at his house evidently with the intention of having a serious conversation with him. "*A Dhòmhnuill,*" arsa Eachann, "*tha mi fhéin a' dol a dh' fhaotainn a' bhàis.*" "*Ma ta*

Eachainn," arsa Dòmhnull, "cha'n'eil duine ann an sgir Dhiuranais a bu duiliche leam a dh' fhaotainn a' bhàis na thusa." "Cha robh fios agam," arsa Eachann, "gu'n robh an urad sin de ghaol agad orm idir." "Cha'n'eil sin agam ort," arsa Dòmhnull, "gaol 's am bith, ach tha fios agam ma gheibh thu 'null air thoiseach orm nach e 'n cliù is fheàrr a bheir thu orm thall, agus mar sin b' fheàrr leam gu mòr thu bhi air dheireadh orm." ["Donald," said Hector, "I am going to die." "Well, Hector," replied Donald, "there is not another man in the parish of Duirinish whose death I should regret more than yours." "I did not know," answered Hector, "that you had such great love for me." "Neither I have," Donald said, "but I know that, if you get across before me, it is not the best account of me you will give in the other country; therefore, I would much prefer that you should die after me."]

From this anecdote it may be surmised that the bard's religion was not up to the stringent Calvanistic standard of the Duirinish Free Church elders. Possibly not; still he was a moral, honest, and industrious man.

It is now necessary to refer very briefly to the merits and characteristics of Macleod's poetry. I have already stated that at the age of twenty-three he published a collection of Gaelic songs, containing seventeen pieces by himself. In 1871 he published a booklet of songs— all his own work. Both these books are out of print. The bulk of his songs have never been printed, and the manuscripts of many of them are in the possession of his widow, who is still living, and occupying with her family the bard's house in Glendale. For obvious reasons any comments offered, or quotations given, must be limited to those songs which have been printed. His first poetic effort, already referred to, is entitled *Rann moluidh do thigh ùr.* It is, for a boy of fifteen, a very creditable attempt indeed, at descriptive poetry. But his admiration for the new house led him into extravagant praise and exaggerated description, and the last three verses drift into the character of a burlesque.

Reference has already been made to the romantic incident of his love for Miss Stewart, and his disappointment at finding the lady's friends object to his suit, has been the cause of one of his best love songs. It is the plaintive, despairing cry of one in deep mental distress, and depicts his own misery rather than the charms of his lady-love. It is pathetic and tender, and being wedded to a mournful but beautiful Gaelic air, cannot fail to deeply affect the sympathetic reader—

> O's tu, 's gur a tu th' air m' aire,
> O's tu, 's gur a tu th' air m' aire,
> 'S tusa rùin tha tigh 'n faincar dhomh,
> 'S gur tric do shugradh na mo shealladh.
>
> Mo chridhe leòinte fo spòig gach galair,
> O chaill mi 'n dòchas gur tu bu bhean domh.
> 'S o thraigh mo shùilean tha 'n ùir ga 'm tharruinn,
> 'S gur geàrr an ùine gu 'n dùin' i farram.
>
> Ge math na sùilean an cùil 's an solus,
> Gun d' fhàg iad brùite air bheag sùgh mo choluinn,
> 'S gu 'm b' fheàrr dhomh dùinte iad na meud an cron domh
> Mu 'n d' leig iad ùmpa' cho dlùth na ghon mi.

It would be possible to take up and criticise each piece *seriatim*, but as the attempt to do so would be very tedious and undesirable, I must content myself by briefly noticing some of the most characteristic ones and making a few general remarks. In his *Sàr-obair nam Bard Gaelach*, John Mackenzie has a short account of Donald Macleod, and gives two songs —*Oran do Reiseamaid Mhic-Shimidh*, and *Smeorach nan Leòdach*,—as good specimens of his work. No doubt they are representative pieces, but some of the shorter songs are, in some respects at least, equal to, if not superior, to these. Macleod is at his best when he is humorous and sarcastic, and evidently he felt, when composing these two somewhat ambitious songs, that it was necessary to keep his humour and sarcasm in abeyance. Mackenzie observes that these two "possess some genuine strokes of grandeur." *Reise-amaid Mhic-Shimidh* is very vigorous, somewhat martial in its spirit, and well exemplifies the rare richness of the author's vocabulary. One verse may be quoted.—

> Bidh slàinte Mhic-Shimidh
> Na cairdeas dha 'chinneadh,
> 'S an t-al nach do ghineadh,
>   Bidh sireadh roi' chàch orr';
>
> 'S àrd ann an spiorad e,
> 'S làidir an gillean e,
> 'S bàrr air an t-Siorrachd e
>   'S teine e nach smàlair !
>
> 'S gàradh ro ghioraig e,
> Sàbhaladh chinneach e,

Slàinte bho thinneas e,
  'S tuilleadh air àird air !

Bho 'n thàr e mar ghibhtean,
An aird 's a aird sliochda'
Buaidh-làrach biodh tric leis,
 Mu 'm brist' iad am fàra.

Of his humorous songs, *Mhurchaidh Bhig* is the best, and probably the most popular. Its inimitable drollery reminds one strongly of the misadventures of John Gilpin. The subjects of the pieces are somewhat similar. "Little Murdoch" was a herd, and came to grief while riding a saddled horse belonging to his master, who was an elder of the church. He was well accustomed to riding, but seldom used a saddle. The horse apparently understood the cause of his rider's awkwardness, and managed to give Murdoch a bad fall. The following verses will give a fair idea of the merits of the *Oran*:—

Thuirt esan is e 'g éiridh—
"Mo léir-chreach mar phranuadh mi;
Cha dean mi tuilleadh feuma,
'S a bheist, bheir thu ceaunach air ;
Ge d' tha thu leis an éildir,
Cha 'n éirig air m' anam thu,
'S ma 's e mo ghalair bàis e,
Gu 'm pàigh thu ri m' aillir e."

The horse replies—

"A Mhurchaidh Bhig, na 'm biodh tu glic,
Cha b' ann ré sud a dh' fhanadh tu,
Ach dhol dachaidh gun aon each
O chleachd thu bhi t-fhear cairiste.

> Bha m' eòlas ort dà bhliadhna,
> 'S tri miosan a bharrachd air,
> 'S cha 'n fhaca' mi each dialta
> Dol riabh gu do dhorus leat."

His boat song, or *Rann molaidh*, is very spirited. The measure and rhythm are not original, but admirably adapted to a poetic description of the peculiar motions of a skiff scudding before a stiff gale. Although not very long the song contains exquisite touches of vivid word painting, and one occasionally detects the latent but impressible humour of the author, which he is evidently trying to hide. His praise of the boat and the crew are, however, sometimes too transparently ironical. Immediately following these remarkably graphic verses we have *Rann firinn do' n bhàta cheudna*, in which he dispraises the same boat with equal vigour and eloquence. Perhaps he did this in imitation of *Mi-mholadh Moraig le Mac Mhaighstir Alasdair*. Two verses may be given as a specimen, which are almost a perfect picture of an old, dilapidated fishing skiff. The metre, it will be observed, is the same as that of Macdonald's *Birlinn Chlann Raonuill*—

> "Bha i sgallach bhreac mar dhéile
> Air dhroch lochdradh ;
> Bha sruth dearg bho cheann gach tàirne
> Mar a chorcair ;
> Mar a bha mheirg air a cnàmh
> 'S a làr 'ga grodadh,
> Bha neid nan corraichean-còsaig
> Na buird mhasgain.
>
> An fhardoch is aognaidh 's is measa
> Chaidh fo' endach ;

An fhardoch is trom 's is tric ultach
Air fear taomaidh ;
Rachadh an eultaidh air h-iteig
Romh gach taobh dhi,
'S ghearradh tu dh' fheur innte na dh' itheadh
Mart 's an Fhaoileach."

Sixty years after the appearance of his first volume, and two years before he died, he published in pamphlet form a selection from his later poetic efforts. The booklet bears on the title-page "*Dain agus Orain le Domhnull Mac leoid's an Eilean Sgiathanach.*" It may be asked—Why did he not publish a bigger book? During these sixty years had the Muse forsaken him? These questions are pertinent enough, but admit of a simple answer. The Muse had not forsaken him; from time to time he composed odes and lyrics as occasion and opportunity presented themselves, but very few of these he committed to paper. Moreover, he had to work hard for his living, and his large and young family necessarily engrossed his attention, and deprived him of the leisure which those who marry young generally possess in their old age. Even with abundant and good material, the publication of a considerable volume of Gaelic poetry would have been a very hazardous undertaking for a man in better circumstances than Macleod. He could not afford to suffer a financial loss. It may be here observed that it is not altogether the apathy of Highlanders that prevents Gaelic books from paying, but the limited constituency to which such works appeal.

The *Orain* and *Dàin* in this booklet are far

superior to the sporadic productions of the bard's early manhood. Doubtless they lack some of the old dash and vivacity, but they gain in the force, quiet dignity, and keen insight into human nature which they display. The poet feels that he is getting old—that his sun is setting, and he turns his attention to loftier themes. He gives full scope to his active imagination. He inclines to be didactic and religious, and to moralize. His *Dàn do'n Ghrein*, *Dàn a' Bhreitheanais*, and *Dàn do'n Uaigh* are sombre and sad in tone. Then his appreciation of nature seems stronger and keener. His sadness vanishes and his soul expands with exuberant delight at the teeming life and beauty of nature under the glorious sun of a May morning.

Rann do dh' éildeirean an Lòin Mhoir is the best known of the songs in this small collection, and a verse or two of it may be quoted:—

>Ged 'tha ùpraidean an t-saoghail
>A' cumail dhaoin' air bheagan tàmha,
>Cha 'n urrainn mi gun bhi smaointinn
>Air na laoisg a chaill an nàire—
>Eildeirean dubha 'n Loin Mhoir
>Nach d' fhuair eòlas air an àithne :
>Bhi 'n an suidhe an cathair binn
>Air aghaidh muinntir a fhuair tàlannt.
>Ma gheibh thu drama bho dhuin' uasal
>Tha thu 'n uair sin air do mhàbadh :
>Ma chuir thu car na do ghuaillean
>A' sealltuinn bh' uait le feithe ghàire,
>Bheir Iain Mac Alastair suas thu :—
>Leubh thu 'n "Cuairtear"* air an t-sabaid,

---

* *Cuairtear nan Gleann*, 1840-43.—A monthly Gaelic magazine edited by Dr. Norman Macleod.

Fuiling a nise do bhinn
Bho Chalum seang 's bho Eòghan tàillear.

'S fìor choltach iad ris na h-òighean
'Thainig le'n cleòchdanan àluinn
A'n coinneamh an Fhir nuadh phòsda ;
Co bu spòrsaile na àdsan.
'N uair thàinig feum air na lòchrain
Bha iad dòlum agus tràighte,
'S fhuair iadsan taobh 'muigh na còmhla,
Far'm bi 'n seòrsa dheth 'm bheil àdsan.

Oran an Uillt Mhòir and *Oran do Thungaig* are productions of exceptional beauty. "Tungag" is a grassy hillock in Glendale, and the Allt-Mòr is one of the streams which drain the glen. The *Orain* describe, with much animation and minuteness and in glowing language, the scenery of the district, and the summer loveliness of nature. It is unnecessary to give quotations.

One feels inclined to ask what rank or position should be assigned to Donald Macleod as a poet. Before one could answer such a question satisfactorily, he would require to have among other qualifications, an intimate acquaintance with the works of all our Gaelic bards—and to the possession of such knowledge I make no pretence whatever. No person claims for Macleod a place among our first-class poets, such as *Mac Mhaighstir Alasdair*, or *Donnachadh Bàn*. Had his published works been more voluminous, or had his old book been better edited, he would have received more general public recognition. That he had poetic genius of a high order is beyond doubt or cavil. Even with the literary disadvantages mentioned, he has secured for himself a very creditable position among our Gaelic bards. We should like to see a complete and carefully revised edition of his poems. It would not only do justice to Macleod's memory and rare gifts, but would form a valuable addition to the literature of the Gaelic language.

[24TH APRIL, 1888.]

The annual meeting of the Society was held on this date, when interesting reports were submitted by the Secretary and Treasurer. Thereafter office-bearers for the succeeding session were elected.

SESSION, 1888-89.

[30TH OCTOBER, 1888.]

The first ordinary meeting of the Society for this session, was held on this date, when the Hon. President. Professor Mackinnon read a paper on "Loan words from Gaelic." At this meeting reference was made to the loss which the Society had sustained in the death of Rev. Alex. Cameron, LL.D., Brodick.

[27TH NOVEMBER, 1888.]

At the meeting of the Society held on this date, Mr. Colin Brown, Ewing Lecturer on Music, Andersonian University, read a paper on "Old Celtic Music."

[24TH DECEMBER, 1888.]

At the Meeting of the Society held on this date, Mr. Alex. Carmichael, Corr. M.S.A., Scot., Edinburgh, read a paper entitled "Uist Old Hymns." As a collection of these Hymns will shortly be published, the whole lecture is not available, but we submit the following report of it, which appeared in the newspapers—and which has been revised and extended by Mr. Carmichael.

UIST OLD HYMNS.

Mr. Carmichael commenced by reading a quaint and beautiful Christmas Hymn or *Duan Nollaig*, as being appropriate to the season. The first verse he translated.—

> Ho, King! Blessed is He,
> Blessed the King
> Of whom we sing,
> Ho, ro! let there be joy!

He remarked that just as the ancient Gael had a song suited to every occupation in which he might be engaged, so also had their pious ancestors in the Western Hebrides a hymn or prayer applicable to the various duties belonging to their economy. These hymns were to form the subject of his observations that evening. He would endeavour to arrange them in some sort of order so that they might easier see that they were suited to the round of duties of an insular dwelling. He would begin at the evening duties of the family which was the "smooring" of the fire before retiring to rest. This simple duty was never performed without the following prayer being recited by the performer.

AM BEANNACHADH SMALAIDH

Tha mi 'smàladh an teine,
Mar a smàlas Mac Moire ;
Gu ma slàn dha'n taigh 's dha'n teine,
Gu ma slàn dha'n chuideachd uile.
Có siod air an làr ? Peadair agus Pàl !
Có air a bhios an fhaire an nochd ?
Air Moire mhin gheal 's air a Mac.
Beul De a thubhradh, aingeal De a labhradh.
Aingeal an dorus gach taighe,
'Ga r còmhnadh 's 'ga r gleidheadh,
Gu'n tig là geal am màireach.

[*Translation.*]

THE SMOORING BLESSING.

I am smooring the fire,
As it is smoored by the Son of Mary.
Blest be the house, blest be the fire,
And blessed be the people all.
Who are those on the floor ? Peter and Paul.
Upon whom devolves the watching this night ?
Upon fair gentle Mary and her Son.
The mouth of God said, the angel of God tells.
An angel in the door of every house,
To shield and to protect us all,
Till bright daylight comes in the morning.

Before going to bed the devout Catholics of South Uist recited :—

AN T-ALTACHADH LEAPA.

Tha mise laidhe 'nochd, le Moire 's le 'Mac,
Le Màthair mo Righ, tha 'g am dhion o gach lochd
Cha laidh mi leis an olc, cha laidh an t-olc liom,
Ach laidhe mi le Dia, is laidhe Dia liom.

Lamh dheas De fo mo cheann,
Soillse an Spioraid os mo chionn;
Crois nan naoi aingeal tharam sios,
O mhullach mo chinn gu iochdar mo bhonn.

. . . .

Guidheam Peadar, guidheam Pòl,
Guidheam Moir' Oigh agus a Mac,
Guidheam an dà ostal deug,
Gu 'n mise a dhol eug a nochd.

A Dhia agus a Mhoire na glòrach,
Ios' a Mhic na h-Oighe cùbhra,
Cumaibh sinne 'o na pianntaibh diolta;
'S o'n teine shiorruidh mhùchta.

[*Translation.*]

THE BED BLESSING.

I lie down to-night, with Mary and with her Son,
With the Mother of my King, who shields me from harm:
I shall not lie down with evil, nor shall evil lie down with me,
But I shall lie with God, and God will lie down with me.

The right hand of God under my head,
The light of the Spirit Holy shining over me,
The cross of the nine angels along me, down
From the crown of my head to the soles of my feet.

. . . .

I pray Peter, I pray Paul,
I pray Mary, Virgin, and her Son,
I pray the kind Apostles twelve
That I may not die this night.

Oh God! Oh, Mary of Glory!
Oh, Jesus! Thou Son of the Virgin fragrant,
Keep ye us from the pains avenging
And from the everlasting suffocating fire.

These Islanders had also their Morning Lesson known as *Beannachadh Eiridh* or Rising Prayer. It was as follows :—

AM BEANNACHADH EIRIDH.

Dia liom a laidhe,
Dia liom ag éiridh,
Dia liom gach aon rà soluis,
Gun an aon rà son' às aonais,
Gun an aon rà son' às aonais.

An Dia 'g a mo stiuradh
An Dòmhnach 'ga m sheoladh,
An Tighearna Dia 'ga m riaghladh,
A nis agus gu siorruidh, Amen!
Triath nan Triath. Amen!

which might be rendered :—

[*Translation.*]

RISING PRAYER.

God with me lying down,
God with me rising up,
God with me in every ray of light,
Nor a ray without Him.

The God directing me,
The Lord protecting me,
The Spirit of God governing me
Now and for ever, Amen!
The Lord of Lords, Amen!

Just as they had an appropriate invocation when "smooring" the fire at night, they had also a suitable petition when kindling it in the morning, known as *Am Beannachadh Beothachaidh*, or the Kindling Blessing.

AM BEANNACHADH BEOTHACHAIDH.

Togaidh mi mo thein' an diugh
An làthair ainglean naomha nèimh,
An làthair Ghabriel is àilde cruth,
An làthair Mhicheil nam milte sgeimh.
    Gun ghnù, gun tnù, gun fharmad,
    Gun ghiomh, gun gheimh, romh aon fo'n ghréin,
    Ach Naomh Mac De bhi m' thearmad.

Dhé fadaidh féin 'n am chridhe 'steach
Aiteal gràidh do m' choimhearsnach,
Do m' nàmh, do m' dhàmh, do m' chàirde,
Do 'n t-saoidh, do 'n daoi, do 'n tràille.
    O! Mhic na Moire mìn-ghile.
    Bho'n ni is isle crannachaire,
    Gu ruig an t-Ainm is àirde.

[*Translation.*]

THE KINDLING BLESSING.

I will kindle my fire this morning,
In presence of heaven's holy angels,

In presence of Gabriel of loveliest form,
In presence of Michael of the myriad charms.
 Without malice, without jealousy, without envy,
 Without fear, without terror of any one under the sun,
 But God's own Holy Son to shield me.

O! God kindle Thou in my heart within
A lowe of love towards my neighbour,
Towards my foe, towards my friend, towards my kindred all,
Towards the brave, towards the knave, towards the thrall.
 O Holy Son! of the loveliest Mary,
 From the lowliest thing that liveth
 To the Name that is highest of all.

They had also a suitable prayer when going to a Court of Justice—known as *Eolas Ceartais*,—an example of which was submitted by Mr. Carmichael. They had numerous milking croons or *Orain bhleoghain*, such as—

BANACHAG NAM BO.

 O, m' adhan! hó m' adh min!
 M' adhan cridh, còir, gràdhach,
 'An ainm an Ard-Righ,
  Gabh ri d' laogh!

 An oidhche bha am Buachaille muigh,
 Cha deachaidh buarach air boin,
 Cha deachaidh geum a beul laoigh,
  A caoiueadh Buachaille 'chruidh!

 Thig a Mhoire 's blith a bhó,
 Thig a Bhride 's comraig i;
 Thig a Chalum Chille chaoimh,
  'Us iadh do dhà laimh mu m' bhoin!

Mo bhó lurach dhubh, bó na h-àiridh
Bó a' bhà-thigh ! màthair laogh !
Lùban siamain air crodh na tire,
    Buarach shiod' air m' adhan gaoil !

'S a bhó dhubh sin ! 's a bhó dhubh !
'S ionnan galar dhòmhs' is dhuits'
Thusa caoidh do cheud laogh caoin,—
    Mise 's m' aona mhac gaoil fo'n mhuir !

[*Translation.*]

THE MILK-MAID OF THE COWS.

O, my heifer ho ! my gentle heifer,
My heifer so full of heart, generous and kind,
In name of the High King
    Take to thy calf.

That night the Herdsman was out
No shackle went on a cow,
Nor ceased a low from a calf
    Wailing the Herdsman of the flock.

Come Mary (Virgin) and milk the cow;
Come Bridget and encompass her,
Come Calum Cille the beneficent,
    And wind thine arms around my cow.

My lovely black cow, thou pride of the sheiling !
First cow of the byre, choicest mother of calves !
Wisps of straw round other cows of the town-land,
    But a shackle of silk on my heifer so loved.

Thou lovely black cow ! mine own gentle black cow !
The same disease afflicts thee and me;

Thou are grieving for thy beautiful first calf,
And I for mine only beloved son under the sea!

The reference in the first verse was to the *Laoicionn* "Tulchan" substituted for the real calf. The term "Tulchan" was now applied to a bishop who was a bishop in name only, while others drew the pay.

Mr. Carmichael then referred to certain hymns which the people of Uist recited—intended to consecrate the seed before putting it in the soil. The person reciting the Consecration Hymn went sun-wise *(deiseil)*, and chanted,—

"Théid mise mach a chur an t-sil,
An ainm an Ti a bheir air fàs,
Cuiridh mi m' aodann anns a' ghaoith,
'Us tilgim baslach caoin an àird."

[*Translation.*]

I go forth to sow the seed
In name of Him who makes it grow.
I will set my face to the wind,
And throw a gracious handful on high.

Having given several interesting examples of "Blessing the sea, and ships"—some of which reminded one of the "Blessing of the Ship," by Alex. MacDonald, the bard—the lecturer quoted a rhyme associated with the warping of cloth—an operation always performed on a Thursday, because it was *Là Chalum Chille chaoimh* (The gentle S. Columba's day.) He then referred to the custom once so common in the

Highlands of taking the cattle to the summer sheilings. *Fèisd na h-àiridh*, or sheiling feast was prepared, after which they dedicated themselves and their flocks to the care of Israel's Shepherd. The following dedicatory hymn was used in Uist and Barra :—

LAOIDH NA H-AIRIDH.

A Mhicheil mhin ! nan steud geala,
A choisinn cios air dragon fala,
Air ghaol Dia 'us Mhic Muire,
Sgaoil do sgiath oirnn, dion sinn uile.

A Mhoire ghràdhach, màthair Uain-ghil,
Cobhair oirnne, Oigh na h-uaisle ;
A rioghainn uaibhreach, a bhuachaille nan treud !
Cum ar cuallach, cuartaich sinn le cheil.

A Chalum-Chille chàirdeil, chaoimh,
An ainm Athair, Mic 'n Spioraid Naoimh,
Trid na Trithinn ! trid an Triath !
Comraig sinne, gleidh ar triall.

Athair ! A Mhic ! A Spioraid Naoimh !
Bitheadh an Tri-aon leinn a là 's a dh'oidhche ;
'S air machair luim, no air roinn nam beann,
Bidh an Tri-aon leinn 's bidh a lamh fo 'r ceann.

[*Translation.*]

THE SHEILING HYMN.

Thou gentle Michael of the white steeds
Who subdued the Dragon of Blood,
For love of God and of Mary's Son
Spread over us thy wing, shield us all!

Mary beloved! Mother of the white Lamb
Protect us, thou Virgin of nobleness,
Queen of beauty, Sheperdess of the flocks!
Keep our cattle, surround us together.

Thou Columba, the friendly, the kind,
In name of the Father, the Son, and the Spirit Holy,
Through the Three-in-One, through the Three,
Encompass us, guard our procession.

Thou Father! Thou Son! Thou Spirit Holy!
Be the Three-in-One with us day and night,
On the machair plain, on the mountain ridge,
The Three-in-One is with us, with His arm under our head.

Mr. Carmichael also referred to several hymns and rhymes connected with the industry of cloth-making. When the process known as "waulking the cloth" was completed it was followed by a Hymn of Consecration, an interesting example of which was submitted. The lecturer next quoted a beautiful composition part of which he had received from the valuable collection of folk-lore belonging to the Rev. John G. Campbell, Tiree. It was known as *Ora nam Buadh* or "The Invocation of the Graces." It was usually recited to a bride. Some of the similies were exceedingly beautiful, such as—

> Is eilean thu air muir,
> Is caisteal thu air tir.
> Is fuaran thu am fàsach,
>   Is slàint' thu dhuine tinn.

An là a's feàrr 'san t-seachdain dhuit,
An t-seachdain a's feàrr 's a' bhliadhna dhuit,
A bhliadhna 's fearr an domhan Mhic De dhuit.

[*Translation.*]

Thou art an island on sea,
Thou art a castle on land.
Thou art a fountain in the desert
Thou art health to the man of sickness.

. . . .

The best day of the week be thine,
The best week of the year be thine,
The best year in the Son of God's domain be thine.

Mr. Carmichael concluded a most interesting and valuable lecture by quoting a beautiful Hymn used before retiring to rest. It would be observed, he said that all these Hymns belonged to the Roman Catholic times, but they had been admired and considered of great value by such Protestant Divines as the late Rev. Dr. MacLauchlan, Edinburgh; the late Rev. Dr. A. Clerk, Kilmallie; and the late Rev. Dr. Cameron, Brodick, and many others.

Rev. Robert Blair, Cambuslang, said they indeed enjoyed a treat that was but seldom got. He had never listened to hymns more touching or beautiful, and they certainly threw much light on the Celtic character. Despite the many references to Angel and Saint worship, of which they as Protestants might not approve, these hymns and prayers proved conclusively that our Celtic forefathers were a deeply religious people. It seemed to him that in consecrating every duty of the day with a suitable prayer or hymn, and so carrying their religion into every detail of life, they proved that they were a cultured people. He was of the opinion that the Highlanders had not yet been properly understood by their Lowland brethren. He had held and maintained that the Highlanders were far ahead in the olden times of those who declared them to be nothing but naked savages and barbarians, and the fine tone and culture of these hymns certainly went a long way to prove all that. He would almost defy any people to produce more beautiful prayers or finer hymns. Mr. Carmichael had put all Highlanders under a deep debt of gratitude to him by collecting these exquisite specimens of our ancient lore. These things were fast passing away, and very few of the rising generation felt much interest in them. The spread of English, through our schools and School Boards, was hastening the disappearance of our Celtic folk lore. He felt personally indebted to the lecturer for the intense pleasure he had afforded himself, as well as all present, by the choice selection of Uist old hymns.

Dr. MacNicoll, Dalmally, said that he knew there was a treat in store for him when he came from Dalmally to hear Mr. Carmichael. He had not been disappointed. It said much for Mr. Carmichael that he, a person different in religion and from a different part of the country, should have been able to collect these hymns from the Catholic Celts of Uist. Mr. Carmichael had, however, by his gentle manners and kindly feeling, overcome not only the natural diffidence of the Celt, but also the caution which a person of one religion maintains towards one holding a different creed.

Rev. William Ross, Glasgow, said he came to show that he was deeply interested in the subject under consideration that evening. They were all much indebted to Mr. Carmichael for the intellectual treat he had provided for them. Referring to a remark made by the lecturer in regard to sanctuaries, or places of refuge, called in Gaelic *comaraich*, Mr. Ross stated that there were several of these in the Highlands, and that after they were superseded as places of safety they became the common pastures of the people. He also remarked that it was interesting to note that the custom of surrounding the marches, or *cuartachadh*, chanting a suitable hymn, and confiding the flock to the care of the Great Shepherd of Israel during the silent watches of the night, had caused the pious peoples of Caithness, Sutherland and Lewis, to apply this term *cuartachadh* to the act of family worship.

Mr. Jolly, H.M. Inspector of Schools, who occupied the chair, in conveying the thanks of the meeting to Mr. Carmichael, said that no one could but observe the practical nature of the religion of the composers of these hymns. It was not intended merely for church on Sundays, but was one continued round of religious aspirations, from the time when they woke till they sought repose at night.

He was sure it would be interesting to the meeting to hear that a cultured English gentleman, on the shores of Loch Maree, was so impressed with the beauty of these old hymns that he had offered to bear the whole expense of publishing them.

Mr. Carmichael thanked the meeting for the manner in which they had listened to his address, and for their appreciation of his labours in collecting these Hymns.

[29TH JANUARY, 1889.]

At a meeting of the Society held on this date, Mr. Duncan Reid, read a paper entitled "Sketches of Kintyre." Mr. Duncan Whyte also read a Gaelic paper, entitled "*Sgeulachdan Ghlinndaruail.*" We submit the principal portions of Mr. Reid's paper, as follows :—

SKETCHES OF KINTYRE.

The written history of Kintyre is but meagre; and like many others of our Highland districts, many important events, interesting folklore, and other valuable information, are, I fear, entirely lost, for want of being preserved in writing. There is a booklet, entitled "The History of Kintyre," by Peter MacIntosh, to which I am indebted for a few scraps of information; but its contents are so limited that it can scarcely be called a history.

North Britain was inhabited by twenty-one tribes of Aborigines when Agricola, the Roman General, invaded it about the year 80. Those of them who inhabited the south west of Argyllshire, from Loch Linnhe on the north to the Firth of Clyde, and the

Irish sea on the south, including the peninsula of Kintyre, were called the Epidii; and what is now designated the Mull of Kintyre was then called the Epidian Promontory. Their eastern boundary was the country of the Albani, now called Lochfyne. Chalmers informs us that the Dalriada of Ireland were the ancestors of the Dalriada of North Britain.

About the middle of the third century the Irish made incursions against North Britain, to which Kintyre, from its proximity, was specially exposed. The northern parts of Ireland were at that time in a most unsettled and turbulent condition, owing to the claims of rival tribes. Those of them who were known by the name of the *Cruithne* were by far the most powerful tribe of the north-western territory. Cormac was then supreme King of Ireland; and it is related that his cousin and General Cairbre Riada conquered a territory of about 30 miles in the north east corner of Ireland, which was possessed by the *Cruithne*. This part was called after the conqueror, *Dal Riada*, the portion of Riada. (*Dala* is an old Gaelic word, now obsolete, signifying a share or portion, and *Riada* is a contraction of *Righ jada*, the long King—hence the origin of the word Dalriada).

Cairbre and his posterity continued to rule over Dalriada for a long time, under the protection and subordination of the sovereigns of Ireland. As the population increased, a desire to extend their territories increased also ; and at the commencement of the sixth century (503) Lorn, Fergus and Angus, three sons of Erc, a descendant of Cairbre Riada, crossed, or as some suppose, re-crossed to Scotland, and the first part of Scottish soil on which they set their feet was Kintyre. Their landing place was at Dunaverty, a precipitous rock at the south of the peninsula. They continued till the time of Bede to be called after their original district the Dalriadini, or Dalriadii. The northwestern part of Campbeltown is still called Dalaruan, from Dalriada. At that time Kintyre was but sparsely inhabited, and the Epidii were little connected with the more inland clans. These three sons of Erc divided the country among them. Kintyre was appropriated as the portion of Fergus, who afterwards became the acknowledged King of the Scots: Lorn got the romantic territory, which still bears his name; and Angus received as his portion the bonnie Island of Islay. As the population increased, their settlements were extended; and other districts, including the neighbouring islands, were merged into the Dalriadian Kingdom.

It seems to be pretty much a matter of conjecture what wave of west-ward movement impelled the Celts through the Continent of Europe; and it seems equally doubtful whether they had crossed from ancient Gaul into England, and moved northward; or whether they had left Spain, and by a more circuitous route, landed in Ireland, and thence crossed to Scotland. Whatever differences of opinion may exist as to whether the Celts had been forced to leave the Continent of Europe by a stronger power than themselves, or had made a voluntary movement northwards, or whether they landed first in England or Ireland, there can be no difference of opinion that the Irish, Scotch,

Welsh, and Cornish are of one and the same race. However much they differ in manners, customs, and character, yet their language is from the same root. The chief difference between the Scottish Gaelic and Irish Gaelic is that caused by the dialectic provincialism, and that distinction is to be found among ourselves within a radius of but a few miles.

Kintyre signifying the head or end of the land, from *Ceann*, head, and *tir*, land—Latin *Finis terræ*—is a peninsula about 42 miles in length, and about an average of 7 miles broad, and situated at the south of Argyllshire. The isthmus of Tarbert connects it in the north with the main portion of Argyll; West Loch Tarbert separates it on the north from that part of Argyll known as Knapdale; on the east it is bounded by the Sound of Kilbrannon; on the west and south by the Atlantic Ocean and Irish Sea.

It is rightly considered among the foremost and most important of our Highland districts, for with it are associated many events of real historic interest. Not only is it among the largest of our Scottish peninsulas, but it has been the nursery of that race of Scottish kings and people that afterwards made Scotland so glorious. It was also among the first places in our land to adopt the principles of Christianity. It is supposed that the Gospel had been first introduced into Kintyre about the middle of the fifth century. St. Kiaran came from Ireland and erected a church at a place now known as Kilkerran—the church of Ciaran—the dark complexioned. In 1261 this church was placed under the control of Paisley Abbey. But tradition has it that St. Colum, a pupil of St. Kiaran, was the first to preach the Gospel in this district, and that he and his companions landed at a place now called "Kiel" on the south end of Kintyre, in a boat or *Curragh* made of wicker and covered with hides. A church had been erected on the shore there by St. Colum—the first which he erected in Scotland—and which still bears his name *Cill-Chalum Chille*, and the walls of which are still standing. St. Colum seems to have founded churches throughout the whole of Kintyre—from Kiel on the south, to Skipness, the northmost point. At this latter place is a chapel built by him, and still in a fair state of preservation. There are few districts (if any) in Scotland which contain so many names of places with the word *Kil* prefixed as Kintyre; and this of itself is evidence of the christianizing influence exercised by St. Colum in this district.

The modern name of the capital of Kintyre is Campbeltown; and the change of name, which appears to have been made either out of compliment to the Argyll family, or an endeavour to anglicise the district by the change of the name of its chief town, took place in connection with the Expedition of Argyll in 1661.

In Gaelic it retains the one half of its original name—*Ceann locha*, the head of the loch. The ancient name was, *Ceann locha Chille Chiarain*, the head of the loch of Kilciaran, so named from St. Kiaran.

To show how some Gaelic names become so distorted as to be almost unrecognisable, I may mention that the name *Ceann locha Chille Chiarain* has been called "Loch Kinkerane" in the 60th Act of James IV. Part of the Act is as follows:—" Because there had been great abusion in the north partes and west partes of the realme, sik as the North Iles and South Iles, for lack or fault of justiciars, and therethrow the people are almost gane wild; it is therefore statute and ordained for the acquieting of the people to justice that there be in time to cum justices and scherells depute in thay partes, as after follows: that is to say, that the justices and scherells of the North Iles have their seats and place for administration of justice in Inverness or Dingwall, as the matteres occurris to be decerned by the said olliciars: and that other justice and schereff be maid and deputes for the South Isles and they partes and to have his place and seat for the administration of justice in the Tarbar or Loch Kinkerane."

I may now refer to one of the circumstances which led to the passing of the said Act, viz., the time (1461) when Henry VI. of England had secured the assistance of the Scots against his rival Edward IV.

The latter, in order to counteract King Henry's policy, formed a league with John of Islay—Earl of Ross and Lord of the Isles—in Feb. 1462; and by this treaty, Ross and numerous vassals became the subjects of Edward, who, on his part, agreed that if Scotland should be conquered by this alliance, Ross should get for his services the country to the north of the river Forth. A few years later (1475) it was resolved to take vigorous proceedings against Ross, and he was accordingly summoned to appear for several acts of treason, among which was his seizing Rothesay and ravaging the island of Bute in 1462. On account of the formidable preparations made against him, Ross became so alarmed that in the succeeding parliament (1476) he appeared and submitted to the will of the King. It was not, however, deemed polite to crush him entirely, and a middle course was adopted. He was deprived of Ross, the castles of Inverness and Nairn, and the districts of Knapdale and Kintyre. On his submission, and engagement to keep the peace and maintain the laws of the land, the title of "Lord of the Isles" was confirmed to him. His submission, however, was only temporary, for in 1480 he entered into another treaty with Edward IV., but was afterwards forfeited in 1490. Angus, natural son of John of Islay, was then declared Lord of the Isles, if his father had no legitimate issue; but a son of this Angus, also illegitimate, usurped the title, but was forfeited in 1503.

I have already referred to the Rock of Dunaverty, as being the landing place of the three sons of Ere when they crossed from Ireland to Kintyre. Dunaverty is a stronghold on a precipitous rock at the south end of the peninsula, which was in the possession of the Macdonalds for generations. During the reign of Charles I., when the King and Parliament were at war, Macdonald, the Lord of the Isles, and some minor clans, joined themselves to Montrose, who was of the royalist party. The King in 1646 issued orders to Macdonald to lay down his arms, but this the latter refused. His forces at this time were estimated at 1400 foot and two troops of horse.

The Earl of Argyll, who was a Covenanter and had much land in Argyllshire, joined General Leslie in an engagement against Macdonald, who was defeated at Rhu-na-haorin, in the parish of Killean, and mid-way between Campbeltown and Tarbert on the west side of Kintyre.

Macdonald and his men were obliged to take refuge in Dunaverty Castle, which they held against the Covenanters for some time; but on the water which supplied the fort being cut off, the Macdonalds had to surrender. On promise of quarter by Leslie, they gave up their arms; but the General did not keep his word, for finding them all disarmed, they were treated with the utmost cruelty by the Covenanters—butchered without mercy, and thrown over the precipitous rock into the sea. Three hundred perished in this way.

The General Assembly of the Church appointed a national thanksgiving for the important service rendered by Leslie. Dunaverty is supposed to have derived its name from this bloody event, but I am of opinion that it was known as *Dunaberte* prior to this event.

Leslie's action was approved of by Parliament, and the " massacre of Dunaverty " was interpreted as being a retribution on the Macdonalds for their own unmerciful conduct in plundering and devastating the district.

By some means or other a nurse and child managed to escape from Dunaverty. She was, however, in great distress, for she knew not whither to go for safety or protection ; but she was determined, at all hazards, to protect her young charge from the sword of the Covenanters. Travelling by all the unfrequented paths and resting in the most secluded nooks she could find, she clung to her charge, and to the hope that she might still escape. But the Covenanters were scouring the district ; and just as she had sat down to rest, she was suddenly confronted by a band of those she dreaded. She was minutely searched, and on being asked if she was the mother of the child she replied in the affirmative. They, however, doubted the truth of this statement, for there seemed to be no maternal likeness between her and the child ; and one of the men gruffly remarked—*Có air bith màthair an leinibh, tha sùilean Mhic Dhòmhnuill aige*, (whoever is the mother of the child, he has Macdonalds' eyes). They did not molest her farther, but allowed her to depart. This child turned out to be Ranald Macdonald, a nephew of the Lord of the Isles, who was afterwards married to Annie Stewart, sister of the first Earl of Bute.

ASPECT OF KINTYRE.

The general aspect of Kintyre is hilly, though none of the hills attain to any great altitude—the highest, *Beinn-an-tuirce*, being about 1500 feet above sea-level. Stretching along almost the entire length of the peninsula is a double chain of hills, running parallel through the centre from north to south, forming extensive glens between, and here and there intersected by deep gorges and passes, and gradually sloping towards the sea on both sides. The scenery, especially around the coast, is beautiful and grand.

Travelling by steamer along the east coast, an excellent view is obtained both of the Arran and Kintyre shores. On leaving Tarbert, the north-east portion, for about seven or eight miles, is rugged and somewhat barren. When rounding Skipness, the ancient castle, church, and burying ground are seen, and stretching along a beautiful sandy bay is the picturesque village of Skipness. Between this point and Carradale Point, a distance of about 14 miles, is a fine stretch of shore ground, with heath-clad slopes in the rear, studded with farm steadings and beautiful patches of arable land. Sailing further down the Sound of Kilbrannon, the scenery becomes more attractive. Five miles south from Carradale is Saddell, and on a beautiful plain at the head of a sandy bay is the mansion house; a little further west is the old castle where once dwelt the "Great Macdonald" or "*Righ Fionnghal*"; and in this neighbourhood wandered the Bruce, nearly 600 years ago, when a fugitive in his own country from the sword of the Sasunnach.

The west coast of Kintyre, facing the Atlantic, is no less attractive. The distance between Campbeltown and Tarbert is 38 miles, and there is daily communication between those two places by coach. West Loch Tarbert, which separates Kintyre from Knapdale, is particularly noted for the grandeur of its surrounding scenery. Studded with beautiful islets near its head, and girt on either side with hill and glen, forest, copse and heath; its shores indented with creeks and bays, with a promontory jutting out here and there, it has no rival for the beauty and grandeur of its varied scenery among its numerous sister lochs of the West.

At the entrance of the loch, stands the hill of Dunskeig—among the highest in the district—like a majestic sentinel guarding the inlet. This hill is worthy of the attention of archæologists. On its summit—accessible only from two points—there is a vitrified fort of large dimensions; and from it can be seen on a clear day the Isle of Rathlin, over 40 miles distant. The walls of the fort are of great thickness, and built of very large stones—so large indeed, that the wonder is how they have been conveyed thither. Dunskeig signifies the hill of mockery, and there it stands with its massive and impregnable masonry facing the Atlantic, and guarding the entrance to West Loch Tarbert with a look of stern defiance and proud disdain at any unfriendly intruder who may attempt an entrance. Travelling by road between Tarbert and Campbeltown, excellent landscape and sea view can be obtained. Not only is the west coast of the peninsula seen to advantage, but the Knapdale hills to the north, and Jura, Islay, Gigha and Carra to the west. The road for the most part lies along the west shore until within a few miles of the peninsular capital, it verges to the east. That portion of it between Tarbert and Clachan, a distance of 12 miles, is very hilly, and may be compared to a gigantic " switchback railway." The rest, for about 26 miles, is very level.

TARBERT.

The village of Tarbert, next in importance to Campbeltown, is situated on the eastern part of the narrow isthmus (¾ of a mile broad) which separates the east loch from the west.

The village has within recent years thriven and increased considerably. It now has many beautiful modern villas, and is a favourite summer resort of visitors. On a hill to the rear of the village is situated the Castle of Tarbert, built in the 14th century. During a visit which King James IV. made to Kintyre in 1498, he occupied Tarbert Castle, and there granted by a charter dated 5th August 1498 the heritable keeping of the Castle of Rothesay to Ninian Stewart, then Sheriff of Bute. It was during this visit that King James held a Parliament in Campbeltown, in order, if possible, to restore order among contending clans.

Tarbert, it is said, derives its name from the Gaelic *tarruing bàta*, dragging a boat, and the incident from which this name originated is as follows:—When Donald Bane, brother to Malcolm Canmore, aspired to the throne of Scotland in 1040, he got the assistance of Magnus, King of Norway, on condition that he would get possession of all the Western Isles or places he would surround in a boat. The condition granted, the King of Norway had recourse to the following trick. He sailed up Loch Tarbert until he reached the end of the Loch, then retaining his position in the boat, he gave orders to his men to carry the boat across the narrow isthmus to the sea on the other side and sail round the peninsula. Thus encompassing Kintyre in a boat, he claimed it as part of his contract—hence its name *Tairbeart*, dragging a boat.

At a later period when Haco, King of Norway, invaded Scotland, he sent a squadron of fifty vessels against Kintyre, which was soon conquered. Two of the most powerful chiefs delivered it up to the Norwegians, swore fealty to Haco, and gave 1000 bullocks for the use of his army. Haco also sent a fleet of sixty vessels and a numerous body of land forces, under Magnus, the King of Man, and Dugal, Lord of the Isles, into Loch Long. These forces crossed the isthmus of Tarbet from the head of Loch Long to Loch Lomond by dragging their boats to the latter lake in like manner. They laid waste a large portion of the country; and Sturtas, the Norwegian bard, records the exploits of his countrymen thus:—" The persevering warriors of the whizzing spear, drew their boats across the broad isthmus; our fearless troops, the exactors of contributions with flaming swords wasted the populous islands in the lake and the mansions around its winding bays."

It is probably to this event that Sir Walter Scott refers in his " Lord of the Isles," when he says—

" Ever the breeze blows merrily,
But the galley ploughs no more the sea.
Lest, rounding wild Cantyre, they meet
The Southern foemen's watchful fleet,
They held unwonted sway ;
Up Tarbat's western lake they bore,

> Then dragged their bark the isthmus o'er
> As far as Kilmaconnell's shore
> Up on the eastern bay.
> It was a wonderous sight to see
> Topmast and pennon glitter free,
> High raised above the greenwood,
> As on dry land the galley moves,
> By cliff and copse and alder groves,
> Deep import from that Selcouth sign
> Did many a mountain seer divine;
> For ancient legends told the Gael
> That when a royal bark should sail
> O'er Kilmaconnel moss,
> Old Albyn should in fight prevail,
> And every foe should faint and quail
> Before her silver cross."

Throughout the whole district of Kintyre are to be found many remains of ancient buildings, stone monuments, and other relics of antiquarian interest. Some of the former are of circular shape, and are principally to be found on elevated ground. They are supposed to be either Druidical remains or commemorations of battles fought at the places in which they are to be found. Numerous stone cairns are also to be found in the district; these had been erected for various causes; as, where a fatal accident occurred, or where a murder had been committed. These places were marked out by stone cairns being erected, and every future passer-by contributed towards the erection by placing a stone there as he passed. It was also customary at Highland funerals, (when the funeral procession had to go a distance, to the burying-ground) for each member of the funeral party to place a stone on the spot where the coffin was deposited, while the party rested and partook of a refreshment of oat cake, cheese, and *uisgebeatha*. Sets of four took their turn in carrying the coffin, and when these became tired, the coffin was laid on the ground, the refreshment operation repeated, and another cairn erected.

Carradale takes its name from the stone monuments which are to be found in this glen—*Carragh*—a stone placed on end in form of a pillar, and *dail*—a field, hence Carradale, the field of monumental erections. This glen, which is about 15 miles north of Campbeltown, on the east side of Kintyre, is about five miles long, running partly from west to east, and then verging towards the south, and facing the Sound of Kilbrannon.

At the graveyard of Bracal, in this glen, is a *Carragh*, consisting of three large stones, where, according to tradition, the Arch Druid is buried. This man's power and influence must have been very great. He was law-giver as well as spiritual adviser, and must have imagined that the Mosaic mantle had fallen upon him. He made a law that no criminal—even a murderer—who came to him for pardon (and pardon granted) could be apprehended or held liable to punishment. For a long time after his death, his grave was to the criminal what the Cities of Refuge had been to the man-slayer in Mosaic times, and he left a law that any one guilty of a crime would be pardoned, if the guilty person were fortunate enough to reach a consecrated space near his grave before being overtaken.

These consecrated places, or sanctuaries, several of which exist throughout the Highlands, were called *Comraich*, which means an asylum or place of refuge. We find this word used in Ossian—*gabham do chomraich*—that is, "I claim thy protection." There can be no doubt but the Druids instituted those customs in imitation of some of the Mosaic institutions.

This sanctuary, to which I referred, lay between two places, designated *Slighe aoraidh*, and *Dail sleuchdaidh*; the former meaning "the way to worship," and the latter "the field of prostration," and are known to this day by these names.

Carradale glen was in possession of *Clann-Mhaoilein* (the Macmillans), for many generations; and like other clans, many a fierce struggle and bloody encounter they engaged in, in defence of their cattle and other property from the greedy grasp of the free-booter, who was ever on the search for "*creach*" or plunder. It was related that on one occasion, when these depredators had carried away the Macmillan's cattle, that the father and his three sons went in pursuit, and though greatly out-numbered, succeeded in recovering their property, after a desperate fight in which many of the free-booters were killed. But the youngest son, who was called by his father *an gille donn* (the brown lad), and who was the ancestor of the Browns of that place, not satisfied with the victory they had obtained, followed alone, after the cattle stealers and killed some more of them, taking off their heads, stringing them together and carrying them home to his father. The old man was so rejoiced at the safe return of his son, and of the additional trophy of his victory, that he exclaimed—

> "Mo laochan, mo ghille donn
> 'S tu féin an sonn a chuireadh riu."

Some time after this, the *gille donn* took ill, and his illness having affected his brain, he wandered from the house to a hill in the vicinity called *Sroin-na-h-eanachair* (the point or nose of the sagacious old person), so called from an old creature who was supposed to have inhabited the hill for generations, and whose lamentations preceded the death of members of a certain clan.

On the hill was a pit, said to be a subterraneous passage, three miles long, into which the *gille donn* fell, and was either killed or drowned; and from that time, before the death of one of his offspring, the cries of the *gille donn* were to be heard, mingled with those of the *caointeach* referred to—their united wailings causing the hill to tremble. From that day to this, *Bodach Shroin-na-h-eanachair*, is a term commonly used in the district to frighten unruly bairns.

SADDELL.

About ten miles to the north of Campbeltown is Saddell, noted for the beauty of its scenery, as well as for the associations of the remote past.

The name is supposed by some to be of Norse origin—from "Sandell," a sandy dale; but I am inclined to believe that it is made up of *samh* quiet, and *dail*, a field or plain—hence *samh-dail* a quiet or peaceful plain—a signification not inappropriate to this quiet and retired spot. In the graveyard of Saddell are buried the remains of many important personages of olden times, among whom are the great Macdonald, the mighty Somerled, and other distinguished warriors. The remains of a monastery still exist there. This monastery, which was under the jurisdiction of the Pope, was finished and endowed in 1261 by Ranald, son of Somerled, a descendant of King Kenneth. Somerled became Prince of Argyll, Lord of the Isles, and Thane of Kintyre. It was from Ranald, who had a son called Donald, that the Macdonalds sprung.

This monastery at Saddell was inhabited by Monks of the Cistercian Order, who had 13 monasteries throughout Scotland. These Monks, who were exempted from paying tithes by Pope Adrian IV. were very wealthy, and, no doubt, imposed on the credulity of the people, who entertained a high estimation of their piety. To the Monks of Saddell belonged at one time the island of Inchmarnock to the west of Bute, and now forming part of the Bute estate; but after the Reformation when the power of the Monks was suppressed, the monastery at Saddell was annexed by the Crown to the Bishopric of Argyll—the Bishop becoming proprietor of Inchmarnock.

On the island they had a Chapel and burying-place, both of which have disappeared about 50 years ago by the vandalism of a tenant farmer who appropriated part of the burying-ground as a stackyard; and the stones of the old chapel to the erection of some outhouses. A large quantity of human bones, including many entire skulls were unearthed during these operations, but they disappeared in a single night, and it was said that they were carted into the sea. I have seen, not many years ago, portions of stone coffins forming part of the structure of dykes on the same farm. The adverse fortune which followed this farmer ever after, has been attributed to his vandalic propensities.

The traditional history of the origin of Saddell Monastery is, that a certain individual had murdered a near relative, whose ghost haunted him night and day; and do what he could, he was unable to get rid of this unpleasant visitor. He at length resolved to seek the assistance of the Pope, in the hope that His Holiness might be able to remove the cause of his troubles. The Pope, of course, granted him absolution, and promised to free him from the visits of his relative's ghost, on condition that he would build a church to be consecrated by the Pope; and the site on which the church was to be built was to be between two hills and two streams. The man accordingly selected this spot at Saddell, and there erected the church according to the Pope's instructions, and it is said that his evil conscience troubled him no more. Between two burns and two hills seemed to be a favoured spot for the erection of churches in the Highlands in those days. What the hallowed influence of this situation may have been, I cannot say.

E

The church at Clachan is one of those built in a similar situation, and I have heard it said that its present is not the original site on which it was intended to be built. The original site had to be departed from, as an unseen hand, as often as a portion was built, demolished at night the work of the preceding day. This operation of erecting, re-erecting, and demolishing went on for some time until a wiser voice had guided them to the present site—then the work progressed without further interruption.

Though the power which these monks had over the people was great, yet it was not universal; and as an illustration of this, as well as of their craftiness, I may relate the following incident which, according to tradition, is associated with this locality.

THE BEADLE WHO IMPERSONATED THE DEVIL.

Among a number of others who refused to accept the Popish principles, there was one man in particular, whom the monks by much persuasion and many threatenings, endeavoured to convert; but in vain. He was, of course, denounced as a heretic, and was told that he would meet the heretic's doom—that not only would his soul be lost but that his body, after his death, would be taken possession of by the devil.

On his deathbed, this man sent for a friend in whom he had every confidence, and requested him as a last favour to watch his body carefully after he died, until he was buried—not that he was afraid of his Satanic Majesty's personal interference, but to guard against the intrigues of the wily priests, who, he knew, would practice every deceit in bringing about their own wicked designs.

His friend promised that he would faithfully perform all that he had desired. The man died, and as was the custom, his body was laid in the church previous to burial. The friend of the deceased having provided himself with some victuals, and a drop of whisky—the liquid spirit, no doubt, to aid in counteracting the advances of the ethereal spirits—and having armed himself with a gun and sword, took up his position beside the body, which he was determined to protect from the clutches of the "old fellow." For two successive days and nights, nothing extraordinary occurred, but on the third night—about midnight—he was startled from a peaceful slumber by the church door being opened. By the dim light of his candle, he perceived an object entering the church and slowly approaching him. As it drew nearer, he observed that the object presented a grim, shaggy and uncouth appearance, with two large horns projecting from the head. This answered to his own ideal of the personal appearance of his Satanic Majesty, and being fully convinced that this was no other than the devil in person on his unearthly mission, he raised his gun and challenged the intruder. He received in response a hollow sepulchral sound, accompanied with a loud rattling of chains Nearer the object approached—again it was challenged, and received the same response, only more audibly. "Another step and I'll fire, be you man or devil," said the body-watcher. Another step advanced the unearthly looking monster. The man levelled his gun and took steady aim. Click, went the flint—the powder flashed—and with a heavy thud and deep groan, down fell the horned monster to the floor. "A good shot and as good a riddance," thought the man, as he resumed his seat beside his charge, with the consciousness that he had done his duty, and as unconcerned as if he had just shot a deer on the hill.

When morning dawned, the priests jubilant of their anticipated success, entered the church, to find to their horror, that the beadle of the church, whom they had hired to personate the devil, was shot dead. They clad him in a bullock's hide, thinking that this disguise would frighten the body-watcher, and enable them to secure the body. The man was apprehended and charged with murder, but in his defence he stated that he thought it was the devil, and he considered that he was doing good service by killing him. He was accordingly acquitted.

STRANGE CUSTOMS.

Many curious customs prevailed in some of the Highland churches of those days. At this one of Saddell a human skull was suspended in a conspicuous place, the idea being to keep the congregation in remembrance of death. It was also customary (at least in some of the churches) to administer public rebuke, before the congregation on the Sabbath, to any one guilty of misconduct, and not unfrequently did it happen that the "gentry" and lairds had to submit to this mode of castigation, which, however ridiculous it may appear, no doubt had a salutary effect.

More strange still was the custom which was introduced into the church at Kilkivan, four miles west from Campbeltown. It appears that the priest or pastor, in order to settle disputes which might arise between husband and wife, had made a law that an annual meeting be held in the church, at which meetings all husbands and wives who were dissatisfied with each other were to appear. All the malcontents being assembled, the priest or pastor who presided, ordered the lights to be extinguished. This being done, they were to grope for partners until they were all paired, and when the church was again lit, as they stood paired, thus were they to live together till the next annual meeting, when a similar "grab in the dark" was resorted to. Were this practice adopted by those who maintain that "Marriage is a failure," they might be able to find a remedy.

Kilkivan, the church referred to, is said to be the last of those ancient churches in Kintyre in which public worship was held before the Reformation. The name is derived from Cill-Chaomhain, the church of the gentle or meek.

About three miles N. E. of Campbeltown are the old church and burying-ground of Kilchusalan, so named, according to tradition, from Cusalan, a daughter of a King of Spain, who died on board of one of her father's vessels which was cruising around the Sound of Kilbrannon, and was buried in this place. In this church is a large stone with a hole in the centre, called the " stone of reconciliation" (*cluch-na-reite*), as through it, eloped lovers were reconciled to their offended parents and friends. If the eloped pair were successful in reaching the church, and grasping hands through the hole in the stone of reconciliation (*clach-na reite*) before being overtaken, the offence was pardoned, and it was held unlawful to prevent the marriage.

[12TH FEBRUARY, 1889.]

At the meeting of the Society held on this date, Rev. Mr. Blair, M.A., read a paper on *Oidhche air Chéilidh*. Mr. Blair's paper was as follows:—

OIDHCHE AIR CHEILIDH.

Is "oidhche air chéilidh" a thug mi air an òraid agam, a chionn 's gu bheil a mhiann orm a leigeil ris duibh mar a b' àbhaist do na seann Ghàidheil an geamhradh a chur seachad ann an dòigh bhuannachdail agus aighearaich; 'us cha 'n urrainn domh so a dheanamh air dòigh a b' fheàrr na luchd-na-céilidh a chruinneachadh ann an tigh aoin de na coimhearsnaich agus leigeil leotha féin an sgeul innseadh.

Bha a' chéilidh a' teagasg nan Gaidheal agus 'g an deanamh fiosrach an uair a bha cothromanna eile a dh' easbhuidh orra. Tha e iomadh uair ag cur ioghnaidh air muinntir cia mar a bha e comasach do na Gaidheil, an uair nach robh sgrìobhadh cho coitcheann 'n am measg, cuimhne a bhi aca air seann bhàrdachd agus sgeulachdan; ach tha a' chéilidh a' mìneachadh a' ghnothaich. Aig a' chéilidh bha sgeulachdan air an aithris, bàrdachd air a cur an céill, agus toimhseachain 'us beuradaireachd a' dol, a bha teagasg an dà chuid

geurachd inntinn agus eòlais nach bu bheag. Cha b'
urrainn muinntir a bha aineolach air a' chleachdainn
so, a thuigsinn cia mar a bha còlas a' teachd a nuas le
beul-aithris a bha ach beag cho neo-chaochlaideach 'us
ged a robh e air a sgrìobhadh. Deir cuid—"Cia mar
a b' urrainn maitheas no eòlas a bhi aca agus gun a'
Bheurla aca!"—mar gu'm b' i a' Bheurla an aon
chànain a bha air an t-saoghal—"cha robh sgoilean aca
'us cha robh paipear-naigheachd a' tighinn a stigh gach
latha: cia mar a b' urrainn iadsan eòlas ni air bith a
bhi aca?"

Ach ged nach robh sgoil anns gach dorus, agus
paipear-naigheachd agus leabhraichean anns gach tigh,
bha iomadh dòigh air fòghlum fhaotainn agus air
geurachd a chumail beò. Bha e 'n a chleachdainn,
mar a tha fhios agaibh, aig na Gaidheil cruinneachadh
ann an tigh na céilidh; agus tha sinne an nochd a' dol
a shuidheadh cùl an doruis a dh' éisdeachd ris na bheil
a' dol aig a' chéilidh, agus an oidhche a chur seachad
le òrain, le sgeulachdan, le cleasan, le naigheachdan,
agus le feala-dhà. Theagamh gu 'm biodh Niall
sunndach, an tàillear, an sin, a bha còlach air gach
seanachas a bha dol feadh na dùthcha; oir cha robh
suiridh no pòsadh eadar dà chlach na dùthcha air nach
biodh Niall min-eòlach. Mur a biodh esan an sin
bhiodh Dòmhnull frionach an greusaiche ann le
freagairtean cho geur ris an sgian-leathraich aige, agus
cho biorach ris a' mhinidh. Timchioll air an tàillear
chruinnicheadh gillean agus nigheanan a' bhaile gu
léir. Bhiodh Eóghan airean ag càradh acfhuinn nan

each ; Alasdair iasgair a' tapadh dhubhan, no a'
deanamh mhaothar ; Calum clobair a' cur suas air
cromaig aluinn, chuilinn ; Baldi buachaille ag
uidheamachadh camain sheilich ; Pàruig mór, an
sgalag, a sgrìobadh shlat air son cliabh mòna ; agus
Gibi nan gèadh 'n a shìneadh ann an cùil na mona 'us
ag cur caorain thioraim an dràsd 's a rithist air teine,
agus ag cumail nam madadh fo smachd. Bhiodh na
mnathan le an obair féin aca ; bean an taighe a
snìomh ; Mór ruadh ag càrdadh ; Ceit Bhaldi a'
Chladaich a' fitheadh stocaidh ; agus a' bhanarach mhòr
ag càradh an t-siolachain.

'Nuair a bhiodh iad mar so cruinn gus am biodh an
cidsean mór farsuinn cho làn 'sa chumadh e, 'us na h-uile
garrach 'us patach balaich a b' urrainn faotainn a stigh,
le a shùilean 'us a chluasan fosgailte, a' faicinn 's a
cluinntinn gach ni a bha ri fhaghail, thòiseachadh an
seanachas. Bhiodh freagairt gheur shìos ; agus radh
tapaidh shuas ; toimhseachan agus sean-fhacal ; òran
agus ùr-sgeul ; gus an saoileadh tu gur ann a bha thu
ann an Oil-thigh nan Druidhean, agus Niall sunndach
an tàillear 'n a àrd-fhear-teagaisg ann. "C" uin a
chuala tu fios o d' mhac a tha 's an arm, a Pheigi ?"
arsa fear-an-taighe ri seana mhnaoi chòir a thainig a
stigh. "Ma ta, dhuine, fhuair mi litir an dé uaith,"
arsa Peigi. "Am bheil e gu math ?" "'S e a tha, 'us
a' faotainn air aghaidh gu math. Saoil sibh féin nach
d' rinn iad *admiral* deth." "*Admiral*!" arsa fear-an-
taighe, "nach ann 's an arm a tha e, agus 's ann air
muir a tha *admiral*" "Ma ta, dhuine, cha 'n 'eil mise

cinnteach ás an ainm ; ach 's e thuirt Seumas anns an litir gur e *admiral*, no *general*, no *corporal* a bh' ann— 's e *ral* a bh' ann co-dhiù."

Bha 'm feala-dhà a nis air saod. "Cha mhór" arsa Niall sunndach "nach 'eil Peigi cho dona 's a bha Cairistìona mhór a bha 'n Tormasdadh, 'nuair a chaidh i mach do Ghlascho 's a thug i dhachaidh an sgeul gu 'n do rinneadh *General* do mhac Bhaldi ruaidh a bha 'n Grùillean. Bha bùth aig mac Bhaldi ann an sràid ris an abradh iad am Margadh Salainn, crioman beag o 'n each odhar. Bha na h-uile cothlamadh aig mac Bhaldi anns a' bhùth ; agus chuir e os cionn an doruis aige ann an litrichean móra, buidhe, còmhla r' a ainm féin, na facail *'General merchant.'* Bha cuid de sgoil aig Cairistìona ; agus leugh i so. 'Ubh, ubh' ars ise, 'nach e Glascho fhéin an t-àite gu faotainn a suas anns an t-saoghal ! Ma ta, ma ta, cha 'n 'eil neach 's am bith gun dà latha, 'n uair a rinn iad *General* do mhac Bhaldi ruaidh !" " An cuala tu" arsa Calum ciobair, "mar a rinn iad breitheamh de Chairistìona aon uair air a' Ghalldachd ?" "Cha chuala mi fein" arsa Niall, "tha mi cinnteach gu 'm b'e sin lagh Chill-ma-cheallaig, an lagh a dhèanadh ise." "Ma ta, thug i binn gle mhath a mach ; cha b' e lagh nam ban mu 'n teallaich a bh' ann." " 'N ann an Glascho a bha sin ?" "O, cha 'n ann. 'S ann a bha e ann an Cill-Mhaol-Chaluim, no Govan, no aon de na h-àitean fada ás sin. Tha fhios agaibh tha bùthan aca air Ghalldachd anns am faigh thu ni air bith a thogras tu r' a itheadh—tighean itheannaich, their iad riutha. Bha Cairistìona mhór ann an aon diubh so ag gabhail a dinneir aon uair—buntàta 'us sgadan, agus marag dhubh a ghabh i. Coma co dhiù thàinig duine bochd a stigh aig nach robh ach glé bheag 'n a phòca. Sheas e greis mhath a' mealltainn fàile chùbhraidh an lòin nach robh e an comas da a cheannach. An déigh dha seasamh tacan, thug e làmh air falbh. Rinn fear a bhùth greim air, 'us cha leigeadh e mach e gus am pàigheadh e air son an fhàile a fhuair e. Dhiùlt an duine so a dheanamh, 'us bha iad brath dol thar a' chéile 'n uair a chòrd iad gu 'm fàgadh iad an gnothach gu binn Cairistìona. 'Am bheil bonn idir agad?' ars ise ris an duine bhochd. 'Tha dìreach dà sgilinn agam,' ars esan. 'Dhòmh-sa iad' ars ise. 'Nall a nis dà thrinnsear' ars ise ri fear a' bhùth. Fhuair i so. Chuir i an dà sgilinn eadar an dà thrinnsear, 'us chrath i iad ri cluais fear a' bhuth. Thug i 'n sin an dà sgilinn air an ais do 'n duine bhochd, ag ràdh 'so t' airgiod; o 'n a bha thusa air do bheathachadh le fàile a' bhìdh aige-san, tha esan a nis pàighte le fuaim t' airgid-sa.' Nach math a' bhinn a thug Cairistìona a mach!" "Ma ta, seadh" ars Alasdair iasgair, "thug i leasan do fhear a'-bhuth co dhiù, a cheart cho math 's a thug Gaidheal aon uair do mharsanta Sasunnach. Bha aodaichean an crochadh aig dorus bùth an t-Sasunnaich agus mir paipeir air a cheangal riù ag ràdh 'an t-aodach so air leth phrìs.' Chaidh an Gaidheal a steach 'us dh' fheòraich e 'Ciod is prìs do 'n bhall so?' 'Tha dìreach cóig tasdain' ars am marsanta. 'Ceangail suas air mo shon-sa e' ars an Gàidheal. 'N uair a fhuair e fo achlais e, chuir e sìos bonn leth-chrun. ''S e cóig tasdain a phrìs.' 'Tha fhios agam air sin; ach thubhairt thu gu 'n robh

iad air an reic air leth phris, agus 's e leth-chrun leth
cóig tasdain.' Chaidh iad gu lagh 'us thugadh binn ás
leth a' Ghàidheil ; 'us chaidh comhairle a thoirt air a'
mharsanta gun a ris 'leth-phris' a chur air aodach."

"Tha sin a' toirt a'm chuimhne" arsa Baldi buachaille,
"nì a chuala mi Blàir ann an Glascho aon uair ag innseadh
aig an t-*Soirree* Ileach. "Dé tha ann an *soirree*?" arsa
Gibi nan gèadh. "Tha" arsa Niall taillear, "an t-ainm
Frangach air son suiridh." "Ciod mar bhitheas iad 'g a
dheanamh?" arsa Gibi. "Cuist, a gharraich! 'us bi
a 'd thosd" arsa Ceit Bhaldi a' Chladaich. "Dé an
gnothach a tha agadsa a bhi cainnt air nithean de 'n
t-seòrsa sin?" "Cuist, a Cheit" arsa Mór ruadh, " 'us
leig leis a' bhalach tàmh. Air leam gu 'm bu mhaith
a bhi ann ma bhiodh an t-suiridh a' dol : nach eil
fhios agad gu 'm biodh na h-uile ni ceart, neo cha
bhiodh am ministir Blàir e fhein ann. Nach innis
thu dhuinn a Neill dé a tha ann an *soirree*?" "Tha
coinneamh mhór far am bheil na ceudan cruinn ag òl
tea 'us ag itheadh arain mhilis 'us *raisins* 'us ùbhlan ;
agus òraidean air an toirt seachad ; 'us òrain ghasda
bhinn air an seinn." "N e sin e uile?" arsa Ceit.
"Ma 's e cha 'n eil an gnothach idir mar a shaoil mise
a bha e." "B' iad na *raisins*, agus na h-ùbhlan a b' fhèarr
leam fhéin deth" arsa Gibi. "Ach dé chuala tu Blàir
ag ràdh?" "Ma ta, 's iomadh rud a thubhairt e, oir 's
ann air an teanga aige a tha 'n ruith. Cha teid tàmh
oirre. Ach 's e an ni a bha mi dol a dh' innseadh
dhuibh," arsa Baldi, "ni a dh' innis e mar dhearbhadh
air geurad nan Gaidheal. Bha balach Ileach aon uair
ag iasgach, 'us chaidh e suas gu tigh tuathanaich.

"Ach!" ars' Eòghan airean, "tha Blàir daonnan ag innseadh na naigheachd sin." "Air t' aghaidh a Bhaldi," arsa Niall. "Cha mhisde sgeul math innseadh dà uair. Cha chuala mi fhèin riamh e." "Chaidh an gille suas. Bha toil aig an tuathanach fhaighinn a mach prìs a' bhuntàta. 'Dé a tha agaibh air a' bhuntàta 's a' bhaile mhòr?' 'Tha rùisg.' 'Cha 'n e sin a tha mise ciallachadh, ach dé a th' agaibh air a' bharaille?' 'Tha cearcaill.' 'Uds! cha 'n e sin a tha mi ag ràdh, ach dé a tha am baraille ag cosd?' 'Tha an t-eàrrach?' 'Cha 'n e sin a tha mise ciallachadh ach dé prìs a' bharaille?' 'Tha prìs nan clàr, nan cearcall agus saothair a' chùbair.' "Nach bu gheur am balach" arsa Calum ciobair. "Cha mhòr nach robh e cho math ri Iain Mac Còdruim am bàrd Uidhisteach. Bha esan ro ghéur, 'us tha mòran de 'n t-seanachas aige air chuimhne ann an Uidhist fathast; agus 's mór am beud nach robh iad air an cruinneachadh agus air an cumail air chuimhne mu 'n teid an call uile gu léir." "Innis duinn cuid diubh, a Neill."

"Chuala sibh mar a labhair e ri Mac-a'-Phearsoin a bha ag cruinneachadh sgeulachdan Oisein. Chuir e corruich nach beag air Mac-a'-Phearsoin, 'us cha 'n 'eil teagamh agam nach do chaill e iomadh rann 'us dàn air tàilleamh' àrdain. Thachair Mac-a'-Phearsoin air a' bhàrd. 'Am bheil dad agad air an Fhéinn,' ag ciallachadh an robh sgeulachdan air bith aige mu 'n déighinn. 'Ma ta, cha 'n 'eil' arsa Iain, a' toirt seadh eile as a' bhriathran, 'us ged a bhitheadh 's beag a b' fheaird mi dol g' a iarraidh an diugh.' Cha d' fheòraich Mac-a'-Phearsoin tuillidh de Iain."

"Tha e air a ràdh gu 'n deachaidh Mac Mhaighstir Alasdair aon uair a dh' fhaicinn Iain. Thachair e air beagan astair o 'n dorus aige féin. 'An aithne dhuit Iain mac Còdruim?' ars an Domhnullach. 'Is aithne gu ro-mhaith' ars Iain. 'Am bheil fhios agad am bheil e stigh?' 'Ma ta, bha e stigh an uair a bha mise steach, 'us cha d' rinn mi ach tighinn a mach.' 'Caithidh mi an oidhche nochd maille ris ma 's àbhaist aoidhean a bhi aige.' 'Tha mi ag creidsinn nach bi e falamh dhiubh sin cuideachd ma bhitheas na cearcan a' breth'—a' deanamh cluich air an fhacal *aoidhean*."

"Bha e uair eile ann an Tobar-Mhoire a'm Muile. Thàinig muinntir a' bhaile a nuas gus a' chladaich a dh' fhaicinn ciod e am bàta coimheach a thàinig gu port. 'Co ás a thug sibh an t-iomram 'illean?' arsa fear de na Muilich. 'Thug ás na gàirdeanan' ars Iain. ''N ann o thuath sibh?' 'Cuid o thuath 's cuid o thighearnan' fhreagair am bàrd."

"Thug Donnachadh bàn Mac an t-Saoir bàrr air sin" arsa Calum ciobair. "Dh' fheòraich neach dheth aon uair—'An tusa rinn Beinn Dòrain?' 'Ud, ud, cha mhi; ach thug mi greis air a moladh.' 'Tha thu geur 'ille; is mòr am beud nach robh an dà theanga a' d cheann.' 'Ma ta, nam biodh an dà chànain anns a' bhun a th' agam, dheanainn feum,' arsa Donnachadh."

"Cha chreid mi," arsa Para mór, "nach robh am pìobaire càm, Mac Eachainn a bha 'n Ile, cho geur ri aon diu." "Dé thubhairt esan?" arsa Niall. "Bha siod uair a bha beagan iorguill ann an Ile mu chur buntàta ás an dùthaich 'n uair a bha e gann anns an eilean. Chaidh cuid a thoirt gu mòd a thaobh na cùise.

Am measg nam fianuisean a bha air an ceasnachadh bha am pìobaire càm. 'Am faca tu soitheach buntàta air a leithid so de latha ann an Loch a' Chnoic?' 'Co leis a chithinn i?' 'Nach fhaiceadh tu le 'd shùilean!' 'Cha 'n 'eil sùilean agam' (cha robh aig Iain ach leth-shuil). 'Am faca tu le 'd shùil, ma ta, soitheach buntàta a leithid so de latha ann an Loch a' Chnoic?' 'Ma ta, cha 'n fhaca mise' ars Iain. 'Ciod a tha thu ag ràdh! cuimhnich gu 'm bheil thu air do mhionnan' ars am fear-lagha. 'Tha mi ag ràdh siod' ars Iain. 'Nach fhaca tu,' ars am fear-lagha a rithist, 'soitheach buntàta ann an Loch a' Chnoic?' 'Cha 'n fhaca mi fhéin' ars Iain. Bha am fear-lagha a' fàs mi-fhaighidinneach 'us mhaoith e Iain a chur ann am prìosan air son tàmailt a thoirt do 'n chùirt Ach bha Iain gun eagal gun fhiamh. Thug am fear-lagha ionnsaidh eile air, 'us mu dheireadh, an déigh móran ceasnachaidh, fhreagair Iain gu ciùin réidh—'Ma ta, cha 'n fhaca mise soitheach buntàta riamh; ach chunnaic mi soitheach fiodha luchdaichte le buntàta." 'Chaidh na bha 's a chùirt 'n an tridheanan ag gàireachdaich, agus cha deachaidh ceisd tuilleadh a chur air Iain." "Ma ta," arsa Baldi buachaille, "chuala mi na bheir bàrr air sin. Bha aon de na Morairean dearga aig an robh droch rùn anabarrach do na Gaidheil, aig mòd ann an Ionbhar-aora. B' e barail a' Mhoraire so nach d' innis Gaidheal an fhìrinn uair air bith ach 'n uair nach rachadh aige air amas air breug; agus eadhon, an uair a dh' innseadh e an fhìrinn, gu 'n rachadh e fada timchioll an tuim mu 'n chùis. Bha aig an àm Morair Cholasa 'n a dhuine òg, 'us bha e ag eadar-theangachadh fianuis seann duine a bha air a cheasnachadh a thaobh tabaid eiginn. Bha fhios aig Donnachadh Cholasa air barail a' Mhoraire a thaobh nan Gaidheal, agus rùnaich e gu 'n cuireadh e dorran air a' Bhreitheamh. Faodaidh sinn a bhi cinnteach, ma ta, nach do rinn e na freagairtean aig an t-seann duine a bheag ni bu ghiorra mar a dh' eadar-theangaich e iad. Am measg cheistean eile dh' fheòraichteadh de 'n t-seann duine— 'Cia mar a bha e teachd beò?' Chuir Donnachadh Cholasa a cheisd ris an t-seann duine agus fhreagair esan—'Ma ta, abradh sibhse ris gur iomadh sibht agus seòl a dh' fheumas duine bochd a dhèanamh mu 'm faigh e aran.' 'Ciod a tha e ag ràdh?' ars am Moraire. Dh' innis fear Cholasa sin da. 'Nach d' thubhairt mi riut' ars am Moraire, 'nach do fhreagair Gaidheal ceisd gu dìreach riamh. Abair ris—am faca e le a shùilean féin am prìosanach a' bualadh an fhir eile.' 'Ma ta, a Mhaighstir Donnachadh ars an seann duine, 'am feòraich sibhse dheth—mur am faca mi le 'm shùilean féin e, cò na suilean leis am faicinn e."

"Cha 'n 'eil sin ceàrr;" arsa Niall sunndach, "cha mhòr nach robh e cho gèur ri Para buidhe, Mac-'Ill' Andrais. Bha Pàruig dèigheil air a' ghunna ; agus is iomadh coileach dubh a thug e dhachaidh gun fhios do 'ı mhuinntir a bha dìon na frìth. Ach mu dheireadh rinneadh greim air Pàruig. Chaidh a thoirt gu cùirt. Thug am forsair a mhionnan gu 'm faca e Pàruig a' losgadh air tunnaig fhiadhaich agus 'g a marbhadh. Rug e air 'us an tunnag aige air spàig. 'Stad, stad, a dhuine choirbte!' deir Pàruig: 'tha thu an dèigh mionnan-eithich a thoirt; 's ann a bha ann *dròc*.'

Bha Pàruig uair eile air a thuras 'us thachair ministir na sgìreachd air. Cha robh Pàruig anabarrach dèigheil air a' mhinistir. Bha am ministir air a bhi cur air chois mòran riaghailtean ùra, 'us bha mòran de 'n t-sluagh car diombach dheth air son a bhi cho cruaidh orra. Bha Pàruig a' dol a ghabhail seachad gun urram an latha a thoirt do 'n mhinistir; ach cha do leig am ministir seachad e. 'Co ás a thug thu a' choiseachd, 'ille?' 'Thug ás mo chasan.' 'Co ás a thàinig thu?' 'Tha sin a' m dhéigh.' 'C' àit am bheil thu dol?' 'Tha sin romham.' 'C' àit am bheil thu fuireachd?' 'Ann am bothan eadar dhà uisge.' 'C' àit am bheil am bothan sin?' 'Eadar talamh 'us athar.' Chaidh an seanachas mar so air aghaidh, 'us dh' fhairtlich air a' mhinistir am fiosrachadh a bha dhìth air fhaotainn. Ghabh e corruich nach bu bheag. 'Tha thu briathrach 'ille; ach bheir mise gu cunntas fhathast thu.' 'Ma ta, le 'r cead,' arsa Pàruig, 'ma tha bheag agaidh orm, deanaibh a mach 'ur cunntas agus pàighidh mise sibh."

"O 'n a thug thu iomradh air ministir" arsa Baldi, "an cuala tu an fhreagairt a thug Baldi burraidh air a' mhinistir mhòr 'n uair a chaidh e a dh' iarraidh baistidh air?" "Ma ta, cha chuala; ach tha mi cinnteach gu 'm biodh i ait." "Tha fhios agad tha Baldi bochd gu math aineolach, 'us cha robh na ceistean gu ro mhath aige. 'N uair a dh' fheòraich am ministir dheth—'Co dhà is còir am baisteadh a fhrithealadh?' 'Dhòmh-sa, dhòmh-sa' arsa Baldi. 'Ud, ud,' ars am ministir còir, 'Cha 'n eil thu comasach an leanabh a chumail ri baisteadh.' 'A chumail ri baisteadh! Chumainns e ged an robh e cho trom ri gamhainn tairbh.' Bha Baldi cho aineolach ri cailleach chòir a bh' ann am Meadar-loch. Bha am ministir ag ceasnachadh, 'us chuir e a' cheisd so oirre-sa—'Co a thug thu á tìr na h-Eiphit agus á tigh na daorsa?' 'S i an fhreagairt a fhuair e—'Och, och, mo mhalachd air luchd nam brèug 'us na casaid a thog a leithid de thuaileas ormsa! Sin àite anns nach robh mise riamh. O'n a rugadh mi cha robh mi ni b' fhaide deas na baile an Obain."

"An cuala tu riamh iomradh, a Nèill" arsa Calum Ciobair, "air Pàl a bha 'n a ghille, ri linn do sheanair, aig ministir na Cille-moire?" "Ma ta, 's mi chuala," arsa Niall; "nach ann ann an tigh piuthar-màthar do 'm sheanair a bha e féin 's am ministir ag cur seachad na h-oidhche 'n uair a chaidh iad thar a chéile. Cha robh ach aon leabaidh chòrr anns an tigh; 'us chaidh Pàl 'us am ministir a chur innte. Luidh iad cas m'a seach, ceann Phàil ri casan na leapa. An déigh dhoibh dol a laidheadh, ars' am ministir ri Pàl—'am bheil thu gu math aig mo chasan, a Phàil?' 'Tha le 'r cead,' arsa Pàl—'am bheil sibhse gu math aig mo chasan-sa?' Ghabh am ministir an gnothach cho àrdanach, gu 'n robh esan 'n a laidheadh aig casan Phàil, 'us gu 'n do bhreab e Pàl a mach às an leabaidh. Bha uair eile a thachair ni a chuir am ministir gu nàire nach bu bheag. Bha e car déigheil air an deoch. Cha robh deur 's an tigh. Bha e domhain am fiachaibh do bhean an tigh-òsda. Cha tugadh i tuillidh air dàil do 'n mhinistir. Chuir e, air maduinn na Sabaid, Pàl far an robh i dh' fheuch am maothaicheadh e i gu aon leth-bhodach a

F

thoirt dà air dàil. Dh' fhuirich Pàl fada. B' éiginn toiseachadh air an t-seirbhis mu 'n do thill Pàl. 'N uair a thàinig e stigh air dorus na h-eaglais bha am ministir a' labhairt air puing éiginn, 'us bha e dol a thoirt seachad barail an Abstoil mu 'n chùis. 'Cluinnidh sinn a nis ciod a tha aig Pàl ri ràdh mu 'n chùis.' Arsa Pàl 's e toirt sùil suas air a' chrannaig— 'Cha 'n 'eil diog aig Pàl ri ràdh ach nach toir bean an tigh-òsda deur tuillidh dhuibh gus am pàigh sibh na bheil oirbh.' Tha mi làn-chinnteach gu 'm b' fheàrr leis a' mhinistir gu 'n robh teanga Phàil air leantainn ri ghial mu 'n do labhair e."

Mar so bha beurachd agus feala-dhà a' dol air an aghaidh ann an tigh na céilidh gus an robh an t-suipeir deas. Chaidh am buntàta a chur air saod; 'us thug na coimhearsnaich a bha stigh làmh air falbh. "Ud, suidhibh" arsa fear an taighe "'us gabhaibh roinn de na bheil a' dol. Cha 'n 'eil sinn air fàs cho Gallda fhathast 'us nach toir sinn comaidh do charaid. Deanaibh suidhe; 's gann an t-earrach anns an cunntar na faochagan." Shuidh iad 'us rinn fear an taighe altachadh snasmhor sòlumaichte; ach cha do chuir sin tosd air beul Nèill. "An cuala sibh" ars esan, "mar a rinn gille Ileach air bodach Gallda ann an àm an fhoghair? B' àbhaist do 'n bhodach altachadh gu math fada a dheanamh; 'us bha leisg air urrad ùine a chosd 'us latha ceutach ann air son na buana; 'us iarrar e air a' ghille Ileach. Thòisich am balach Ileach air Beinn Dòrain a ghabhail le guth stolda, sòlumaichte; 'us 'n uair a ràinig e air a' chrìch, thòisich e aig an toiseach a rithist. Theid mise am bannaibh dhuibh nach d' iarr an Gall air Dòmhnull altachadh a dhèanamh 'n a dhéigh sin."

"Ag iomradh air altachadh, tha sin ag cur a'm chuimhne" arsa Calum Ciobair "ni a thubhairt caileag Ghaidhealach aon uair ri seana mhaighstir a bha aice. Chaidh i a choinnhead a seana mhaighstir aon uair, seachd no ochd de bhliadhnaichean an déigh dhi fhàgail. Thug iad oirre fuireach r' a dinneir. Bha ise airson a bhi anabarrach modhail agus ni eiginn gasda a ràdh ri a seana mhaighstir. An déigh an altachaidh,—'A dhuine,' ars ise, 'nach ann agaibh a tha chuimhne mhath: 's e sin dìreach a cheart altachadh a b' àbhaist duibh a ràdh 'n uair a bha mise an so o chionn ochd bliadhna."

"Chuala sibh" ars Alasdair iasgair "achuinge a bha do ghnath air a cur suas le ceann-feadhna àraidh. Bha e air a shàrachadh le cuid d 'a choinnhearsnaich, 'us ghuidh e—

    O shannt nan Caimbeulach,
    O fhearg nan Drumonach,
    O uaill nan Greumach,
    'S o sgleò nam Murraighean,
    A Thì mhóir dìon sinn."

'N uair a chaidh crìoch air an t-suipeir rinn iad riombal mu 'n teine 'us thoisich iad air cleasan gun lochd. Bha greis air a thoirt air toimhseachain agus air cleasan a bha freagarrach gu fòghlum a thoirt. 'S e "Ceann a chapuill bhàin" a cheud chleas air an d' thug iad làmh. "Seachad so" arsa Niall. "Dé tha so?" arsa Calum. "Ceann a' chapuill bhàin" arsa Para mòr. "C' àite 'n robh i 'n raoir?' ars' Alasdair iasgair.

"Bha i 'n raoir an Cille-Chiarain" arsa fear eile. Agus mar so chaidh an cleas mu 'n cuairt, ag cur ceann a' chapuill bhàin do gach Cill an Albainn 's an Eirionn gus an fairtleachadh air neach Cill ùr air bith ainmeachadh. An sin rachadh geall a thoirt uaith 'us dh' fheumadh e peanas éiginn a sheasamh mu 'm faigheadh e air ais an geall. Theagamh gu'm b' e am peanas rann a dheanamh ; no ùrsgeul a ghabhail ; no òran a sheinn ; no ni éiginn de 'n t-seòrsa sin. Bha, trid a' chleas so, eòlas air ainmean agus suidheachadh àitean, neo mar their sinn anns a' Bheurla, "Geography" air a chur a 'm meud.

Cleas eile car de 'n cheart seòrsa air an robh greis air a thoirt d' am b' ainm "Laora-pocan." Ghabh Para mòr slat 'n a làimh agus bhuin e ri glùn gach aoin 's a' chuideachd ag ràdh an rainn so—"Laora-pocan, lara-pocan ; pocan seipein ; seipein Seòmaid ; dà mheur mheadhoin ; meur mhic Iain ; Dùghall glas nach leigeadh às, a cheann 's a chaola ; caol na slaite ; dhuine so, a dhuin' ud eile ; fhir so bhos na coise deise, stoc a stigh an dalmag." Am fear air an tuiteadh an stoc a stigh, na 's lugha na gu 'n glaodhadh e mach "hura, hura" mu 'm bualadh an t slat e, rachadh geall a thoirt deth. 'N uair a bha fear an déigh fir dhiubh a mach, chaidh ainmean a thoirt orra—"Slabhruidh òir" no "Slabhruidh airgid." Chaidh an sin ceangal a chur air sùilean fir dhiubh 'us chaidh e air a ghlùinean 'us geall a chumail os a chionn leis a' cheisd—"Ciod a nithear ris an neach d' am buin an geall so ?" Bheireadh esan an sin a mach am peanas a bha ri dhèanamh air: air-neò chumadh fear an geall os a chionn a' feòraich na ceisde mar so—

"Geall, geall bòidheach; geall, geall briagha!
"Tomhais cò d' am buin e,
"'S gheibh thu as a' chliabh.

Bheireadh esan oidhirp air so a dhèanamh. Theireadh e "do Shlabhruidh òir." "'S brèugach dhuit e"; 'us rachadh peanas èiginn a dhèanamh air.

Mar so chaidh an fheala-dhà air a h-aghaidh. Bha rannan eile a bha air an cur aig àm an àite "Laorapocan" mar a bha an rann so. "A hipill, a hapuill; a chaorain, a chapuill; a sheana mhaol iaruinn; fiacail Fhaolain; buille muigh, buille stigh; co meud mac a rug thu 'n raoir? Mac an dì, mac an dò; buille bò, beucan; buille beag a chionn na slaite; crup a stigh an dalmag." Neo bhitheadh an rann so air a ràdh. "Laorabuin, làrabuin; buin iall; iall a bhreabain; breabain sùileach, sùileach; sgilleam, sgilleam bheireach; thor na caillich; port Aonastail, port Anastail; port Mhic Guaire; Guaire eeiteach, fear Dhun-Eidinn; giobastanach, gobastanach, cleit."

De 'n cheart seòrsa bha an rann air am bheil sinn uile eòlach—ris an abrar "Murachadh 'us Mionachadh." Ach cha cheadaich an ùine dhuinn labhairt orra so, 'us feumaidh sin tarruing gu codhunadh: agus ni sinn so le deoch an doruis a thoirt seachad. Mar a bha a' chluich seachad agus a bhitheadh a' chuideachd a' sgaoileadh— gu sònruichte na 'm b' e cuideachd òil a bha ann— theireadh fear an taighe—

"Nis is mithich sgur de 'n òl
"Fhad 's a tha ciall againn gu sgur;
"'Us mur 'eil sibh toilichte le òl,
"Tha 'n amhainn mhòr am muigh.
"Deoch an doruis, deoch an t-sonais,
"Deoch an deagh thurais.
"Ni-math gu 'n robh againn;
"Ni-dona gu 'n robh uainn;
"Air ghaol sith 's air sgath sonais,
"Thugaibh deoch an doruis dhuinn."

Ach ged a fhuair sibh deoch an doruis, leigibh leam, ann an aon fhacal, a ràdh gu 'n robh buaidh mhath aig na coinneamhan so air na Gaidheil. Faodaidh e bhi gu 'm bheil a nis tuillidh eòlais againn na bha acasan: ach 's i mo bharail gu 'n robh moran tuillidh blàthais 'us caoimhnis, seadh 'us fearalais 'n am measg na tha 'n ar measg-ne. Agus, ged nach robh na cothroman aca cho lìonmhor ris na sochairean a tha againne, cha 'n 'eil mi cinnteach nach robh urrad de thoradh na fìor dhiadhachd ri amas orra 's à tha 'n ar measg an diugh. Tha e fìor nach robh srannail an eich iarrainn ri chluintinn mar a th' ann an diugh air leitir Chruachain agus fuaim rothan a' charbaid a' dùsgadh mac-talla à sgàrnaich nan garbh-chrioch. Cha robh bàta smùid anns gach port agus fios-dealain anns gach ceàrn. Ach "bha aiteas 'us àgh feadh nan gleann." Mur an robh mòran beartais aca, bha aca nì nach ceannaich òir a' chruinne ché: bha caoimhneas ri bochd agus iochd ri uireasach; bha braithreachas agus toileachas inntinn ri amas orra anns na glinn.

Bha na tighearnan fearainn, mu 'n d' fhòghluim iad gnàthan Shasuinn, a tuinneachadh mar athraichean agus mar bhraithrean am measg an t-sluaigh, ag aoradh anns an aon eaglais leò, a' measgadh leò 'n am fearas-cuideachd, 'us a' deanamh co-fhaireachduinn riu 'n am bròn. Bha, mar so, ard agus iosal air an aonadh ann an dàimh dhlùith agus chairdeil. Bha mòraltachd àrd 'n am measg. Bha barail air lagh 'us air ceartas aca a chum iad gun aramach air bith a dheanamh an uair a thàinig cruadal, fuadach 'us deuchainn orra. Ged a chaidh iomadh gleann fhagail fàsail agus iomadh srath tarbhach a lomadh de shìol nan curaidh a sheasdlùth mar lèine chneis air taobh an cinn-fheadhna, gidheadh, cha chualas mort a bhi air a dhèanamh air tighearna fearainn no maor grùinnd. Cha 'n ann mar a tha muinntir eile a' deanamh a rinn na Gaidheil; dh' fhalbh iad le cridheachan brònach agus spioradan dubhach, ach dh' fhalbh iad gu ciuin gu dachaidhean ùra a dheanamh deas dhoibh fein 'us d' an sliochd ann an dùthchannan cèin. Agus an uair a thàinig bochdainn 'us gainne ghoirt 'n an caramh, cha robh éiridh a mach air bith 'n am measg; cha robh goid chaorach no bristeadh bhùithean; cha robh meirleadh no spùinneadh 'n am measg. Ged a bha cuid diubh cho bochd nach robh aca ach duileasg a' chladaich neo bàrr an fhraoich bhadanaich ri àm na cruadail ud mar lòn, gidheadh, le faighidinn, ghiùlain iad an deuchainn. C' àite air aghaidh an domhain mhòir am faigheadh sibh sluagh a dh' fhuiling mar a rinn iad 'us a ghiùlain e le leithid de fhaighidinn! Cha 'n aithne dhòmhsa! Is i mo bharail gur iad

"Fineachan tìr ghairbh a' chuain
Broilleach uaill an domhain fharsuing."

Cha 'n aobhar nàire idir an cliù, an cleasan 's am fealadhà a chumail air chuimhne.

Oigridh na Gaidhealtachd! biodh agaibh cuimhne air na daoine o 'n d'thàinig sibh; 'us na leanaibh gnàthas air bith a bheireadh tàmailt do 'r dùthaich. Biodh stuamachd 'us fearalas 'us deagh bheus an còmhnaidh ri fhaicinn oirbh. Iarraibh gu 'm bi maise na naomhachd air a cur ri buadhan nadurra, a chum 'us nach e a mhàin gu 'm meal sibh cliù o dhaoine ach gu 'm bi fàbhor an Ti ud agaibh aig am bheil a chaoimhneas gràidh ni 's feàrr na beatha.

[26TH FEBRUARY, 1889.]

At the meeting of the Society held on this date, Mr. David Ross, M.A., B.Sc., LL.D., read a paper on *The Relation of Celt and Norseman in Saga times*. Mr. Dugald MacFarlane, B.A., also read a paper on *The Science of Thought exemplified in the Gaelic Language*.

Mr. MacFarlane's paper was as follows:—

THE SCIENCE OF THOUGHT EXEMPLIFIED IN THE GAELIC LANGUAGE.

Man is pre-eminently the thinking and speaking animal. So much so, that unless in the very widest sense of the term, other animals may be said to be unable to think. Their modes of expression by vocal sound or gesture, are very limited, and must be taken as the measure of their thought-power. If we judge their thinking capacity by their power of expression, as we do man's, we must conclude they do not carry on mental processes analogous to his. But it is possible they may have highly-developed modes of thought of their own in accordance with a mental constitution altogether different from that of the human species.

The power to think is a function of the brain. This organ is, material though it may be, by certain operations capable of producing the result we call mind. What these cerebral operations are—motion of material particles, currents or what—we must not wait to consider. To the full study of thought, a thorough knowledge of the physical organ whose function is thought, is imperative; and much light is thrown upon the subject by investigations of the whole nerve system, and more especially by the pathology of the brain.

Many speak of mind as an entity, a being independent of the brain tissue, and using it only as the material index on which to read certain changes, which it afterwards translates into thought. Careful observation, however, and scientific investigations lead to a very different conclusion, namely, that the mind is the self-consciousness of varied movements and impressions in the brain matter, perceived and combined by itself into percepts, that is, the results of the perception of material objects. These percepts lead up to concepts of things and acts. By combining and separating a comparatively limited number of primary concepts, thought is built up, and reason evolved. The mental recognition of concepts is by some sign inseparably present when a particular concept arises in the brain.

With man in his normal condition words are the signs, simple in their primitiveness as the concepts they represent. Such simple primary words are supposed to be the root sounds from which all the words of a language are developed, just as thought is evolved from the primary concepts. Both processes advance *pari passu*, and are inseparable. The thought and its representative word are the same cerebral operation; and they may be communicated audibly, or otherwise, to the minds of others. The audible or visible expression of the thought is, however, caused by another set of brain operations, which stimulate the organs of speech, or the hands, to motion. We have great difficulty in distinguishing between the two sets of operations. But the pathology of the brain shows that man may be able to think correctly, while, in the expression, he is quite unable to say the words which are in his mind, or says others he does not wish to say.

By this theory words and thoughts are identical. If such be the case—and I believe it practically is—by the study of words as to their historical descent and current use, we may get closer to that intangible mystery called thought. Regarded from this standpoint, any language may supply matter sufficient to occupy many minds in examining its numerous strata. We find, as we pursue our investigations, many a line of fault which brings us to a full stop, as when we trace a word back to a point beyond which we cannot go. Yet in a far off language we may pick up the sequence, and arrive at the primary root and concept which ultimately expanded into the particular word. We come across many evidences of disturbance, much that is metamorphosed; here, tokens of the violent irruption of a foreign element; there, a much-worn fragment of an age long gone by. Such an investigation has all the charms and all the toil of a geological survey, and requires much plodding patience to piece the data. I do not for a moment pretend to any such lofty attempts in what I have to bring before you this evening. The task I have set before myself is rather to play the rôle of the gold prospector, and to indicate to others more fitted by wealth of talents, where a vast and almost untouched gold field lies. My essay will be rude, but, I hope, will serve to encourage some bold adventurer to search the Gaelic field. In it are to be found many a nugget—rough, it may be, on the exterior, but of purest gold within.

My first point will be the evidence our language throws upon the physical basis of thought.

A brain cut off from the outer world, however great might be its potentialities, could produce a mind of only a very low order. It could have no stimuli to set it agoing except those uncertain ones from within, resulting in mere subjective sensation. Now, mere sensation could never result in the sublime power we know as thought. All evolution of thought depends on the stimuli from without, which are conveyed to the brain by the senses. Of all the sense organs the eye produces the most vivid and accurate impressions on the sensorium. Consequently, the percepts thus created have a corresponding definiteness—aided and corrected as they are by the other perceptions. It is by the eye principally, we get our impressions of relative local position. We get the near, the far, the yonder, in relation to that of which we are most conscious, namely, *self*. Hence, demonstrative words play a most important part. In Gaelic we have *so*, *sin*, and *siod*, as demonstratives. Close inspection shows them to be in reality namewords (nouns) as is seen in *An so* (the here), *An sin* (the there), *An siod* (the yonder). *An* is the mental index-finger pointing to some individual object which can be definitely localised, *e. g.*—*An duine so*. Here the concept *duine* is of an individual object. *An* is, as I said, the mental index-finger pointing to it; while *so* marks its relative position with regard to the thinker. When we rise to higher stages of thought-development, and conceive of *duine* as a species, we drop *an*. *Duine* now is an abstraction, and can no longer be pointed to. It cannot be localized, consequently, *so*, *sin* and *siod*, are no longer applicable.

The noun force of these demonstratives is still further shown by the readiness with which prepositions can be attached to them, as—"*Ann an so*,"—"*As an sin*," "*Bho 'n so suas*" &c. These demonstratives are derived from one original root. The same root furnishes formative particles, as in "*Mise*," "*Thusa*," "*Ise*," &c. Here emphasis is laid upon the personal pronouns by affixing the demonstrative particles, and thereby intensifying the conception of local position occupied by the person represented.

In Gaelic thought time is conceived of as space, having its *so* and *sin*. Here we see a tendency at work to endow the abstract and immaterial with the properties of material objects. It is a rudimentary process of mythology, which obtains very extensively in Gaelic. Time is regarded as an entity, and the mind thinks of its relations and points as perceptible objects to which the mental finger "*an*" can be pointed. The "*an sin*" of locality becomes the "*an sin*" of time—the remoter point—"the then." The expansion of this conception of time has given rise to such modes of expressing points of time, as—"*An nochd*," "*An raoir*," "*An diugh*," "*An dé*," "*An niridh*," &c. Here we have the same usage exactly as in dealing with concrete objects. We see constantly at work a mental tendency to endow what we cannot perceive with the properties of perceptible things. Hence it is that, in expressing thought in the Gaelic language, the noun plays so important a part. The noun takes the most prominent place, even to the subordination of the verb. In many instances the latter is dispensed with altogether, especially in asking questions, e.g.—"*Cò e?*" (who he), "*Ciod fàth do thurais?*" (what the object of your journey), "*Gur còir urnuigh a' dheanamh*" (that right prayer to making), "*Cha luchd-brathaidh sinne*" (not folk of betraying we), &c.

Gaelic grammars set forth paradigms of the verb with nearly as many tenses as the Greek. But upon inspection we find that most of them really consist of the verb "to be," and nouns governed by appropriate prepositions. A few examples will illustrate this.

(1) *Tha mi ag bualadh* (lit.—I am at striking); (2). *Bha mi 'g a bhualadh* (lit.—I was at *his* striking); (3).

Bithidh mi iar (air) mo bhualadh (lit.—I shall be *after* my striking); (4). *Bithidh sinn ag bualadh a' bhùird* (lit.—We shall be at striking *of the table*), &c. In each instance the noun force of what grammarians call the infinitive is obvious. It is governed by prepositions, has possessive adjectives attached to it, and also governs other nouns in the genitive. The preposition *iar* (after) is worth noticing, as we shall later on find it employed in a special use. When we remove from the verb paradigm this method of expressing action, we find that the Gaelic verb proper is not prolific in inflection. It is very remarkable how strongly local the conception is in this mode of representing action. The verb "to be," denoting existence, is what suffers inflection, while the rest of the work is performed by the noun. In this again we see the abstract conception "striking" endowed with a shadowy substantial existence.

In Gaelic there are very few words of the type designated adverbs. There are no prefixes or affixes of a formative nature wherewith to construct such a class of words.

I have already referred to the mode adopted to represent points of time, namely, the use of *an* and the noun. Where the period or portion of time cannot be reduced, as it were, to a definite conception, the *an* is omitted and the noun alone, or preceded by a preposition, is employed; *E.g.* "*Fad an là*" (lit.—length of the day); "*Rè seal*," (lit.—duration of a glance); "*Rè tamuill*," (lit.—duration of a short space), &c.

The mind cannot conceive very clearly the limits and conditions of many time references. The vagueness of the conception is portrayed in the very terms employed. "*Gu siorruidh,*" (lit.—to evergoing) ; "*Gu dilinn,*" (lit.- to end of age) ; "*Gu ball,*" "*Gu suthainn,*" &c.

In combining concepts of "How" with concepts of action, Gaelic proceeds after a peculiar fashion. Concepts of "How" are based on concepts of qualities. "*Duine math,*" (A good man) ; "*Rinn è è gu math,*" (He did it well—lit.—he did it towards good), as if *math* were an entity towards which the act proceeds. "*Gu cinnteach*" (towards certain) ; "*Gu fior*" (towards true). The quality is set up as a standard, as it were, and the "How" is regarded in relation to that standard.

But we must hasten on. The strong mythological tendency and vivid local colouring of the Gaelic mind is beautifully illustrated by the way in which expression is given to a very great variety of abstract conceptions having reference to a man's position as a living being among his fellows. His existence in this present life is presented to us as "*Ann*" (in it); "*Tha e ann*" (lit.—he is in it); "*Cha 'n 'eil e ann*" (lit.—he is not in it—he does not live—he is not). By thought expressions founded on this conception of "being in" while we exist in this world, is figured forth a man's position from a national, racial and social point of view ; his professional status is set before us, and his bodily, mental, and spiritual characteristics are predicated. For instance,—*Tha sinn 'n ar n-Albannaich*—*'n ar Gaidheil*—lit.—we are *in our* Scots—*in our* Gaels. *Tha e 'n a athair*—he is *in his* father. *Tha am paisde 'n a nighean*—The child is *in her* girl. *Tha an duine 'n a shaor*—*'n a chroitear*—*'n a mhinistear*—*'n a amadan.*—

the man is *in his* wright—*in his* crofter—*in his* minister—*in his* fool, &c. The nouns *athair, nighean, saor, amadan,* are used in the sense of genus; and the individual is spoken of as being in its own proper class.

When the possesssion of property is the subject of thought, the Gael says his belongings are *at* him, just as his Latin and Greek brothers did—*Est domus mihi—oikos 'emoi esti—tha tigh agam*—a house is *at* me. Here local position is the image employed to represent the relation of the thing possessed to the *self*, which to the mind is the central fact of the Kosmos. What one has near at hand is more or less under his control. Mere proximity, however, does not ensure against the possibility of something intervening and lessening the control exercised by the *self* over it. Consequently, we find, generally, that this " At " thought is attached to what, in the course of circumstances, we may lose. Our legal, inalienable rights, our opinions, our likes and dislikes are conceived of as *with* us. They go where we go: they are inseparable appendages. We see this in—*Tha airgiod gu leoir agam, ach cha 'eam fein*—lit.—plenty of money is *at* me but it is not *with* myself. *Cha toigh leis duine a tha " leam leat."*—he does not like a trimmer—lit.—a man is not pleasant *with* him who is "*with* me, *with* thee."

Of course this method does not obtain invariably. No one method does in any language. We do not think by one fixed mechanical rule forced upon us by necessity. A language is not the outgrowth of a compelling instinct.

It is very strange that our fitful and changing

passions, such as hatred and malice, are *at* us. What we voluntarily induce and cherish is for the most part spoken of as *with us*; while rage and the violent paroxysms of insanity are *on us*. Disease, sickness, sorrow, pain, joy, hunger, and thirst, are *on us*. Even *death* is said to come upon us. These latter are all conceived of as visitations from, as it were, some power or place exterior to ourselves. They are burdens, not as a rule pleasant to bear, to him who is *under* them.

The time at our disposal could easily be taken up with the examination of these peculiar idioms; and their proper employment goes far to distinguish good from bad Gaelic; but enough, possibly too much for your patience, has been given to show how imagery based on percepts is employed to portray conceptions of what is abstract.

I have endeavoured to illustrate within brief compass the prominent part played by name-words in the expression of thought, and especially how largely conceptions of locality bulk. The verb does not figure so conspicuously in Gaelic, although its position in a sentence is always near the beginning, and, as a rule, before its subject. So also, in passing, I may just mention that words denoting quality, as a rule, follow the words which they qualify—just the reverse of the position some eminent authorities say they ought to occupy for clear thinking. Be that as it may, one can hardly get over the fact that the perception of material objects as such must precede the perception of the properties in them which the mind conceives of as qualifying words. Nevertheless, to know objects we must appreciate first the properties which constitute their distinctive features. In the Gaelic mode one might almost venture to say he saw traces of the primitive order of the evolution of thought. Certain it is that in most of the Aryan tongues the same order is very general, as if they all still retained the impress of a common primary impulse.

By considerations such as the above, we come to see the simplicity of the Gaelic mode of thought reflected in the equally simple collocation of the words. Its style is more primitive than that of the Latin, Greek, or Sanscrit, where an extensive system of grammatical inflection is employed to guide the sequence of thought. Yet Gaelic is not destitute of those word changes which are designated grammatical inflections. It has its cases, tenses, and its formative affixes to indicate the relation of words to one another in the web of thought. But its genius as a language is emphatically the portraiture of thought in the guise of pictures drawn from the outer world; more especially as received through the eye. To this is possibly due its directness, its vivid statement, its nicety of distinction, and its poetic tendency. For mind marks distinctions most clearly while the concrete is before it, and popular poetry is based more on an appreciation of the outer world than on what we perceive by introspection. The Gaelic mind always operates as if it were directly stimulated by the actual presence of external entities. "Intellect creates words and words intellect," and any primary impulse may in the evolution of thought be transmitted with an ever increasing intensity from generation to generation, unless interfered with by influences from other sources.

Let us now proceed to consider another striking feature in the development of Gaelic thought-words. With us the names of the cardinal points of the heavens—and it will not be difficult to "box" the Gaelic compass, as we have not got much beyond the cardinal points—are determined by the position of the thinker, just as with the Jews of old. Our Keltic forbears, like all primitive peoples, looked with feelings of adoration and awe upon the sun, especially at its rising. By a step upwards from mere word-mythology, the glorious and mysterious luminary was, along with other powers of Nature, elevated to the dignity of a God. In this we have the germ of religious thought. Of course the religious instinct must have been latent in the race before any special development could take place. In addressing the sun God, our Gaelic poetry rises, like that of most other peoples, to a pitch of sublimity.

> "O, thusa féin a' shiubhlas shuas,
> Cruinn mar làn-sgiath chruaidh nan triath!
> Cia as a tha do dheàrrsa gun ghruaim,
> Do sholus tha buan, a ghrian!"

Again at its setting—

> "An d' fhàg thu gorm astar nan speur,
> A mhic gun bheud, a's òr-bhuidh ciabh?
> Tha dorsan na h-oidhche dhuit réidh.
> Tha pailliunn do chlos 's an iar.
> Thig na stuaidh mu'n cuairt gu mall
> Ag coimhead fir a's gloine gruaidh,

> A' togail fo eagal an ceann.
> Theich iadsan gun tuar bho 'd thaobh.
> Gabhas codal ann do còs,
> A Ghrian, is till bho 'd chlos le aoibhneas."

The ancient Kelt, standing in rapt adoration of the rising sun, faced to the *Ear* (east). Hence, when the Gael gives close attention to ought—*Bheir e fa 'n ear e* (lit.—he brings it under the east); *i.e.* he brings it under notice. The west he styled *Iar* (behind or after), a word we have already noted as helping the verb "to be" to form the perfect tense of the verb. The south he named *Deas* (the right hand), a word cognate with Latin *dexter*. *Deas* is parent to a numerous progeny which elucidate the gradual evolution of thought from a central germ. Like *dexter*, it meant clever. I am ready—*Tha mi deas* (lit.—I am right-handed). *Deas-fhocal*—a right-hand word—a repartee. He who has right hand speech—*Deas chainnt*—or *deas-briathrach*, is eloquent. A suit of clothes is *deise*, through the idea of trimness or neatness. We speak of right-handing food *Deasachadh*, just as in English we speak of dressing it.

In the phrase *Dol deiseal mu chárn*, we have a condensed account of the religious processions of our fathers, as they followed the course of the sun, round the sacrificial cairns. The observance of this rule was supposed to propitiate the deities and procure luck. Hence *deiseal* conveys the idea of luckiness. *Tuathal*, meaning northward, indicates misfortune. Even in taking a drink the liquid goes *tuathal*—northward—when it goes the wrong way.

Let us take another word of which the changes serve to illustrate the gradual evolution of thought from a central nucleus. Often, as the ever-growing ripple widens on the mental pond, the original idea, though never entirely lost, grows more vague and shadowy, while the actual word itself suffers but little from the phonetic decay inevitable in the course of time. " Words are nothing in themselves; but depend on what we put in them."

Tigh means a house and is derived from the older *Tig*. From it we have *Teaghlach*—the household—the *familia* of the Roman. At the head of the *Teaghlach* was *An tighearna*—the householder—indicative of the patriarchal form of government. It will be interesting to compare the course of this word with the English *Hláford*—the loaf provider—we might say the loafer, but in a very different sense from the modern acceptation of the term. Both *Tighearna* and *Hláford* show in an interesting way the gradual change of thought put into these words at different times, and under changing circumstances. Superiority was the dominant idea in both. When the patriarch no longer ruled his *Teaghlach*, and the *Hláf* (loaf) was no longer doled out to the poor serf, this idea still clung to both words, and *Tighearna* and " Lord " became titles of the feudal superiors of the land. "Lord" still keeps its place as a title of distinction, although the holder of it now rather *receives* than *gives*, the loaf. On the other hand, *Tighearna* as a mark of rank is practically dead. Lastly, both are with great appropriateness given to the " Lord of lords "—*Tighearna nan tighearna*—who is assuredly the great loaf-provider and householder of the human race.

In regarding words referring to colour, we see portrayed very strikingly the operations of primitive minds receiving their impressions from the general features of Nature. Art with them, had not yet multiplied shades, and nice mental distinctions had not, therefore, grown. In Gaelic we have for most colours two distinct sets of terms—one to mark intenser; the other, the less pronounced shades. E.g., *Geal* and *bán*; *gorm*, *uaine* and *glas*; *buidhe* and *odhar*; *dearg* and *ruadh*. I have not observed any word falling in with this classification in the case of *dubh*, black.

Let us look at some of these words indicative of colour more in detail, and let us begin with *Gorm*. In its use we find a manifest mental confusion based on an ocular defect, not uncommon among people, namely, the inability to distinguish between green and blue. This indicates the existence of a partial colour-blindness among the Gaels, due probably for the most part to the circumstances of their position. For example, we speak of the *Gorm thalla*—the *blue* hall—the sky spreading like a great hall-roof over *An tír ghorm shleibhteach* the *green* mountain land. *Gorm phreas* is a green bush; while *Gorman* or *gille guirmean*, is a weed whose blossom is a decided *blue*. The ghastly pale shades of green are *uaine*. Another term applied to certain shades of green is *glas*, taken into Gaelic from the Norse *glös*, from which is derived also the English word "glass." In that language we speak of *bottle* green from the colour of the glass. *Buidhe* (yellow) for some reason or other has come to be regarded in the Gaelic mind as the emblem of beauty and propitiousness; and this has given rise to peculiar modes of expression. *Latha-buidhe* (lit.—a yellow day) is a lucky day. For favours received, and a sense of satiety, we say we are *buidheach*— yellowed in mind; and when one asks a "blessing" on food, it is termed *Am buidheachas*—the yellowness. Again, our bodily complexion may have the same tinge when over satiety has induced *A' bhuidheach*—"the yellowes"—the jaundice. Just a word or two upon *dubh* (black), and the ramification of thought displayed in its usage. By Aryans in general, black is regarded as the emblem of "dule and wae." *Dubh là* is the opposite of *latha buidhe*. In Gaelic *Dubh* is taken as a fitting emblem of mystery, as "dark" is in English. *An dubh aigein*, the black, mysterious abyss. *An dubh fhocal*—the black word—puzzle. In the expression *Dubh-leus* (a cloud shadow—lit.—a black light), we have a strange application. Still more curious is the use of the word in denoting family relationship. A great grandson's grandson (what people but a Keltic would ever have had a special name for such a connection) is *Dubh-ogha*—a black grandson. *Fionn-ogha*—a fair grandson—is grandson's grandson. In the former the relationship is black, that is to say, obscure enough most assuredly.

We have *Dubh-bhròn*, deep sorrow, and a fit of the "blues" in Gaelic is *Dubh leann*—a black brewing—melancholy due to an overflow of bile—atrabiliousness.

In common parlance many of the Gaels speak of "Nicky-ben" as *Dòmhnull dubh*—black Donald.

Deary is the word for vivid red; *Ruadh* for duller shades. From the last we have Rob Ruadh—Rob Roy—and the surname Roy. *Deary* is used to denote intensity without reference to colour, as in *Dearg ruisgte*, (lit.—red naked, meaning stark-naked). A vivid impression is *Air a' dheargadh air m'inntinn*—reddened upon my mind—a locution remarkably like the English "branded," *i.e.* burned upon my mind. The Gaelic hunter went a-hunting *An dearg*—"the red," meaning deer; while his agricultural brother, tilling the strath with plough or *Cas-chrom*, called the soil he had turned over *An dearg* to distinguish it from that not yet turned over, *Am ban*—"the white gowan lea."

In the above instances we see displayed in the terms of the language, how thought grows and expands from a conceptual nucleus. However numerous and peculiar the progeny which has grown around any such parent, we are able, as a rule, to trace in each descendant some likeness to its progenitor. But if we take any one of the nuclei themselves, and trace *its* history, we find its origin in a simple concept. This we cannot do without the aid of the expert. Of course it is not to be expected that, in tracing historically the words of a language, we shall not encounter many gaps in the genealogy and many anomalies difficult of explanation. Nothing, however, is surer than that language is developed from a comparatively few roots representative of concepts. Professor Max Müller affirms that most of the originating concepts of language relate to acts.

It is in tracing words back to roots that the philologist has discovered the common paternity of the Aryan tongues. Gaelic is one of the noble sisters, and one which retains much of the primitive mould in which was first cast the Aryan mode of thought. Yet, this language, while it preserves the stamp of primitiveness, shows a decided tendency to profit by borrowing from its neighbours. This is shown by the shoals of loan words from Latin, Norse, later English and French.

It would be beyond the compass of this paper to notice these in much detail; but perhaps a glance at the development of thought as indicated by the great group of Latin loan-words, which refer to religious matters, may be permissible. The fact of their existence in Gaelic whould have enabled the comparative philologist, unaided by history, to deduce the introduction of a new department of thought amongst the people speaking that tongue. I refer to Christianity. Its propagators used Latin as a sort of sacred language. New thoughts require new words. So the Latin terms were adopted by the Gaelic folk from their teachers. Time has gradually changed their native dress till now in the "Garb of old Gaul," they have all the appearance of genuine Kelts.

Like most heathen peoples the Gaels had a conception of a God. Hence the native word *Dia* (cognate with "Deus, Dios, Divas") is retained. More, however, is put into its Christian use than its heathen use. The Gaelic *Flath* (noble) after death existed in *Flaitheanas*.

(lit.—the place of nobles) a Gaelic Elysium, or happy hunting-ground. To-day it means Heaven. These nobles would exist in *Flaitheanas* in material form. The spirit world in the Christian sense was beyond them. Consequently we finds words introduced such as *Spiorad, Aingeal*, &c. The general term for the worship paid to God is *Aoradh* from the Latin *Adorare*. Its history is a strange one. Christians borrowed it from the language of heathens, and afterwards bestowed it as a legacy to another heathen race, and so it flourishes now in the house of the Gael.

The "Satan" of the Semitic races became the *Adversarius* of the Latin-speaking Christian, and now the latter bears the Gaelic form *Abhairsear*. The history of words such as these is just the history of thought. A word may change its exterior form, so to speak, and we may put into it more or less new, but still in essence it survives the same as it was centuries ago.

Religious affairs were administered by the *Easpuig, Sagart, Abba*, &c. *Easpuig* is derived from *Episcopos*, which is also the original of English Bishop and French Evêque. Each of these is *Episcopos* in disguise, and behind them is the same originating conception—an overseer. His Crozier was *An bachall* from *baculum*; but later times put it to meaner use, or rather restored it to its pristine significance as we see in *Bachull sealgair*—a hunter's staff.

From *Easpuig* we have Gilleaspuig, bishop's man—anglicised Gillespie. The common expression of familiarity, *Laspi Ruadh* would scarcely suggest a high ecclesiastical origin.

Sagart is from *Sacerdos*, one who attends to holy things. Our Gaelic *Sagartail* is exactly the English Sacerdotal. The English of King Alfred's age had Sacerd (with hard c) but the word has given place to priest derived from presbyter.

Abba gives the name *Mac an Abba*—MacNab, a name which figures in modern comic literature. Now, however, from being attached to high monastic rank it adheres to a not over-respectable presbyterian elder, and friend of Ally Sloper.

At parting to-night, when we bid each other "good-bye" in the kindly Gaelic phrase *Beannachd leat*, we assume ecclesiastic dignity without any investiture, but that of hearty good will. *Beannachd* is benediction, and *leat* (with thee) in Gaelic, indicates that we wish it to be more than a passing blessing. In Presbyterian phrase, we pronounce the "benediction" in these words.

A Frenchman once said to an Englishman:—The Hell you English have has more it it than our *Enfers* (lit —the lower world). The same remark is true, as far as derivation is concerned, of our Gaelic *Ifrinn*. Both have the same origin, *Infernus*—the place beneath.

Even the home-made *Coinneal* (Latin *candela*) which illuminates the crofter or fisherman's humble cot, when the Gael spends *Oidhche air Cheilidh*, is a true descendant of the Church.

Beurla is a term whose history is interesting. For instance, in literature we say *Gnath beurla na h-Eirionn—na h-Alba*—the mode of speech of Erin—of Scotland; *a' bheurla leathann* or *a' bheurla Ghallda*—the broad Scotch or the language of strangers or foreigners; yet in every

day speech we call the English language *A' Bheurla*—
the speech. In this we acknowledge the predominance
of the language of the Teutonic invaders, and reduce
the term to a specific use. At the same time *Beurla*,
as a general term for language, is almost gone into
disuse.

In this hurried and disjointed sketch I have
endeavoured to indicate some features of the thought
system of the Gael, and I trust to see the same subject taken up and dealt with in a systematic and
thorough manner, by some one with plenty of leisure,
and the command of the best sources from which to
draw the necessary materials.

[26TH MARCH, 1889.]

At the meeting of the Society held on this date, Mr.
W. Jolly, F.G.S., F.R.S.E., H.M. Inspector of Schools,
read a paper on '*The Feeling for Nature in Gaelic
Poetry.*'

THE FEELING FOR NATURE IN GAELIC POETRY.

Mr. Jolly introduced his subject in these words:—
"Have Scottish Celts possessed, and have they
shown in their literature an appreciation, of the scenery
of their beautiful country, any love of Nature?"

Hill Burton's answer to that question is, decidedly,
No! He declares "that the Highlanders have ever
shown themselves peculiarly unconscious of the merits

of their native scenery, and that a passion for it is an emotion of recent growth, growing up in the bosom of the Saxon Lowlander, who visits it as a stranger !"

The true answer to the question, despite Hill Burton, is, emphatically, Yes !

However eminent Burton's authority on some matters may deservedly be, here he is utterly and absolutely wrong ; as Professor Mackinnon expresses it, his opinion on this subject is "as ludicrously inaccurate as can well be conceived." (*Scotsman*, January 12th, 1888.) It needs not the testimony of Matthew Arnold, Principal Shairp, Robert Buchanan, Alexander Smith, Professor Blackie, and a host of others, Highland and Lowland, to shew this. It is simply a matter of historical proof, for evidence, which surely a historian would have considered adequate; and the proofs are super-abundant and conclusive, that the Highland race has been exquisitely and poetically sensitive to natural influences, to the beauty and grandeur of landscape, so abundantly exhibited in their native land.

The evidence is mainly, if not solely, one of fact, of the contents and character of the literature, and not one of opinion, except as far as opinion is needed to interpret the literature. This is the only proof required; and it is surely one that should convince the most matter of fact of men, such as Hill Burton, who was merely a learned specimen of the unimaginative, hard and dry Lowlander, who neither loves nor understands the emotional and sentimental Celt, nor, for that matter, cares much to do either. Such evidence it is the purpose of this paper to adduce, at least, so much of it as will prove the thesis maintained which is :—That the Scottish Celt has for centuries been a child of Nature, appreciative of her varied forms and influences as exhibited in his mountainous home ; that he has also had some glimpses of the deeper relations of man to Nature ; and that, to use the words of Principal Shairp, "some features of their country's scenery, and some human feelings and habits which it has fostered, have expressed themselves in songs of the native Gaelic speaking bards, which, for force and vividness, no foreign language can equal," ("Aspects of Poetry," p. 258).

In selecting specimens of this naturalistic poetry, I have, of purpose, confined myself almost entirely to poetry produced before the early part of the present century, to make the proof more convincing, in order to present it in its native purity, without inter-mixture of foreign elements, which the growing intercourse between the Highlands and the Lowlands may have introduced into its literature, and which doubtless it did introduce, though much less than might be supposed ; for much of modern Gaelic poetry is as genuinely native and purely Celtic as any that every gushed from the Highland Castaly. I have also quoted nothing from Macpherson's "Ossian," on account of the long continued and still existing controversy, even among Celtic students, regarding the historical value of that remarkable book, of whose literary and poetic merit, and remarkable influence on English literature, there cannot be a moment's doubt.

My acquaintance with Gaelic Literature, I am sorry

to say, has been made entirely through translation, and not, like that of our friend, Professor Blackie, and the late Principal Shairp, from personal study of the Gaelic tongue. But such knowledge as I have been able to acquire, through the numerous and rapidly extending renderings of Celtic poetry into good English, is sufficient for my present aim. This is, to give an estimate of the character, history and value of the naturalistic poetry of the Highlands; just as it would be sufficient for a similar inquiry into Hebrew, Icelandic or Vedic poetry, where access can be had to worthy translations from these literatures, without personal knowledge of these little known languages, so rich in native poetry. Happily for English readers, the gems of Gaelic literature are yearly becoming more available for general study by Lowlanders, whose accident of birth and breeding has prevented their imbibing the ancient language of the hills in childhood's home, from a mother's lips, where alone, it would seem, it can be genuinely absorbed. A band of capable Gaelic scholars, possessing the requisite skill in the use of both tongues, have yearly, especially of late, added to the treasures of Gaelic literature that exist in an English dress.

At the same time, during my study of Gaelic literature, now extending over many years, I have more and more felt how much I have lost in having been prevented, through various causes, chiefly pressure of work, from acquiring a knowledge of that literature, in its native mellifluous and expressive speech. But that acquisition is now, alas, impossible. I have, however, been increasingly impressed with the importance of Gaelic literature, especially its poetry, as a moulding influence in the future development of English literature. I would here express my strong opinion of the desirability of having more of the treasures of Celtic literature made accessible to English readers; and I would urge those Highlanders who have the capacity, to labour, even more assiduously than they have yet done, at this patriotic and pleasant task.

Mr. Jolly then proceeded to give abundant criticism and examples from Gaelic poetry, of Celtic insight into Nature and appreciation of her varied aspects, as exhibited in that beautiful land. The Highlander had always been a keen observer of natural phenomena. This was proved by his place-names, which are remarkably descriptive and exact as to form and colour; and by his literature, where almost every feature, as exhibited in his country, is described with fulness and fidelity, and with high perception of its varied phases, from the terribly wild to the sweetly beautiful. Gaelic literature exhibited none of the fear of the greater and fiercer aspects of Nature which so long pervaded the poetry of the Lowlands; and this from the earliest times—showing a catholic sympathy with Nature, centuries before it was born into English or Scottish literature. Mountain scenery was a special element in the life and poetry of the Celts. This formed a marked contrast to its treatment in Scotland and England, up to the middle of last century. In proof of this, he quoted from Mary Macleod, who flourished from 1569 to 1674. This "passion for mountains" reached its height in *Donnacha Ban*, of whom Mr. Jolly expressed the highest opinion, as one of the greatest and freshest examples of poetic genius unspoiled by books, who possessed Walt Whitman's "dew-scented illiteracy," and who was thus able to nestle closer to the heart of Nature and hear her finer strains, without any traditional blindness engendered by book learning. Mr. Jolly quoted largely from "Ben Doran," as translated by Shairp and Blackie.

The glens were also pictured as variedly as in Nature, which is well shown in the old address to Glenshee and other valleys, preserved by the Dean of Lismore, in 1512; and in Duncan Ban's "Misty Corrie." The streams were well described, as exampled in Alister Macdonald's "Sugar Brook." Even the plains were not forgotten, as proved by MacCodrum's account of the Uist machars. The sea appeared in many moods, from calm to storm, so ably given in "The Birlinn" of Macdonald, a great work second to none in its class, and worthy to be classed with Longfellow's "Building of the Ship," Schiller's "Lay of the Bell," and other great technical poems.

Animated nature, in birds, deer, and other creatures, was lovingly described, as illustrated by quotations from Jerome Stone of 1756, MacCodrum, Macintyre, Macdonald, &c. In regard to flowers, which early grew in Gaelic poetry, it was remarkable how very late was the mention of heather in Saxon literature, one of the earliest being by Thomson in 1728. Mrs. Grant, of Laggan, was the first to write an address to it in 1803; whereas in Celtic poetry, it had flourished from the first, hundreds of years before.

Times and seasons, under varied phases, were vividly painted by Gaelic poets. The evening scene in "Findu and Lorma," first published in Dr. Smith's "Sean Dana," in 1789, was read, characterised by Charles Stewart of Killin as "the most beautiful passage in Gaelic poetry," and "inimitable;" certainly, Mr. Jolly held, very fine poetry, shewing wonderful beauty and touching sweetness of feeling, with anticipations, in sentiment, of Burns's "Afton Water." William Ross, the Gairloch bard, was also quoted, in one of his fine bucolic love ditties, describing an autumn evening, with local colouring. The poetical treatment of Winter was a poetical *crux*, a very good test of the possession of deeper poetic perceptions. For generations, it was treated in most literatures in its forbidding, and terrible aspects. Thomson was one of the first to see its real beauty and grandeur; and it was long before poets could rise to the loving admiration of Burns for this season, in which he found "a peculiar pleasure more than the rest of the year." Gaelic poetry had, he feared, not risen above common error in this respect. It described Winter in its trying or repelling aspects only, as exemplified in Dugald Buchanan's poem to Winter, in which there was only one example of the higher touches, where winter was said to "give the stars a new glory."

The use of Nature for purposes of comparison, and for the illustration and adornment of other themes, was next entered on. Gaelic poetry was exceedingly rich in such employment of natural images, from the earliest times: indeed, it had a tendency to overcrowd its canvas with figures. Its comparisons were remarkably apt, rich, picturesque and beautiful. Examples were cited from the Ossianic fragment, *Brosnachadh Catha*; from the "Lay of Oscar," whose death was one of the constant themes of the Celtic muse; from the old ballad in the Dean's book, "The four wise men at Alexander's Grave;" from Ian Lom's "Lament for Keppoch," where he describes himself as "a tree bare and leafless, without nuts, without apples, withering, barkless, sapless and way-gone;" from Macintyre's admirable epithelamium to his wife, "*Mairi Bhan Og;*" from an exquisite passage in the "*Sean Dana*," "the Lay of Dargo;" and from an unpublished poem, finely translated by Mr. Carmichael, "Who is she, the melodious Lady Lord?" full of the delicate local imagery of the Uists. Gaelic poets had such delight in natural imagery that they worked it up into elaborated and striking metaphors—as if they had peculiar pleasure in the movings of their own imaginations, like all true artists who love their work.

What had been gone over had been mainly the external features of nature, and their artistic employment for illustration. The Gaelic muse was capable of still higher flights—of a rare gift of love-song, set in appropriate natural scenery, able to take a worthy place in the gallery of the Scottish love lyrics; perceptions of the nearer relations of nature to man; intense joy in nature for her own sake; and, what might be thought surprising, flashes even of the modern Wordsworthian spirit, as in the ancient poem, one of the oldest in Highland literature, "The wish of the aged Bard," so very finely translated by Dr. Hugh Macmillan, which Mr. Jolly read.

He hoped, at an other time, to exhibit the relations of the literature of the Highlands to those of other lands, especially to that of Scotland and England; its native independence of external influences; and its anticipation, by centuries, of valuable elements in the poetical treatment of Nature, long before these arose elsewhere, especially in Britain.

In conclusion, Mr. Jolly said :—I look upon it as vastly important that the literature, and especially the poetry of the Highlands, should be better known to English readers; and that, for this purpose, a select anthology of its contents should be made by competent Gaelic and Celtic scholars, versed also in the general history of literature, especially of the literature of the rest of Britain. In this direction, eminent service has been done by Professor Blackie for English students, by his bright, able and informing "Language and Literature of the Scottish Highlands," published in 1876. This should be read by all interested, not only in the Highlands and their people, but in the true history of the literature of the British Isles. This history should include Wales and Ireland, whose literature is as rich, if not richer, in many respects, than that of Celtic Scotland.

In the particular field of naturalistic poetry, to which we have turned our attention to-night, I should hope to see a special inquiry made into the subject of the "Feeling for Nature" in Gaelic poetry; and a special anthology formed from it, with similar aims and results to what

Professor Veitch has so ably and interestingly achieved in his important work, lately issued, "The Feeling for Nature in Scottish Poetry." I am convinced that Highland literature, when better known, especially its poetry, is capable of moulding the future development of English literature in no mean degree; and that it should, and will, introduce into it new and fresh, broadening and inspiring elements, which would vivify, strengthen and expand it; as it did more than a century ago, when "Ossian," even with all Macpherson's broken lights, burst like a new star, with lasting power and brilliancy, on the astonished literary world.

What we have already seen, is sufficient to shew that Gaelic poetry admirably illustrates what Matthew Arnold calls the "magic of style," which he strenuously claims as a special characteristic of Celtic poetry in general. This "natural magic" arises from the Celtic "nearness to Nature and her secret," which, he holds, gives the Celt a peculiar power of "bending language at its will, and expressing the ideas it has with unsurpassable intensity, elevation and effect." This power, he argues, Celtic poetry exhibits, "not in its great poets only, in Taliesin, or Llywarch Hen, or Ossian, but in all its productions." It posseses also what Arnold calls "a better gift still, the gift of rendering, with wonderful felicity, the charm of Nature." It is characterised by what he designates a "delicate magic, in the *use* of Nature." This power he contends, and he contends rightly, as now generally and increasingly acknowledged, "it seems impossible to believe did not come into romance *from the Celts*," like the use of rhyme and assonance in poetry. This peculiar genius of Celtic poetry, he maintains, is more than beauty; it expresses "the intimate life of Nature, her weird power, and her fairy charm," a capacity for which there is no other word, as he asserts, than "magic," "the magic of Nature."

And Gaelic poetry exhibits in high degree these most valuable all important elements of general Celtic song, thus eloquently claimed for it by this eminent and competent critic. But here we must leave the remainder of the wide and attractive field.

What we have already traversed, though only the lesser elements of the poetical treatment of Nature, abundantly proves that Gaelic poetry is full of Nature; that Highland poets have been close observers of natural scenes, in an unusually wide range of feature and mood; and that their perceptions of natural facts have been minute, loving and faithful; that these facts they have presented not as mere photographs, truthful but bare transcripts of what they saw; but that they have utilised them for artistic and poetical purposes, with rare and admirable power.

And surely, the pleasant paths of Celtic poesy, which we have travelled and enjoyed this evening, are sufficient to make even the most prejudiced Lowlander agree with Principal Shairp, in his appeal to an Oxford audience of classic dons and Saxon sufficiency:—

"To Lowlanders, accustomed to read the great standard poets, and to measure all poetry by their model, it may be some advantage to turn aside and look at a poetry wholly unlike that of England, Rome or Greece, a poetry which is as spontaneous as the singing of the birds and the beating of men's hearts; a poetry which is, in great measure, independent of books and manuscripts; a poetry which, if narrower in compass and less careful in finish, is as intense in feeling, and as true to Nature and to man, as anything which the classical literatures contain." ("Aspects of Poetry.")

[30TH APRIL, 1889.]

At the meeting of the Society held on this date, Mr. Malcolm Macfarlane, Paisley, read a paper on "*Phonetics of Gaelic.*"

SESSION 1889-90.

[29TH OCTOBER, 1889.]

At the meeting of the Society held on this date, Rev. A. Stewart, LL.D., *(Nether Lochaber)* read a paper on "*Characteristics of Gaelic Poetry.*"

[26TH NOVEMBER, 1889.]

At the meeting of the Society held on this date, Mr. John Mackay, C.E., Hereford, read a paper on "*Folk-Lore of Sutherlandshire.*"

[24TH DECEMBER, 1889.]

At the meeting of the Society held on this date, Mr. John Boyd, H.M. Inspector of Schools, read a paper entitled "*Historical Notes on Education in the Highlands.*" The following is a revised Newspaper report of Mr. Boyd's paper :—

HISTORICAL NOTES ON EDUCATION IN THE HIGHLANDS.

In the outset of his remarks, the lecturer referred to the obscurity of early Highland history, in which, notwithstanding the labours of Dr. Skene, who had done so much to arrange the material and to separate the spurious from the authentic, there was still more to perplex than to satisfy the student. The references to education, in particular, were few and meagre, the light first breaking with the arrival of Columba from Ireland. The monastery at Iona had, it was pointed out, a good deal of the function of a college, the "alumni," one of the three divisions of the community, being students. Latin was the chief basis and medium of their education, but they must have cultivated the native Celtic, at least in its spoken form, with a view to their missionary work. Columba himself wrote hymns in Gaelic, and successors of the early brotherhoods apparently wrote a good deal in the same tongue. The attention to the art of writing, with a view to copying the Bible and other manuscripts was exemplified in the special title of *scribnidh*, which in after times was combined with that of *fear-leighinn (vir lectionis)* conferred on the chief teachers, and implying probably a similar distinction to that of the modern LL.D.

Notices were given of the gradual spread of education accompanying the extension of religious establishments throughout the Highlands, though of course popular education, as the term is now understood, had almost no existence. Scholastic education was confined to those connected with the work of the Church, but through them a leavening influence must have extended to the general population; and it should be remembered that much moral and religious instruction, and much discipline of the memory and understanding, were possible without books. The tenth, eleventh, and twelfth centuries, saw a considerable increase of schools; such College centres as Abernethy, having apparently several in connection with them. Those of each centre were under a 'rector scolarum', who was evidently a man of note and influence, though probably, subordinate to the *fear-leighinn* who was a sort of chancellor or superintendent. The first schools existing separately from religious institutions were the burgh schools, which had arisen as early as the reign of Malcolm IV. (1153–1165), at Perth, Stirling, and other towns. Another great landmark was the founding of King's College, Aberdeen, in 1474, by James IV. and Bishop Elphinstone, which had for its chief motive the extension of learning and civilisation throughout the Highlands, and which, with the Grammar School of the same city, drew many students from, at least, the nearer Highland regions. It was worthy of notice that at the latter institution, while the Lowland vernacular was forbidden, Gaelic was one of the languages, with Latin, French, and others, in which the scholars might converse. Referring to the famous Act of 1496—famous among other things, for its compulsory element—while Mr. Boyd could hardly accept the view of Dr. Hill Burton that it was hortatory rather than legislative, he remarked that the Highland chiefs must have regarded it in the former light, and that few of them gave any heed to the exhortation.

The institution of 'Song schools' was referred to as an important feature of the later pre-Reformation period. At first confined to Cathedral towns and designed to train choirs for the church services, they became by degrees more widely diffused, and their advantages were extended to young people generally. After the Reformation, other subjects were taught in some of these schools, but the first idea survived till a comparatively late period. In 1733 for instance, the salary of a teacher of singing, was found as one of the charges against the revenues of the royal burgh of Tain.

The influence of the revival of learning and of the Reformation on the education of the people was not much felt in the Highlands. It was a common misapprehension that a fully equipped school system dates from the establishment of Presbyterianism. The proposal to have a school in every parish was not realized for many long years after. The Highland barons, whether accepting the principles of the Reformation or not, were not slow to follow the example of their Lowland brethren in seizing the revenues which Knox designed for the support of education, and though many schools were planted in the northern counties by commissions of the General Assemblies, not a few of them soon lapsed, the distance from the central authority, which was itself weakened by struggles against abitrary royal power, leaving little to counteract local difficulty and neglect.

The great educational error, as the speaker held, which had continued to our own day, of trying to root out the native language and impart all culture through virtually a foreign language, was attributed to James I. of England, whose Council, in 1616, issued an order requiring the English tongue to be universally planted, and Gaelic, to be removed and abolished, as one of the chief causes of the continued "barbaritie and incivilitie" of the Highland people. Some of his schemes, however, proved to be wise and beneficial, such as the "Statutes of Icolmkill," by which, among other obligations, every gentleman or yeomen possessed of sixty cattle had to send his eldest son to school in the Lowlands, and maintain him there till he could speak, read, and write English. This order was a few years later made to include all the children of such families over nine years, and in all probability the great change that took place in the feeling of the Highland chiefs towards the Stewart Kings had its origin among those thus educated. After a somewhat detailed account of legislation down to the Act of 1696, the lecturer expressed regret that, except as regards some of the grammar schools, history gave scarcely a single glimpse of school life. No sympathetic spectator had enabled them to look into the ordinary Highland school, with its low roof thatched with heather and fern, its clay floor, its scanty light, or to see the schoolmaster, amid the smoke of his peat fire, leading the little bare-legged Celts up the first steps of the ladder of learning. They were equally unacquainted with the average Highland schoolmaster and his relations to the people, but they knew that unauthorized persons were not permitted to usurp his functions. An amusing instance of this was quoted. About the middle of the seventeenth century a woman from Morayshire established a school in Inverness, and the magistrates met to consider this innovation on the vested rights of the parish schoolmaster. They did not order her to desist altogether, but they enjoined her not to teach 'beyond the Proverbs', which with the Book of Psalms, were considered the easiest and therefore the most elementary reading in the old Testament. An account was next given of the educational work of the Society for Propagating Christian Knowledge. Originating in 1701 among a few gentlemen who had formed a society in Edinburgh for the reformation of manners, it speedily obtained the full sanction and influence of the General Assembly and letters patent from Queen Anne, erecting it into a corporation with considerable powers and privileges. Its capital, which in 1708 was £1000, had risen in 1781 to £34,000 and by that year the schools numbered 180, with an attendance of 7,000 scholars. Its administration was enlightened and beneficent, its encouragement, pecuniary and otherwise, of promising scholars being an admirable feature, and it supplemented the statutory school supply, which was still very imperfect, with equal liberality and discretion. The directors, accepting the common view that the prevalence of the Gaelic language was one of the causes of existing evils in the Highlands, at first forbade instruction in that language, but afterwards the teachers who were Gaelic speaking, were enjoined to teach the meaning of the English lessons, and ultimately Gaelic books were circulated, an edition of the New Testament in that language, translated by the Rev. Mr. Stewart, of Killin, being prepared at the Society's expense. The teachers, not a few of whom were men of university education, had to be duly examined and on passing successfully were rewarded a formal diploma. They received fixed salaries, and were not to exact fees. Sometimes the schools were endowed with 'crofts' by proprietors who sympathised with the Society's aims. Shortly before the middle of the eighteenth century, the society made a notable attempt to establish technical schools. The agricultural schools failed, and the attempts to start linen manufactures, as at Lochcarron and Glenmorriston, met with small success. Spinning schools, however, in which various home industries were taught, were maintained for many years in various localities.

Some account was also given of proposals of the Government to supplement still further the supply of schools throughout the Highlands. After the rising of 1715, Parliament voted £20,000 for the purpose, and commissioners presented a report to the Secretary of State in which they named 151 places where schools were needed, and specified their educational necessities in detail. With this report, however, the matter ended.

Something similar, and equally without result, took place after the "forty-five."

The education of the middle and upper classes in the Highlands was at this period of a very superior kind, being often completed at Leyden, Douay, and other foreign universities. It was said of many Skye gentlemen that they spoke Latin better than English, and there was probably not much exaggeration in the statement, that when the Hessian troops were quartered in Athole, in 1745, the officers found Latin a ready means of communicating with the inn-keepers. The new social and educational conditions brought about by the gradual breaking up of the clan system after Culloden, and the changes which followed, with the story of how they were met by legislation and voluntary effort, were reserved for future treatment, the lecture concluding with a brief estimate of what had been achieved by the end of the eighteenth century. Quoting from Major-General Stewart of Garth, the speaker showed that while many were still unable to read and write and many were unable to understand what they read, in English, the advantages of education were greatly appreciated and had answered the most sanguine expectations, raising the sons of humble cottars to distinguished places in the learned professions, and developing generally, amid poverty and violations of law and regular government, many honourable points of character.

[28TH JANUARY, 1890.]

At the meeting of the Society held on this date, Rev. William Ross, read a paper on "*Our Gaelic Grammar and how to teach it.*"

[25TH FEBRUARY, 1890.]

At the meeting of the Society held on this date, Mr. Henry Whyte, (*Fionn*) read a paper on "*Some ancient Celtic customs.*" Mr. Whyte's paper was as follows:—

SOME ANCIENT CELTIC CUSTOMS.

Any one who has given the least consideration to local or national customs will admit that they are daily falling into unmerited neglect. The same holds good in regard to many of those superstitious rites and ceremonies so closely interwoven with the early history of the Celt, "in ages long ago,"—customs and superstitions tenaciously adhered to by our forefathers long after they ceased to believe in their efficacy—and many of which are still practised and rigidly adhered to by the representatives of modern civilisation, and Nineteenth Century enlightenment. Though a good many ancient customs are still retained in Lowlands and Highlands, it is generally found that their origin and meaning is entirely forgotten or unknown. Some of us unwittingly follow many of those ancient customs, as for instance, if we are quite undecided which of two turnings or roads to take, and there is no one to guide us, we invariably turn to the right, the *làmh-dheas* or south hand of the Celt—who believed that luck followed anything done *deiseil* or sun-wise. I cannot pretend to bring before you anything like a complete or exhaustive treatise on ancient Celtic customs. Every Highland *Clachan* or district, has its own customs, and every community has its own way of performing many of the ancient rites and ceremonies. I have endeavoured to arrange the customs with which I deal in groups under various heads, so that they may prove the more interesting to you.

One word of explanation, regarding the manner in which almost all those rites and ceremonies had to be performed—as this will render it unnecessary, to explain the matter when we come to the description of those various customs. When the Celt took his bearings he faced the East—consequently his right hand was south or *deas*, hence *deas-lamh*, and every thing good and lucky came from that airt. His left hand was *tuath*, and so any thing done awkwardly by a Celt, is called *tuathal* or northward—and so accustomed are we to speak of anything that goes wrong or is done badly, as *tuathal*, that we entirely forget the original meaning of the expression; and when drinking or eating, anything goes down the windpipe, we say *chaidh e tuathal*, it went northward, whereas it went down or southward.

The Gaelic Proverb, "*Deiseil air gach ni*," (The sunward course with every thing)—was firmly believed in, and rigidly acted upon by the Celt, as it is indeed by all the principal races of the world. I may also call your attention here to the fact that *caorunn*, (rowan tree) red thread, and salt, were the most potent charms or protectors against the spells of fairies and witches.

> "Rowan-tree and red thread
> Gar the witches tyne their speed."

In addition to the sign of the cross—and coming down the ages, contact with the Bible, or the repetition of the Lord's Prayer, the Creed and the Ten Commandments, were potent against the wiles of evil-spirits, and every thing uncanny or awful. I shall first deal with the various Celtic Customs associated with births—many of which are still observed in Highlands and Lowlands alike.

CUSTOMS AT BIRTHS.

When a "little stranger" arrived at the castle, or seat of the chief, especially the birth of an heir, the clan piper was called upon to play a *Fàilte* or Salute. In every household, however, the first care was to prevent the fairies or *sithchean* from stealing away the child to their *sithean* or fairy mound. It was commonly believed that the fairies frequently stole away a child, before it was baptized, and left a fairy child in its place, and so, when a young infant showed signs of pining away, the wise old *cailleachs* shook their heads and declared that the real child had been stolen, and a fairy one substituted. To prevent this kidnapping on the part of the fairies, certain rites and ceremonies had to be performed. Fire, say a burning peat, had to be taken in the right-hand (*làmh dheas*) and the mother and young child encircled seven times, going *deiseil* or sun-wise. This had to be performed morning and night till the child was baptized, and the mother churched according to the law of the ancient Church. There seems to have been a doubt as to whether this of itself was sufficient, for a thread of scarlet was tied round the child's wrist, and a Bible was placed in the cradle beside it, while another was placed under its mother's pillow. When the child was to be baptized a cake was baked, called *bonnach baiste*, or christening cake, and this was neatly tied in a white handkerchief and laid on the child's breast when carried to the church. The first person met on the way to church was saluted, and asked to partake of a piece of the *bonnach*. In the Church due care was taken—and is still—that if there were several children to be baptized, a girl did not take precedence of a boy, otherwise it was believed that the girl would have a beard and moustache when she grew up. After the child was baptized a feast was held in the house of the child, to which friends were invited. The first food partaken of was crowdie. *(fuarag.)* The father then placed a basket filled with bread and cheese on the *cromay* or pot-hook, suspended over the peat fire in the centre of the floor, and the child was handed across the fire with the design to frustrate all attempts of evil spirits or evil eyes. This rite or ceremony seems to have been designed as a purification and was of idolatrous origin, as the Israelites made their children pass through the fire.

If twins were born in the family of a dependant, one of them was sent to the chief's house to be brought up and cared for. This leads me to refer to the ancient custom of

FOSTERAGE

which was very common among the Celts. The most minute and interesting account of this very ancient Celtic custom is to be found in the *Seanachas mór*, that valuable record of the Rights and Customs of the Celts of Ireland. Skene* says "there were two kinds of fosterage —fosterage for affection, and fosterage for payment. In the *Seanachas mór* is carefully noted the clothes that were to be worn by the various grades of foster children, as well as the food they were to receive. Porridge—"*lite*" it is termed in the original—was to be given to them all, but the materials of which it is made, and the flavouring vary according to the rank of the parents of the children. The sons of the inferior grades are fed to bare sufficiency on porridge made of oat-meal upon butter-milk, or water, taken with salt-butter. The sons of the chiefs are fed to satiety on porridge made of barley meal, upon new milk with fresh butter. The sons of kings are fed on porridge made of flour, upon new milk taken with honey. The food of all, however, was alike till the end of a year or three years. The price of the fosterage of the son of *Ogaire* is three sids, or three *Samhaises*, that is 3 year-old-heifers, and for his daughter 4 sids, a sid in addition being given for the daughter, because the

* "Celtic Scotland." Vol. III.

household arrangements for her accommodation are more extensive than for the sons. This was the lowest price given and the *Fer Midbuid*, or man of the humblest rank, could not perform the fosterage for less. The boys were to be taught the herding of lambs, calves, kids and young-pigs, and kiln-drying, combing, and wood-cutting, and the daughters the use of the quern, the kneading-trough and the sieve.

"The price of the fosterage of the son of a *Bó-aire*, or cow-lord, was 5 sids or 3 cows. The price of the fosterage of the son of an *aire* was ten sids, and instructions in the usual sciences is given him; that is, the sons were taught horsemanship, shooting, chess-playing and swimming; and the daughters, sowing and cutting-out, and embroidery. The price of the fosterage of the son of a king, was thirty sids, and the foster sons were to have horses in times of races, and the foster father was bound to teach them horsemanship. The children remained with the foster-father till the boys were 17 and the girls 14 years of age. The age of boys was divided into three periods. The first extended till he was seven years old, the second from seven to twelve years, and the third till he was seventeen. During the first period the foster-father might punish him with castigation, and during the second with castigation without food; but for his first fault there were to be three threatenings without castigation. After the age of twelve he had to make compensation in the usual way, with regard to which there are many minute regulations. On the termination of the fosterage, the foster-fathers returned the children with a parting gift, and in return the foster son was bound to maintain his foster-father, in sickness or old age, in the same manner as he would maintain his own father or mother."

A similar system although not quite so complete nor so well arranged, existed among the Scottish Celts, as may be learned from a perusal of Logan's "*Scottish Gael.*"

There are many Gaelic Proverbs which refer to this custom—all of them pointing to the strong attachment existing between foster-parents and their foster-sons and daughters, as well as among foster-brothers.

"An co-dhalta nach dearbh 'àite, 's mairg a dh' àraich duine riamh."—(The foster-child that proves it not, pity him that reared).

"Comh-dhaltas gu ciad is càirdeas gu fichead." (Fostership to a hundred, blood-relations to twenty degrees).

"Is caomh le fear a charaid, ach 's e smior a' chridhe a chomh-dhalta." (Dear is a kinsman, but the pith of the heart is a foster-brother).

LUCKY DAYS.

The Celts like many other peoples, had their lucky days, and children were considered lucky or otherwise, according to the day of the week on which they were born. A Monday bairn was lucky, for *Di-luain* (Monday) was "*Iuchair na seachdain*" the key of the week, and Tuesday, also more or less lucky, being near Monday. Friday, called *Di-h-aoine*, was considered a most unlucky day, for as the name indicates it was a *fast* day, *aoine* being the Gaelic name for a fast. Hence we learn that *"aireamh na h-Aoine,"* (Friday's count) was most unlucky; and to wish any one *"Ruith na h-Aoine,"* was equal to wishing him bad luck. It may be observed that Friday is considered an unlucky day in many countries, that being the Crucifixion day. Saturday was also unlucky being the end of the week, and so children born on these days were to be pitied. The great value set upon the beginning of the week as compared with the end of it is brought out in the rhyme :—

> " Imrich Shathurn mu thuath,
> Imrich Luain mu dheas ;
> Ged nach biodh agam ach an t-uan,
> 'S ann Di-luain a dh' fhalbhainn leis."

(Saturday's flitting by north, Monday's flitting by south ; had I but the lamb to move, 'tis Monday I would go). There is a Lowland proverb much to the same effect—"Saturday flitting, short sitting." The associating of good luck with the beginning of the week and bad luck with the end thereof is not borne out—at least, as regards bairns born on these days, by the following Scotch rhyme which, however, like many others of its kind, contains more rhyme than reason. The rhyme runs as follows :—

> " Monday's bairn is fair o' face,
> Tuesday's bairn is fu' o' grace ;
> Wednesday's bairn 's a child o' woe ;
> Thursday's bairn has far to go ;
> Friday's bairn is loving an' giving,
> An' Saturday's bairn works hard for its living:
> But the bairn that's born on the Sabbath day,
> Is loving an' giving, handsome an' gay."

There are other superstitious customs connected with children, but as they are neither ancient nor Celtic, I shall not refer to them. I must, however, refer to a few of the proverbs and songs or rhymes which illustrate this part of my subject. That the ancient Celt had philoprogenitiveness in a large degree, may be learned from the many proverbs he has placed on record regarding children and their habits. Let me quote a few:—

"Tigh gun chù, gun chat, gun leanabh beag, tigh gun ghean gun ghàire." (A house without dog, without cat, without child, a house without cheerfulness or laughter.) Perhaps the following proverb comes nearer the truth.

"Is truagh an fheadhain aig am bi iad, is truagh an fheadhain aig nach bi iad." (Pity those who have them, pity those who have them not).

That the manner and behaviour of the child were looked upon as a reflection of home life is expressed by the saying, "Aithnichear leanabh air a bheusan." (A child is known by his manners). "An leanabh a dh' fhàgar dha féin cuiridh e a mhàthair gu nàire." (The child that is left to himself will put his mother to shame).

What can be truer, or more necessary to be remembered by parents than this wise old saying, "An rud a chì na big 's e nì na big, na chluinneas iad 's e chanas iad." (What the wee ones see the wee ones do, what they hear they repeat).

There is abundant testimony in the folk lore of the Highlands, to prove a strong belief in the powers of the fairies to steal away children and to substitute others in their places—the substitutes often being very precocious and wise—old heads on young shoulders. Here is a fragment of a very old and pretty fairy song belonging to that class of nursery songs, called in Gaelic *Tàladh* or songs of caressing. It is supposed to have been sung by a good fairy, as she sat hushing to sleep a child whose mother had deserted it. The words are as follows :—

TALADH.

Nam bu leam fhéin thu, thàlaidhinn thu,
Nam bu leam fhéin thu, thàlaidhinn thu,
Nam bu leam fhéin thu, thàlaidhinn thu,
'S a thasgaidh mo chridh' gu'n tàlaidhinn thu.

SEISD—Thàlaidhinn thu 's gu'n tàlaidhinn thu,
Thàlaidhinn thu 's gu'n tàlaidhinn thu,
Thàlaidhinn thu 's gu'n tàlaidhinn thu,
'S a chagair mo chridh' gu'n tàlaidhinn thu.

Chunnaic mi seachad mu 'n taca so 'n dé,
Duine mór foghainteach, làidir treun,
Le 'bhogha 's le 'shaighead, 's le chlaidheamh fo 'sgéith,
'S mór m' eagal gu 'n tachair do mhàthair ris.

The following may be accepted as a free translation of the foregoing verses :—

A FAIRY CARESSING SONG.

Wert thou mine ain I'd fondle thee,
Wert thou mine ain I'd fondle thee,
Wert thou my ain dearie nae ill wad come near ye ;
My heart's dearest treasure I'll fondle thee.

Chorus—Fondle thee ; yes fondle thee,
    Fondle thee; yes fondle thee,
      O sleep noo my lammie, ne'er fash for your mammie,
      My bonnie wee mannie, I'll fondle thee,

    Yesterday even' I heard them say,
    A braw and brave gallant gaed by this way,
    Wi' bow and wi' arrow, an' sword keen and narrow.
    I'm feared your mammie 's awa wi' him.

As an instance where a fairy child had been substituted for the real one—the latter fact being only discovered by a slip on the part of the fairy child which was certainly odd, and old-fashioned beyond his appearance—allow me to quote from the introduction to J. F. Campbell's "West Highland Tales."—*The Herds of Glen Odhar.* "A wild romantic glen in Strathcarron is called Glen Cavaig, and it was through this that a woman was passing carrying an infant wrapped in her plaid. Below the path overhung with weeping birches, and nearly opposite, runs a very deep ravine known as Glen-Odhar, the dun glen. The child, not a year old, and which had not spoken or attempted speech, suddenly addressed his mother thus—

      'S lionmhor bó mhaol, odhar,
      Le laogh 'na gobhal,
      Chunnaic mise 'g am bleoghan
      Anns a' ghleann odhar ud thall,
      Gun chù, gun duine,
      Gun bhean, gun ghille,
      Ach aon duine, 's e liath.

      Many a dun hummel cow
      With a calf below her,

> Have I seen milking
> In that dun glen yonder,
> Without dog, without man,
> Without woman, without gille,
> But one man, and he hoary.

The good woman flung down the child and plaid and ran home, where to her great joy, her baby boy lay smiling in its cradle." So much then for the customs associated with births.

MARRIAGE CUSTOMS.

In treating of the Celtic customs associated with marriages, I shall go back to the time when the clan system was in its zenith. In modern days a more or less protracted courtship, and perhaps a sensational breach of promise with the usual sheaf of love-letters, is frequently the prelude to marriage. Under the clan system, courtship was not always necessary, for the chief provided his clansmen with partners. Martin who visited the Western Isles in 1696, informs us that MacNeill of Barra provided his clansmen with wives, and that when a tenant died, his widow addressed herself to MacNeill, who provided her with a husband. Love-letters were unknown, for Martin remarks " Women were anciently denied the use of writing in the Islands to prevent love intrigues, their parents believed that nature was too skilful in that matter, and needed not the help of education, and by consequence, that writing would be of dangerous consequence to the weaker sex." In the Highlands under the clan system, as well as in the Lowlands and in England, it was customary to exact a fine from the parents of vassals, on the occasion of a marriage. The fine varied according to the rank of the parents, and was usually paid in kind, and we find that when Dr. Johnson visited Ulva in 1773, he found that MacQuarrie, the laird or superior of that island was in the habit of demanding a sheep, but, about the time referred to, five shillings was accepted as the fine instead.

When the consent of the fair one was obtained—when as we say now-a-days, they were "engaged"—the bashful youth went to ask her father's approval, and arrange matters. Shortly thereafter a meeting of friends on both sides was arranged called "*an réiteach beag*, or *an còrdadh beag*, (known in the Lowlands as "the bookin'" or the "bottlin'"), and the prospects of the young couple discussed. After this meeting the lovers were declared bride and bridegroom, and some Tuesday or Thursday "in the growth of the moon," was fixed for the celebration of the nuptials. Thereafter the "cries" were put in, and due care was taken that the marriage took place before the moon began to wane. Then followed the *réiteach mór* or *còrdadh mór* when matters were finally adjusted, and the arrangements for the marriage completed. At this meeting the best-man *(fleasgach)* and best-maid *(maighdean)* were nominated by the bride and bridegroom. A week or so prior to the nuptial day, the partners, with their attendants, perambulated the district inviting the guests. On these visits the bride received many useful presents, while all who were invited were expected to send some contribution in kind to help the marriage feast. When the eventful day arrived, volleys of musketry summoned the guests to the wedding. At the hour appointed the bridegroom selected a party of young men who were dispatched to summon the bride and her party to the marriage ceremony. Their approach was announced by volleys of musketry. Then the bride and her maids prepared themselves for the procession, the bride being usually mounted on horseback. The company being now all in readiness, the bride's party proceed to the place appointed for the marriage, generally the church. The bridegroom's party followed at some little distance, and when both parties arrived at the *rendezvous*, the bridegroom's party stood in the rear till the bride's party entered the church or house, she and her attendants having the precedence throughout the day. This fact is clearly brought out in the story associated with *Cumha Mhic-an-Tòisich** (The Mac-Intosh's Lament). The chief of this Clan was killed on his bridal day, when on his way back from church after the ceremony. The incident which took place about the middle of the sixteenth century may be briefly stated thus:—

It seems there was a prediction (as the Highlander would say, "*Bha èn dàn dha*"), that MacIntosh of the day was destined to die through the instrumentality of his beautiful black steed. Whatever he felt, the chief determined to show his people that he treated the

* For the words and music of this Lament see "The Killin Collection," and MacBean's "Songs of the Highlands."

prediction lightly, and so he continued to ride his favourite notwithstanding the entreaties of his friends to the contrary. On the day of his marriage, the chief rode his favourite charger, which became more than usually restive. He became so restive that the chief, losing control of himself and his horse, drew his pistol and shot him dead. Another horse was at once procured for the chief, and he proceeded to the church. After the ceremony was over, the bridal party set out on their homeward journey. The bride and her maids upon white palfreys preceded, and the bridegroom and his friends followed. In passing, the chief's roan horse shied at the dead body of the black horse and the rider was thrown to the ground and killed on the spot. A turn in the road hid the accident from those in front, and thus the bride, unconscious of the fatal fall of her husband, continued her way home the happiest of brides. Tradition relates that she not only composed the beautiful air of the lament, but chanted it as she moved forward at the head of the bier at her husband's funeral, and marked the time by tapping with her fingers on the lid of the coffin. This, it is said, she continued to do for several miles, from the family castle at Dalcross to the burying ground at Petty, near Inverness, and ceased not until she was torn away from the coffin, when it was about to be lowered into the grave. Her's was no ordinary experience—a maid, a bride, and a widow in one day—and she could sing with her sister of Erin*—

* See Campbell's "Language, Poetry, and Music of the Highland Clans," page 220, where the Erse words, and music, as well as a translation are given.

"A virgin, a widow, I mourn lone and lowly,
This morn saw me wedded in God's temple holy ;
And noontide beholds me a lone widow weeping
For my spouse in the dark tomb for ever lies sleeping.

"On my heart lies a cloud, and will lie there for ever,
Hark, hark to the death-knell that dooms us to sever !
Oh, well may my eyes pour forth tears as a fountain,
While dew gems the valley, and mist dims the mountain.

Arriving at the altar, great care was taken that no dogs passed between the bridal pair, and particular attention was paid to having the bridegroom's left shoe without buckle or latchet, in order to prevent witches from casting their unlucky spells over him and his bride. When the bridal knot was tied, it was customary for the young folk who attended the marriage to compete as to who should arrive first at the house of rejoicing, the first to arrive carrying with them the blessing, and being supposed to be the next to marry. This is called in the Lowlands "winnin' the kail." Meanwhile the young couple come out of the church, and having every knot about them untied, they went three times *deiseil* (sunwise) round the church. Thereafter they each retired, attended respectively by their "best-man" and "best-maid," when knots were retied, and the two parties—the bride's having precedence—hurried on to the place of merry-making. After the feast was over dancing commenced—the bride leading off—amid the shout of "*Bean-na-bainnse air an ùrlar,*" (the bride on the floor), and the piper appropriately striking up the well-known *port*—

"Mo thruaigh mi fhéin ma's droch bhean i,
Mo thruaigh mi fhéin thug dhachaidh i ;
Ithidh i biadh, 's cha dean i gniomh,
Mo thruaigh mi fhéin thug dhachaidh i."

[*Translation.*]
O, pity me if ill she be,
O, pity me that broucht her hame ;
She'll eat her food, and dae na guid,
O, pity me that broucht her hame.

Of course, it was unlucky to marry in May, as the rhyme has it—

"Marry in May and rue for aye."

A sunny marriage day was reckoned a good omen—

"If the day be foul that the bride gans hame,
Alack and alace but she'd lived her lane !
If the day be fair that the bride gans hame,
Baith pleasure and peace afore her are gane !"

Another rhyme says :—

"Happy the bride that the sun shines on,
And happy the corpse that the rain rains on."

During the course of the night the young couple proceeded to their future home, the piper usually striking up "Rach a laidhe 'laochain," (go to bed my hero.) It was generally the case that some one was in the house to receive them, and a bannock was broken over the bride's head for luck as she entered. Throwing slippers or shoes after a bridal party for luck is in accordance with an ancient Jewish custom. On Sunday the young couple were churched, and this brought the marriage festivities to a close.

There are many Gaelic proverbs bearing on marriage such as—

"Na gabh té air bith mar mhnaoi, ach té air am bi athais agad."

Take no woman for a wife in whom you cannot find a flaw.

The Irish say—"Na gabh bean gun locht."—Take no faultless wife.

"Tagh do bhean mar a 's math leat do chlann."

Choose your wife as you wish your children to be.

"Tagh do bhean 's i na currachd-oidhche."

Choose your wife with her night-cap on.

"Tagh nighean an deadh mhàthar, ged a b' e 'n donas a 'b athair dhi."

Choose the good mother's daughter, were the devil her father.

"Thoir eun a nead ghlan."

Take a bird out of a clean nest.

"An uair chì thu bean oileanach,
　Beir oirre, beir oirre,
Mur a beir thus oirre,
　Beiridh fear eil' oirre."

When you see a well-bred woman
　Catch her, catch her,
If you don't do it
　Another will match her.

"Ma's math leat do mholadh, faigh bàs; ma's math leat do chàineadh, pòs."—If you wish to be praised, die; if you wish to be decried, marry.

DEATH CUSTOMS.

On the death of a person in the Highlands, the corpse was stretched on a board, called *an eisinn* or *an eislinn*, covered with a linen wrapper, and the friends laid on the breast of the deceased a wooden platter, containing a small quantity of earth—usually a green sod—and salt. The earth was meant as an emblem of the corruptible body, while the salt was an emblem of the immortal soul. If there was any butter in the house, a nail was put into it, in order to prevent its putrefaction—or as the Celt called it, "*gun dol aog*," death being known as *an t-Aog*. There is a well known "port" which states—

"A' bhean a bh' aig an tàillear chaol,
Thug an t-Aog an ceann dhi."

All fires were extinguished where a corpse lay, and it was counted so ominous of evil for a dog or cat to pass over it, that the poor creature, was instantly deprived of life. Wakes were common, and it was customary for the bards to attend, and recite poems in memory of the departed; hence the origin of the phrase *Moladh mairbh* (praise of the dead), usually applied to undue adulation. It was unlucky to bury on Friday. Of old, coffins were not used, the dead being clad in their tartan plaids, and carried to the church yard on a board. For the poor folk, there was the parish coffin of wicker work, called the *caisil-chrò*, with a bottom that could be opened, as soon as the coffin touched the bottom of the grave. When this was done, the coffin was lifted out of the grave, and was ready for future use. It was probably to cover this *caisil*, that the parish "mort-cloth," or *brat-nam-marbh*, was originally used. A funeral occupied the entire day, it being disrespectful to the dead to undertake any other work on that day. If any of those carrying the bier stumbled, it was considered a bad omen for them. The churchyard had to be watched by the friends of the last person buried, till another funeral took place; hence the *bothain-chaithris* or watch-houses to be found in all old churchyards. In many cases, the family piper attended and played a *coranach* or *cumha*, as the body was being borne to the churchyard. Cairns were raised over the dead; hence the saying "Curidh mi clach a d' chàrn," (I will put a stone in your cairn), and on adding a stone, the wish was added—"A chuid de Phàrras dha," (His share of Paradise to him).

There are many Gaelic proverbs bearing on death, such as—"Cha tig am Bàs gun leisgeul." Death comes not without an excuse., "Cha tig am Bàs gus an tig an t-àm." (Death comes not till the time comes.)

DOMESTIC CUSTOMS.

We shall now consider some customs associated with the domestic life of the ancient Gael. In the pastoral age, when "congestion of population" was unknown, it was customary for a young couple, shortly after they got married, to set out in quest of a place, where they might set up a house of their own. Fate, as it were, was left to determine where the site of that home should be. A good strong withe or *gad*, having been twisted, and two creels *(cliabhan)* attached thereto, these creels, having been filled with stones, were set on the back of a steady horse. The horse, having now been turned round *deiseil* or sunwise, was allowed to proceed in any direction he liked. Roads being unknown, the horse proceeded over moss and fen till the withe or *gad* snapped by the weight of the stones in the creels *(cliabhan)*, and on the most convenient spot near by, the future home of the young people was at once set up. As the proverb says " *An tìr do 'n tigear 's i ghabhar* " (The land we come to will be the land accepted.) Before setting out on such an interesting expedition, the withes were steeped in water to soften them, hence the proverb, " *Is mithich a bhi bogadh nan gad* " (It is time to be steeping the withes, *i.e.*, getting ready for a journey.) In connection with setting up house, as well as at certain seasons of the year, there was a custom called *Dol air faoidh*—(going a-gathering)—called in the Lowlands "thrigging." The bride took a journey among her friends, each of whom presented her with some useful article of house-plenishing. This custom was also practised by widows and old women in reduced circumstances, who went on *Faoidh clòimh* or wool-gathering—this wool they afterwards made into stockings and clothes for themselves and others. It was quite common to go on *Faoidh Nollaig*, a little before Christmas, and on such occasions it was customary to go in couples. There is a Gaelic proverb which illustrates this. It runs—"Bithidh rud uime nach robh mu 'n chùl chàise " (Something will come of it more than the cheese back.) It seems that three parties of the MacDonalds of Glencoe went in different directions on a *Faoidh Nollaig*, or gentle-begging expedition, for the Christmas of 1543. They met by appointment at the Black Mount, and proceeded to divide the proceeds, when it was found, after everything else had been divided, that the remnant of a cheese, was still to be disposed of. From words on the subject, the claimants came to blows,—not with fists, alas! but with dirks, till only one man out of eighteen, was left to tell the tale! A small loch at the spot where this happened, is still known as "*Lochan na fola*," the bloody tarn.

In ancient times, the Celt ground his own meal and baked his own bread. A few good sheaves of corn or barley were taken, and the grain switched out of the ear and put in a pot on the fire to dry—this process is called *earraradh*, while the usual kiln-drying is called *ealchadh*. A quicker process of drying the grain was to set fire to the straw. This was known by the name *gradan*, from *grad*, quick, and the meal thus made was called *min ghradain*. The grain was then ground in the *bràth*, and was ready for use, it being possible to have the grain cut, dried, ground, and eaten in less than two hours. It may be interesting to quote the law enacted in 1284, in the reign of Alexander III, forbidding the the use of handmills or querns in Scotland :—

"That na man sall presume to grind quheit, maisloch or rye, with hand-mylnes, except to be compelled by storm, and be in lack of mylnes quhilk should grind the samen. And in this case if a man grindes at hand-mylnes, he shall give the threittein measure as multer;

SOME ANCIENT CELTIC CUSTOMS.

and gif any man contraveins this our prohibition, he sall tyne his hand-mylnes perpetuallie."

The operation of grinding with the quern, was usually performed by two women, sitting opposite each other on the floor. Underneath the quern was spread a dry hide, called the *craicionn bràthain*, to keep the meal clean. Song was essential to the operation, and several quern songs have been preserved. The following may be accepted as a specimen. It was collected by the late D. C. MacPherson, Edinburgh, the "*Abrach*" of Gaelic literature, and published by him in his collection of Gaelic songs called "*An Duanaire*." The translation is by Mr. M. MacFarlane, a member of this Society.

CRONAN BRATHANN.

Fonn—Hi hòileagan,
Hi hòileagan,
Mu'n cuairt a' bhràth
'S na sòraibh i;
Hi hòileagan,
Hi hòileagan.

O, beannaich am balg,
'Us beannaich an gràn,
A' chnotag* 's gach màm
De'n ghradanadh.†

Beannaich an t-inneal,
'Us beannaich an crann,

---

* *Cnotag.* A block of stone, or wood, hollowed out for unhusking barley. A husking mortar.

† *Gradan.* An expeditious mode of drying grain for the quern by burning the straw. (From *grad*, quick.)

A' bheirt 'us gach ball
A bhuincas di.

Cuir an car deiseal
Am feasda de'n bhràth,
Ma 's math leat min bhàn
'Bhi torrach dhuit.

Mu'n cuairt i 'n a still,
Le luinneagan binn,
'S cha toirear do'n t-sìthean ‡
Deannag dhi.

'N uair a rachadh i ceart 'n a siubhal.

Fonn—Mu'n cuairt i leis a' char dheiscal,
  Mu'n cuairt i gu daingeann trom ;
    Mu'n cuairt i leis a' char dheiscal,
  'S cha 'n eagal di 'dhol do'n tom.

Mu'n cuairt i le ruighe gramail,
  Na caomhain d'fhallus—bleith an gràn ;
Mo mhuirichinn 's iad uile falamh—
  Fear-an-tighe 'chion an tràth !

Na'm biodh agam bò dhruim-fhionn, cheann-fhionn,
  Na'm biodh agam bò chroidh-fhionn, dhoun ;
Cha bhiodh agam fear-an-tighe
  'Bleith na brathann, crom.

Ma's calchadh § a th'agad no gradan ;
  Mas earraradh ‖ e, fair dhomh mam ;

‡ *Sithean.* A fairy-mound.

§ *Ealchadh.* Grain dried in a kiln, or furnace.

‖ *Earraradh.* Parched corn ; corn parched in a pot prior to being ground in a quern.

'S ma 's acras, gur manadh 'g a chasgadh
Fideagan blasda¶—min bhàn !

THE QUERN CROON.

CHORUS—Sae merrilie,
Sae cheerilie,
Ca roun' the quern,
Not sparinglie,
But readilie,
And steadilie.

O, be the grain blest,
The poke and the rest,
Each heap, as it's prest,
O' the gradden grist.

And blest be the quern
The grip and the gearin
And ilka bit airn
Belangs until't.

Aye south about wheel
And a' shall gae weel ;
The bonnie white meal
Will be grand to eat.

Come, gar it spin roun'
Keepin time wi our tune,
And nane shall be stow'n
Tae Fairy Land.

¶ *Fideagan blasda.* I presume this means tasty mouthfuls of unhusked corn, called *sgiolan. Fideag* is a small white worm, just like unhusked corn.

When the speed increases.

CHORUS—The south about gar it gae spinnin';
Fu steadily gar it row;
Aye south about gar it gae spinnin';
And nane shall tae Fairy knowe.

O' ca awa till ye be pantin',
Till the sweat come on your brow;
The bairnies hae lang been wantin,
The guidman has fasted too.

Gin my kye in glens were roamin',
Or browsin' by yonder cairn,
My gudeman nae mair at gloamin'
Need be ca'in at the quern.

Come han' me, afore I famish,
A gowpen my mouth tae fill;
There's naethin' will hunger banish
Like grist frae our wee mill.

It is impossible to give anything like a literal translation of this quern croon. In the first verse a blessing is invoked on the sack containing the corn— or barley—on the grain itself, on the husking-mortar and each heap of parched corn. In the second verse a blessing is invoked on the quern and all that pertains thereto, while in the third and fourth verses, the operator is enjoined to turn the quern in a right-ward direction if he would wish the meal to be nutricious, and if this be done, none will go to the fairy-mound. This belief in turning the quern to right-ward, is not confined to grinding with the quern, but is applied on all occasions as enjoined by the proverb—"*Deiseil air gach ni,*" (The sunward course with everything.) There are several Gaelic proverbs which refer to the quern "*Is feairrde bràth a breacadh gun a bristeadh,*" (A quern is the better of being picked without being broken.) Another proverb runs "*Gun aon tàmh air beul na bràthan, 's gun aon ghràinn' air chionn an làtha*" (Without ceasing of the quern, and not a grain at the end of the day) *i.e.*, the fruit of the grinding or "*torradh*" being carried away by the fairies as fast as it was made. It will be observed that as the speed of the quern increases, the measure of the song changes.

MAIDE-DOICHIOLL.

In days long ago, locks were almost unknown in the Highlands; indeed, the ancient Celt looked upon them as decidedly mean—hence the saying "*Cha mosach ris na glasan,*" (as nasty as the locks.) Doors were seldom closed, but it was customary to place a white stick or wand across the door-way when people were dining, or engaged in any occupation where privacy was required. This stick was called *maide-dvichioll* or stick of inhospitality. Sir Walter Scott refers to this custom in "Rob Roy," when he makes the party in possession of Jean MacAlpine's "Change-house," at the Clachan of Aberfoyle, ask the intruders if they did not observe by the "white wand above the door, that the house was already occupied." Martin found the custom quite common when he visited the Hebrides in 1693.

SLINNEARACHD.

This was a method of divination, in which the ancient Celt placed great reliance. It was called "*slinnearachd*" from *slinnean* a shoulder. It was performed thus—The meat was cleared from a shoulder-blade of beef or mutton, without the assistance of a knife or any other weapon. The diviner carefully inspected the transparent part of the bone, and from the disposition of certain spots, predicted whatever remarkable was to happen to the family, or to any of the relations of the person, from whose flock or herd the animal had been taken.

At feasts or marriages the rump of any animal was called the "Bards' portion," from the fact that whoever got this portion, was expected to compose a verse of poetry, suitable to the occasion. At a wedding party in the village of Cladich, Lochaweside, the "best man" was a Captain Campbell. Sitting opposite him at the supper table, was a worthy representative of the Clan Cameron, whose gathering-tune is "*Thigibh an so a chlanna nan con 's gheibh sibh feoil,*" (Come hither ye sons of the hounds and you will get flesh.) For the purpose of raising a laugh, Campbell handed a well-polished bone across the table to Cameron, and asked him to show his bardic powers. Recollecting the popular belief that the Campbells got their name from *cam*, wry or twisted, and *beul* a mouth, Cameron said :—

"An Sergeant Caimbeul so shuas,
 Duine uasal o bhun nan cnoc,

> Shin e 'n droll dhomh thar a' bhòrd,
> Ach b' ait leis gu leòir e bhi 'na chorp.
> Ged thug sinne spéis do 'n fheòil
> 'S car a bhi 'n ar sròin 'na déigh,
> Tha cuid eile 's caime beòil,
> Cho déigheil air an fheòil rinn féin."

Recollecting that the name *Cameron* is supposed to be derived from *cam*, twisted, and *sròn* a nose, the following free translation may pass—

> "My friend Sergeant Campbell the bravest of men,
> Who lives in yon Clachan far over the ben,
> A well-polished rump-bone has handed to me,—
> The meat that was on it he ate, as you see.
> *Our* love for good mutton acknowledge I must,
> And for *it*, I believe that our nose took a twist,
> But here we have others with mouths all awry
> With eating good mutton, and beef on the sly."

Our forefathers had the good sense not to eat for eating's sake. They had the bards and *seanachies* at their feasts, who recited poems on the valiant deeds of the heroes, accompanying their recital with the harp. The value of a feast was in accordance with the richness of its conversation—their's indeed was—

> "The feast of reason and the flow of soul,"

and hence the proverb "*Cha 'n fhiach cuirm gun a còmhradh,*" (a feast is worth little without its conversation.)

There was another custom common among Highlanders—and with it I shall end my paper. After partaking of any food, the entertainer shook hands with his guests, and wished them health and prosperity.

I was the object of such sincere congratulations the the other year, when I spent a few days under the hospitable roof of my good friend Mr. J. Campbell, the the poet of Ledaig.

I am conscious that I have but touched the fringe of a very large and interesting subject. There is little that is original in all that I have stated, but the recital of these ancient customs may help to perpetuate some of them. I have, in fact, "gathered a posie of other men's flowers, and nothing but the thread that binds them is mine own."

[25th March, 1890.]

At the meeting of the Society held on this date, Dr. A. Clerk, read a paper entitled, 'Notes on Ancient Gaelic Medicine.' Dr. Clerk's paper was as follows:—

NOTES ON ANCIENT GAELIC MEDICINE.

To explain why the first part of this paper is occupied with translations from an old Latin book, I must make a short preliminary statement. In the Advocates' Library in Edinburgh there are twenty or more Gaelic MSS., most of them, I believe, not original, but translated by one of the Beatons or Bethunes, a famous family of Physicians, who settled at first in Argyleshire, but on the invitation of the Lord of the Isles, removed to Skye. They were the descendants of Archibald Bethune of Pitlochy and Coppeldrie, in Fife, 5th son of John Bethune, 5th laird of Balfour, of which latter Cardinal Beaton was nephew. A pamphlet was published in Edinburgh in 1778, giving the genealogical history of the family, which mentions that Angus, 5th descendant from the laird of Balfour, wrote a "system of physic, the *Lily of Medicine*, which he finished at the foot of Montpellier, and after 28 years' study." Of course this is a mistake; the author was a professor at Montpellier University, but not a Beaton, as the title of the book indicates: *Bernardi Gordonii opus, Lilium Medicinae*, &c. What Dr. Beaton did, was to translate the Lily into Gaelic. There is not much known about Bernardus, but his book became an authority in most civilized countries in Europe. It was translated also into Irish Gaelic, and some of the MSS. are still found in the British Museum, with interesting annotations. Dr. Moore of London, contributed a very interesting paper on these MSS. to the St. Bartholomew Hospital Reports, from which I will make a few quotations, to show how highly the *Lilium* was esteemed in Ireland in the 14th and 15th centuries. There is a manuscript copy in the Bodleian Library, Oxford, dated 1505, but it was never printed in English.

The practice of the educated Physicians in those days in the Highlands and in Ireland can be studied in the *Lilium Medicinae* of which we shall give a few samples—the practice of medicine among the common people we must pick up from traditional sayings and proverbs; the latter part of this paper will mention some of these.

The following annotations from the Irish MSS. will show the high esteem in which this book was held.

(1) Aois an tighearna in tam do scriobadh an leabhar so 1482 agus isi an bliadhan sin do marbh Pilib Mac Tomais a Baira Pilib Mac Risdeart a Baira.

The age of the Lord the time this book was written, 1482; and it is this year that Philip, son of Thomas Barry, slew Philip, son of Richard Barry.

Here is another interesting quotation : "A prayer for Gerald the Earl, Lord Justice of Ireland, who bought the book for twenty cows. Two and twenty skins in this book. The tax of Ormond, one hundred and twenty cows, came to the Earl the day this was written. Thomas O Maolchonaire lifted that tax for the Earl. The year of grace, this year in which I am, 1500 of the age of our blessed Lord at this time." The Earl seems to have parted with the precious volume, as a later inscription says : "Charles Hicky is the possessor of this book, and if it be lost I pray God restore it back again, 1680." Another book says : "From the books of Mahon MacMahon, doctor of Physic, after 14 years at the University of Paris, a learned man of France, 1728."

I found a copy of the *Lilium Medicinae* at the Glasgow University, and will give a few translations to show what a mixture of superstition and shrewd sense was in its learned pages.

I will read a part of the preface to explain why books in those days were often called after the names of flowers. "Moreover, in honour of the Heavenly Lamb, that is most shining, and is the glory of God, the Father, I give Lily of the Art of Healing for title to the book. For the Lily has many flowers upon it, and seven white leaves, and seven golden grains in each Lily of them: and it is this shall be the book; for there shall be seven parts in it, and the first part of them shall be golden, shining, lucid, and it shall speak of all diseases, beginning with fevers. Five shall be the other parts, and they too shall be light, pleasing, and shining, and will make everything clear of which they speak. It was in the light, clean University of Montpellier, that, by the aid of Almighty God, this book was begun after the twentieth year of our reading, and the annals of the Lord were at that time 1000 years and 300 and 3 years, and it was in the month of July, that it was begun." Thus finisheth his preface.

I should like now to give you a few specimens of medical literature and the method of treating a subject, before the days of experimental science, and shall I say, before the days of inductive reasoning. Perhaps I had better not affirm the latter, for no doubt, men always reasoned more or less inductively, but you would certainly be much struck with the easy way in which the philosophers of these middle ages drew their conclusions.

INCUBUS. CHAPTER XXIII.

"Incubus is an apparition bruising, and weighing upon the body in the time of sleep, and confusing movement and sleep.

The incubus, moreover, is the name of a demon, and it is therefore, that some people hold, that when this demon is right upon the body of the person, especially when he is asleep, empty because of the corrupt influence he presses upon the body, so that the patient dreams that he is being smothered. And in the case of sucking children, they are often smothered, because they are unable to suffer so much corruption; and this is the opinion of the theologians. Although the laity say that it is a hag that is in it a-jumping about upon the body bruising it, and this is nought, and the physicians have a better opinion.

Incubus either comes from an internal or external cause; if external for example, when the patient is asleep, coldness comes suddenly upon the back of the head, squeezing and shutting it, or when a body sleeps after being filled too much with food and drink. The internal cause, moreover, is corrupt fog arising from the humours closing and oppressing the brain, and the heart, so that spirits are not able to go fully into the body; and thus, since it is in the members that they are soonest at an ebb, therefore, it appears to the sick, that this phantom seems to arise from the feet, and afterwards little by little covers the whole body. . . and, therefore, he speaks grunting, asking help, if he could speak, and is altogether shivering, because of that heavy burden, and in consequence of the shutting up and obscuring of the spirits.

And that sometimes comes from the blood, and sometimes from a great cholera, and sometimes from phlegma, and sometimes from melancholia.

Signa.—The symptoms of this dream are indicated through the suffering of the sick man himself.

Prognostica.—To whoever this often comes, unless relieved, he will fall into one of the following:—Apoplexy, epilepsy, or spasm, or paralysis, or sudden death. And, if it come to a person awake, it is worse; and also if it come with a cold sweat, while awake, and if it come with palpitation of the heart, it is worse of all.

Cura.—First of all, the person to whom this is wont to come, let him have a beloved companion who will waken him when he hears him speaking, like crying, and who will rub his feet and his hands strongly, and will sprinkle his face with rose-water, and will give an emetic, and dianthus with musk or diambra; and in such case it may be well said, that there is always Pylades, who will cure Orestes." I need hardly continue this any longer, as the rest is only various other cures for the nightmare.

Let me read you what he says of a disease which is common enough, namely, epilepsy or the falling sickness.

"Nevertheless I say to you about epilepsy, that I have treated many old, poor, rich men and women, and of almost all kinds of epilepsy, and yet I have not myself, nor have I seen anyone else, cure any patient, who was not young, or one where the disease was due to unhealthy way of life, and had not been long established, though I did my best in every case, and though the patients were obedient. Here I am ignorant, but God has knowledge. And I say this so that when patients come to you, you may avoid disgracing yourselves by empty and untrue promises of curing epilepsy, because every epilepsy is eradicated with great difficulty if at all.

K

When the patient is in the fit, if some one puts his mouth over the ear of the patient, and says three times those three verses :—

> "Gaspar fert mirrham thus Melchior Bathasar aurum
> Haec tria, qui secum porlabit nomina regum,
> Solvitur à morbo Christi pietate caduco."

Without doubt he will get up at once. That this is efficacious when repeated in the ear is true, and it has often been proved, that he gets up at once. And it is said that the same verses written and worn round the neck cure entirely."

As these two specimens of Bernardus may be a little tedious to people, who are not specially conversant with medical subjects, I will give the remaining quotation on a subject with which every person is more or less on speaking terms.

In speaking of Love, Bernardus says :—" Love, which is called *Eros*, is a melancholy feeling arising from love to a woman. The cause of this passion is a false estimate of the form, figure, and manner, which gets fixed in his mind. Hence when anyone is taken captive from love of some particular person, he believes and thinks her to be fairer, better, and more adorable, more pleasing, and higher-endowed by nature and morals than any other; therefore he loves her ardently without mode or measure, thinking that, if he gain his end, he will be happy and delighted. His judgment is corrupted, because he is continually brooding over these things, and dismisses all other considerations. Thus, when anyone speaks to him, he hardly hears what is said to him."

There is a good deal more of this graphic description, but it is too long to insert here. Now for a few of the symptoms of *Eros*.

"They go off sleep, food, and drink, they get thin, their eyes are often tearful; they brood over hidden thoughts with grievous sighs, and if they listen to songs which regret the parting of lovers, they immediately begin to weep and be sad, but if it be of the union of lovers, they begin to laugh, and sing. The pulse is irregular and out of order, but becomes quick and bounding if the name of their sweetheart is mentioned, or should she happen to pass before them. Galen remarks, that you can find out if the melancholy of your patient be that of love, or of something else, by mentioning the names of his lady-acquaintances, and, when her name occurs, up goes the pulse."

Many other symptoms are given, but with these examples, I will give a few of his recommendations for treatment.

"If he will listen to reason let him be done with false imaginings: let some one make him ashamed by instruction and advice of his foolish conduct, showing him the dangers of his time of life, the day of judgment, and the joys of Paradise; and if he is not amenable to reason, and should be young, let him be whipped frequently and severely, until the whole affair becomes disgusting to him. After that you can let him free, as Ovid says:—

Ostia si tollas, periere Cupidinis arus.

"If you open the door the bow of Cupid shall be broken." He also adds, give him something to do, and again quotes Ovid:—

Da vacuae menti, quo teneatur, opus.

"Give work to the empty mind, by which it may be steadied."

Much as Tennyson in Locksley Hall:—

I myself must mix with action, lest I wither by despair.

"Visit beautiful places, mountains, plains, fountains, groves and fine scenery."

I will finish with one more prescription—no doubt efficacious, but the ladies might object—"Admire always two women—more if you like—the more the better. This will keep your love from being so concentrated as to be dangerous." When the venerable old Doctor gave this advice to young men, he evidently was ignorant of damages for breach of promise, or injured feelings.

Let Chaucer finish this very imperfect sketch of Bernardus—

> Well knew he the olde Esculapius,
> And Deiscorides and eek Rufus;
> Old Ypocras, Haly, and Galien;
> Scrapyon, Razis, and Avycen;
> Averrois, Damascien, and Constantyn;
> *Bernard* and Gatesden, and Gilbertyn.
> *Chaucer.*

MEDICAL MAXIMS IN GAELIC.

To leave the book knowledge of those days, and which, no doubt, was considered scientific, let me draw your attention to the knowledge, which existed among the people—knowledge of plants, wells, and incantations. Medicine like all other sciences, and arts, was first cultivated among the people, and there was no class or caste set apart for its cultivation. However, it began to be confined to a special class at a very early period of civilization, as we see that among the savage tribes of Africa, in our own day, the medicine man is both priest and doctor, rolled into one. With us it was quite the reverse, as the practice of medicine was, in the middle ages, confined mostly to the priestly caste, and surgery, till comparatively recent times, was relegated to the barber. You see till this day, the notched plate dangling over the barber's shop. The plate was to hold the blood, and the notch was scooped out to fit the arm. Surgery in our day, is quite the co-equal if not the superior of medicine. The physician in those days, sent for the barber, when he wanted blood drawn, now he sends for—no—he now never draws blood at all.

A great many cures, which are no cures, and incantations, which are ineffectual, are found in every district, but they are not all of this description, and I must say, that many excellent advices, for the treatment, and especially for the prevention of disease, are given in the form of verse. Many of them have acquired the dignity of proverbs. I mean to give a few of those in the following pages, though I fear they may be a little tedious, as good advice very often is—

>An uair a bhios a bhrù làn,
>'S miann leis an t-sùil tàmh.

>When the stomach is full,
>The eye becomes dull.

This hardly needs any commentary, for nearly everyone has experienced the inclination to nod after a heavy meal, especially if near the fire. When the stomach has received food, it requires a large supply of blood to manufacture the gastric juice, as well as for the absorption of the products of digestion, and thus the brain is deprived of its usual supply, and so tends to inaction and sleep.

The next one I quote, shows that the eruptive fevers were not unknown among them—

> Cha luaith a sguireas an tinneas diot,
> Na thoisicheas an tachas ort.

> No sooner does the fever go,
> Than the itch begins.

In fevers accompanied with rashes, the skin comes off, after the rash has disappeared—may be in large flakes as in scarlet-fever, or in fine dust as in measles. This desquamation is often accompanied with itching. I think that is the correct interpretation.

Here is a curious saying: more poetical, I fear, than matter of fact—

> Cha n 'eil caslainte gun iocshlaint,
> Ach cha n 'eil tilleadh air an aog.

> Every disease has its remedy
> But death is irresistible.

But death is usually the consequence of some malady, so that this would hardly hold except all died of old age or accident. However, the expression is beautiful, and we must not be too critical.

The next expresses absolute truth—

> Cha 'n ionann do fhear na neasgaid,
> Agus do fhear 'ga fàsgadh.

> The man who has a boil feels differently
> From the man who squeezes it.

Proverbs, as you know, are only partially true. Perhaps we might say that of everything, as well as of proverbs. The following illustrates this—

> Cuiridh aon tragh air ais laogh is leanabh.

> One meal if it lack, calf or child will go back.

Now-a-days, at least in towns, children are often crammed with food, and would be the better of fewer meals.

> Dian-fhàs fuilt; crion fhàs cuirp.

> Great growth of hair, small growth of body.

In my younger days I thought and indeed had been told that hairy people were very strong, and so some may be, but from observations which I have made since I began to turn my attention to the signs of disease, or tendency to disease, I have often observed, that strumous children are often covered with more hair—generally a fine downy hair—than healthy children. They have often large eye-lashes, and quick growth of nails. You are not for a moment to think, that all who have long eye-lashes are of this constitution—such a belief would mar our appreciation of the beauty of an eye thus endowed. Starvation, or insufficient food, produces, I suppose, the same in animals—small body, long hair and large head. The next is half truth perhaps, but the other half superstition.

> Fear sa bith a dh'òlas bainne capaill le spàinn chriothninn, cha gabh e n'triuth ach aotrom.
>
> He who drinks mare's milk with an aspen spoon, will take the hooping cough lightly.

Of course mare's milk is very nourishing, and perhaps the aspen is thrown in to increase the patient's faith. A mixture of imagination and milk—not by any means a bad composition.

The next maxim is only too true—"Galar fada, is eug na bhun."—a prolonged disease and death at its root. This is so true, that it needs hardly any commentary, but for fear it should be too depressing, let me add, that, as I said before, it is not by any means absolutely true. At the public dispensary of Anderson's College, where large numbers of the poor were treated gratuitously, I often asked,—How long have you had this cough? Ah weel doctor, I hae this hoast for 20 years.

Here are two maxims, which I could make nothing of at first, till I thought them over for a while.

> Fàsaidh an fheòil, fhad 's is beò an smior.
> Gleidhidh cnaimh feòil, fhad 's is beò smior.

"Flesh will grow, while marrow lives," may do as a translation of both. The function of the marrow of bones was for a long time unknown—the spinal marrow of course, we know to be a thick strand of nerves, but not so that of the long bones, which is largely made up of fat. It is now supposed, or I should rather say ascertained to be engaged in blood-making. If that be so, it is a most important function, and no doubt the flesh, as well as other tissues, would suffer, if the marrow was affected. How did the makers of those proverbs know of the importance of the marrow? If a proverb is the wisdom of many, and the wit of one, then the function of the marrow must have been well known to many.

Is mairg do 'n dùthchas droch ghalar.
Sad is the inheritance of a bad disease.

This proverb sums up the doctrine of heredity of disease. There are a few diseases which can be transmitted directly from parents to offspring, but there is heredity in another way, which is not so depressing to the unfortunate, who may have been dowered with this sad inheritance. Consumption and cancer, for instance, are well known to run in families, as the saying is. Though that is so, and is a popular belief, yet it comes about, I believe, only in this way. There are no specific germs of the disease transmitted, but such as the parents are, so are the children. If the parents have a weakness in their constitution, then by the law of heredity, the children will likely be endowed with the same bad qualities. I may put it in another way: that instead of receiving the disease from their parents, they only receive a body, which is not endowed with a strong resistance to this special disease. If that be true, it may encourage all, who have this bad *dùthchas*, to take care of themselves, and they will likely escape altogether the fate of their parents. The next wise saying seems to have been made to show the way out of a bad heredity.

Ruigidh an ro-ghiullachd air an ro-ghalar.

Good nursing (or care) may overcome the worst disease.

So it may, and as families must have acquired a heredity for evil, so, *vice versa*, they may uproot this tendency for a better. These Gaelic sayings are really astonishing. They are pithily expressed, and show a wonderful insight into the subjects of which they treat. I might add many more, but too much wisdom is apt to grow tiresome, so we will leave them and speak for a short time of the more superstitious cures, which were practised, in olden times, in the Highlands, and which have not altogether disappeared yet from among some of the Islands and Glens.

In Martin's book on the Western Isles, published in 1703, is mentioned, among other things, the admirable and expeditious way the Islanders had of curing most diseases by simples of their own product.

For "poor meagre people" whale is recommended— the smaller kind being the most nourishing. In a few weeks, if this treatment is carried out, these same meagre people become plump and lusty. "The natives chase the whales into the bays, and if they wound one mortally it runs ashore, and, what is wonderful, the others follow the track of blood, and run themselves also on shore in like manner." This treatment is on the same lines as our own, when we give cod-liver oil to emaciated people.

They treat jaundice at least with vigour, if not so rationally, as the last. The directions are these:—

"To cure jaundice put the patient on his face, and pretending to look on his backbone, pour a pailful of cold water on his bare back, and this proves successful."

A second method—They make the tongs red hot in the fire, and gently touch the patient along the vertebral column, "which makes him furiously run out of doors, still supposing the hot iron on his back, till the pain be abated, which happens very speedily, and the patient recovers soon after." The hot iron is still used as a method of treatment for various complaints.

For inflammation of the lungs the great remedy was bleeding, the practice of which only ceased a generation back. They bled the cattle in the beginning of summer, from an idea that they fattened better after, and made bannocks of the blood, which they considered of high value when travelling. No doubt they were nourishing morsels, and kept any length of time after being smoked and dried.

The following is an instance of clever surgical ingenuity. The uvula, or little tongue that hangs at the back of the mouth sometimes gets paralysed, and is more than doubled in length. Often it returns to its original size, but occasionally it remains permanently elongated. The operator passed a hair through a quill, so as to form a loop; this loop they passed over the uvula, and by pulling at the ends of the hair they tightened it, and with a pair of scissors, snipped off what was below the constriction. The modern instrument, called the *guillotine*, is much on the same principle.

John Campbell, forrester of Harris, had a very unique treatment for cold. He walked into the sea with his clothes on, and immediately went to bed, wet clothes and all, and having loaded himself with blankets, he soon fell into a profuse sweat, and his distemper disappeared. The late Archbishop Whately hewed wood as hard as he could for some time, then ran to bed, piled on blankets, and, like our friend John Campbell, broke into a good sweat.

A better method however, was common among the Islanders. The earthen floor of the house was heated by a large fire. The fire was then removed, and the floor covered with straw, upon which the patient lay down. He was then covered with blankets, and, in a short time, he perspired freely over all his body.

The Irish improved on this. They built a small circular turf hut, in the centre of which they lighted a fire on a flagstone. When the stone was well heated, they removed the fire, and, as in the last instance, covered it over with straw, on which the sick person lay. The opening was then closed, and, after a certain interval, the patient came out bathed in perspiration, and often left his malady behind. We may see in these three instances the evolution of the Turkish bath, as it exists in modern times.

With these common sense methods were often mixed up superstitions compounded of pagan and christian elements. When the Lewis people wished to look into the future and know the result of the malady, they sent a person to St. Andrew's well, in the village of Shadar, to fetch some water. When the messenger arrived at the well, he softly floated the vessel or dish on the water, and if the vessel turned sunwise in its motion the patient would recover, but if the reverse way the malady would be fatal. This no doubt is a survival of the ancient sun worship, traces of which remain in many of our old customs. Dr. Stewart "Nether Lochaber," that veteran antiquary, relates the following anecdote, which illustrates the same worship.

A messenger was sent to a remote glen, and, when he arrived at the shepherd's house, he found it shut, and no one about. Not far off he saw some smoke rising from a hollow, and thinking that the people were probably washing at the stream, he directed his footsteps thither. What was his astonishment, when he approached the smoke, to find not a washing, but a number of women performing a ceremony, which was certainly not christian. There were five women in all, two of whom held a large hoop between them. This hoop had been covered over with a straw rope wound round and round, and sprinkled with oil in order to make it burn the better. It was then ignited, and soon a complete circle of fire was formed, through which a small rickety baby was passed from hand to hand by two women, who stood on opposite sides, and as many times as it was months of age. The child was supposed to be blighted by an evil eye, and the passage through the fire was believed to thwart this influence.

In Dumfries, which is comparatively Celtic, they often put their sickly children sitting on the middle of a cart-wheel, as the smith was fitting on the iron ring, which is made first red-hot to burn its way smooth on the wooden felloes.

Of all heathen deities the sun is the noblest, if we can call any one of them so. The sun was to the ancients the most powerful force in the universe, and the source of all life, and we can hardly wonder that, in the pre-scientific age, it received divine honours.

[27TH APRIL, 1890.]

At the Business Meeting of the Society held on this date, the various Office-Bearers read reports, satisfactory in every respect. Thereafter Mr J. G. Mackay read a paper on '*Life in the Highlands a hundred years ago.*' Mr. Makay's paper was as follows:—

SOCIAL LIFE IN THE HIGHLANDS IN THE OLDEN TIMES.

It is unfortunate that so little has been written about the Highlands by natives of the country, who being acquainted with the state of society and manners, would be able to give an intelligent and unbiassed account of the social condition of the country in the past, and not left us dependent upon what has been written by strangers, many of whom were prejudiced, and who, even though they would have been incline to treat us fairly, could hardly have done so from their want of knowledge of the language, customs, and institutions of the people. That there were many Highlanders even at a remote period who could have done so, there is not any doubt, for, though there were no schools of learning in the country previous to the Reformation, many of the Highland youth of good families got a fair education in Edinburgh and Aberdeen, and some went abroad, even to France and Italy. Martin, who wrote an account of his tour to the Western Isles about the end of the seventeenth century, says that he was not only the first native, but the *first* who travelled in these islands, to write a description of them. He makes a complaint which might very well be repeated at the present day, "That the modern itch after knowledge of foreign places is so prevalent, that the generality of mankind bestow little thought or time upon the place of their own nativity." and adds, "It is become customary in those of quality to travel young, into foreign countries, while they are absolute strangers at home."

This has left us with very little knowledge of the social life of the Highland people during a very interesting part in their history.

During those years between the Reformation and the "45," the Highlanders occupied a very prominent part in Scottish History, and it is their misfortune to have their deeds recorded by historians who showed no disposition to do them justice. While their bravery and military prowess could not be denied,—as in disparaging *their* bravery that of their opponents would be still further degraded,—the meanest and most mercenary of motives were attributed to them. The chiefs were represented as being actuated not by sympathy or principle, but from their inherent love for rapine and disorder, while their followers were supposed to have no choice in the matter, but to blindly follow their chiefs without questioning the object or cause.

We are not so much concerned in the meantime as to the part the Highlanders took in the events of those stirring times. Many of the facts are recorded in history, and their bitterest enemies cannot deny them the credit which is their due, and we may hope some day to see a History of Scotland that will do them the justice their conduct deserves. Our purpose at present is to give so far as we have been able to gather from the limited sources at our command, an account of the social life in the Highlands during the last century, and the early part of the present, before the great changes consequent on the introduction of the sheep-farming system took place.

Life in the Highlands in those times was very different indeed from what it is at the present day.

In a purely pastoral country like the Highlands, nearly the whole population was necessarily occupied in one way or another about the land, and everyone must consequently have more or less land, according to his station, for the maintenance of his stock, which constituted the wealth of the country. The land was divided in the first instance in large tacks among the chieftains or head men, who occupied what was termed "so many *peighinn*," or penny-lands, and for which they paid a certain tribute annually, partly in kind and partly in money, in support of the dignity of the chief. These men again let out portions of the land to the common men of the tribe, for which they received payment in kind and also in services, such as cutting and stacking peats, tilling the ground, and securing the crops, &c.

These services were rendered according to a regular system, so many days at peat cutting, at spring work, or harvest, &c. When the services were rendered for land held direct of the chief, they were termed *Morlanachd* or *Borlanachd*. When for lands held of the tacksmen, they were termed *Cariste*. So long as the patriarchal system prevailed, these services were neither so severe nor so degrading as they became in later years, when the chiefs lost all interest in their people. When the strong arms and loyal hearts of his clansmen formed his only wealth, the chief was very careful of the comfort of his people, and the tacksman were bound to treat them justly, as the chief could not depend upon the loyalty of an unhappy people. When, however, with altered circumstances, after the passing of the "Hereditary Jurisdiction Act," they lost the power they formerly held, of combining together for the purpose of warfare, their love for their people ceased; farms were let to the highest bidder, and in most instances, south-country shepherds and stock raisers, took the place of the Highland gentlemen tacksmen. Then the position of those who were left as sub-tenants, became uncomfortable in the

L

extreme. The former tacksmen, from their kindly nature and clannish sympathies, would naturally treat them kindly, but the new-comers, whose only interest was the making of money, considered them only as lumber in the way of their sheep and cattle, and services which formerly were rendered as an indirect way of maintaining the dignity of their chief, soon became degrading in their eyes, and very grevious to be borne.

The land held by the members of the clan under the old system, was divided into townships, usually *leth-pheighinn*, or half-penny land to the townships. Penny-lands were of different sizes, probably according to their value, or custom of the district.

Skene says, that the average township in the Mid Highlands consisted of 90 acres within the head dyke, of which 20 acres were infield, 15 acres were outfield, 10 acres meadow, 35 acres green pasture, and 10 acres woody waste, and the moorland behind the dyke 250 acres.

The arable land was usually held on the runrig system, a third of the land being divided by lot every three years, while each had a stated amount of stock on the hill pasture. Besides the regular rent charge, each member of the clan contributed according to his means on great occasions, such as the marriage of a son or daughter of the chief. These contributions, in the aggregate, frequently amounted to a good deal. It was customary, even on the occasion of the marriage of an ordinary clansman, for the neighbours to make a contribution of useful articles so as to put the young couple in a good way of house keeping.

The rent book of a Highland chief in the olden time would be a very interesting study to day, with its payments in kind. In the old "Statistical Account" of Scotland, Dr. Smith, of Campbeltown, gives a most interesting statement of the rental of the district of Kintyre and Islay in 1542, then in the possession of the Lord of the Isles—

North Kintyre.

In money, £105 10s. 0d. Scots.
Oatmeal, 388¼ sts. a st. is ⅛ of a Boll.
Malt, 4 chalders 10 Bolls.
Marts, 6, Cow, 1.
Mutton, 41.
Cheese, 307¼ sts.

South Kintyre.

Money, £162 3s. 4d. Scots.
Meal, 480 sts. 2 pecks.
Malt, 25 chalders, 14 Bolls, 2 Firlot.
Marts, 48, Mutton, 53.
Cheese, 342¼ sts.

Islay and Rhinds.

Money, £45 0s. 1d. Scots.
Meal, 2593 sts.
Marts, 301
Mutton, 301
Cheese, 2161 sts. 3 lb.
Geese, 301
Poultry, 301

TOTAL.

In money,	£323	18 6
Meal, 3061 grs. 3 qr. 3 lb. at 2s.,	366	2 10
Malt, 30 chalders, 8 Bolls, 2s. 4d. at 5s.	122	2 6
Marts, 356 at 2 marks,	553	6 8
Mutton, 559, 2s.,	45	11 10
Geese, 301 at 4, Poultry, 301 at 2,	6	0 4
	£1666	2 11

At the time of which we write there were no slated houses in the Highlands, with the exception of the castle of the chief and chieftain. The common houses were built upon the same plan as many of the crofters' houses of the present day, with the fire on the middle of the floor. Many of them had the cattle in the one end of the building, with only a wattle partition plastered with clay, dividing them from the part occupied by the family. Many more had barns and stables apart from the dwelling, but were irregularly placed. From the ruins of hamlets still easily traceable on every hill side, it can be seen that the habitations of the tenants of former days were built more substantial, and with more ideas to comfort than the huts of their successors the crofters.

One cannot, on examining the ruins of the many castles in the Highlands, but be struck with the extraordinary strength of the buildings, and it is difficult to imagine that they could have been the work of the barbarians our ancestors are supposed to have been, if we believe all we are told by the historians. In order to give them strength they were built on the ledges of rocks, or on the most inaccessible promontories, which would make it a very difficult undertaking, even with all the machinery of the present day. What it must have been in those days it is difficult to imagine. These buildings took such a time to put up, and cost so much labour, that it is not astonishing that the minor gentry contented themselves with houses of a less pretentious kind.

In foretelling the many changes that were to come over the country, *Coinneach Odhar*, mentions among other things, that there would be a "*Tigh geal air gach cnoc*," a white house on each hillock, which has been verified in some districts at least. It is a source of astonishment to strangers visiting the Western Isles, that the people are content to live in such houses, as many of them inhabit. From a careful study of the Highland question, I have become convinced that it is more the misfortune than the inclination of the people, which causes such an apparent want of desire to improve their surroundings. I am satisfied that notwithstanding the insecurity of tenure in the past, they would not content themselves in such houses were it not the great difficulty of procuring timber, there being very little growing timber in the islands. This is easily seen, as in those districts in the Highlands where wood is easily procurable, the houses are of a superior class, and even in the islands, whenever a crofter made a little money, his first care was to improve his dwelling, though frequently at the risk of an increase of rent.

The rearing and dealing in cattle was by far the most important industry in the country, and even the principal gentry were engaged in it. They collected all the cattle, which they bought up usually in the month of September, and drove them to the Southern markets. The transporting of a drove of cattle in those days, was a laborious work, as well as a very risky one. In many cases they had to pay tribute for permission to pass through the land of a clan with whom the owner did not happen to be on good of terms. They often ran the risk of encountering some of the *Ceatharnachs*, or broken men who infested the mountain passes on the road, and losing some of the droves, unless the drovers were strong enough to hold their own.

In many cases the drovers did not pay for their herd till their return, and then they went round their customers, and paid them with scrupulous honesty. Most of them being gentlemen of honour and position in their respective districts, the people considered the transaction safe. When occasionally they were disappointed, the unfortunate thing was that they had no redress—there was no petitioning for cessio in those days. *Rob Donn*, the bard, who was frequently employed as a drover in the interest of his chief, Lord Reay, and others, composed a very scathing elegy on the death of one of these characters, who died at Perth, on his way home from the South.

"Tha Rogairean airtnealach trom,
'N taobh bhos agus thall do na Chrasg
O 'n chual iad mu 'n cuairt an Ceann-cinnidh,
Gu 'n do dh 'eug e an Siorramachd Pheairt.
Dh' aindeoin a dhreuchdan 's a chiall
Cha do chreid duine riamh a bha ceart

> Aon smid thàinig mach air a bheul
> 'S cha mho chreid e féin Righ nam feart."

From the want of roads, cattle was the only commodity that could make its own way to the market, the small Highland breed of sheep which was reared in the country at that time, was not usually sent to the Southern markets—this breed of sheep which is now nearly extinct, with the exception of some few still reared by the crofters in the Island of Uist, is a hardy little animal, the wool of which is very fine, and the mutton exceedingly sweet and tender. I have seen some rams of this breed, with as many as four, or six horns.

The honourable profession of "cattle lifting" was not classed as a common theft—far from it. Many a Highlander is still proud of his "cattle lifting" ancestors. It was customary for a young chieftain before being considered capable of taking part in the affairs of his clan, to make a raid upon some other clan with whom they were at feud, or into the low country, whence they considered every man had a right to drive a prey. Some clans obtained a greater notoriety than others as cattle lifters. The MacFarlans were such adepts at the work, that the sound of their gathering tune "*Togail nam bò,*" was enough to scare the Lowland *bodachs* of Dumbartonshire. The MacGregors, again, had a world wide reputation in the profession, while the MacDonalds of Glencoe and Keppoch, and the Camerons in the Mid Highlands, were not far behind them in excellence, and my own clan in the North rejoiced in the flattering patronymic of "*Clann Aoidh nan Creach.*" It so happened that those clans who bordered on Lowland districts, were more given to pay their neighbours those friendly visitations. In several districts there are corries pointed out where the cattle used to be hid; as a rule they are inaccessible, but from one narrow opening, which could easily be defended against any rescuing party. It is peculiar that a very high code of honour obtained among even the most inveterate reivers. A Highland reiver would never stoop to anything less than a cow from a rich man; the property of the poor was always safe from them. Private robbery, murder, and petty thefts were hardly known. It may be said there was nothing to steal, but there was comparative wealth and poverty as elsewhere, and the poorer the people were, the stronger the temptation to steal, and the stronger the principle must have been which enabled them to resist it.

This scrupulous honesty was not confined to the property of their own kinsfolk, the effects of strangers who might happen to be among them were equally safe. They were most scrupulous in paying their debts, and such a thing as granting a receipt or a bond for money lent, would be considered an insult—*Dh'fhalbh an latha sin!*

There was an old custom of dealing with people who did not pay their debts. The neighbours were convened and formed into a circle with the debtor in the centre. He was there compelled to give a public account of his dealings, and if the judge considered that he had not done fairly, a punishment called "*Tòin chruaidh*," was administered to him. He was caught by two strong men by the arms and legs, and his back struck three times against a stone.

The instruments of husbandry in those days were of the rudest description. With the smaller tenant the greater part of the tillage was done with the *cas-chrom*, same as now used by the crofters in many districts. The plough then in use was entirely of wood, with perhaps an iron sock, and was drawn by four, and often by six horses. The horses were yoked abreast, and were led by a man walking backwards, another man held the plough, and a third followed with a spade to turn any sods which might not happen to be turned properly. The whole arrangement was of the most primitive description, and would look very amusing at the present day.

The harrows had wooden teeth, and sometimes brushwood in the place of the last row, which helped to smooth the ground. There being no roads in many districts, carts could not be used, so that goods had to be carried on horse back, in two creels, hung upon a wooden saddle with a thick rug made of twisted rushes neatly woven together. The burden had to be divided, so as to balance on the animal's back—if this could not be done it was put on one side, and stones put to balance it on the other. There was also a form of sledge used for carrying any heavy article; it was shod with iron, and dragged after the horses like a harrow; another form had trams like a cart. The first was called *Losgunn*, the latter *Carn-slaod*. These are still used in districts where there are no roads.

Such a thing as a gig or carriage was, of course, out

of the question in those days; indeed, there are people living, who remember when the first spring conveyance came to Skye. The remains of this ancient luxury are still to the fore. It has had an eventful history, first in the honored services of the laird, when it carried the *élite* of the island, and was the admired of all beholders. Then it became the bearer of the laird's factor; from that it came down the hill to the service of a tacksman, and finally settled with a small country innkeeper, where it ended its busy days.

Before the erection of meal mills, the corn was all ground with the quern, two flat stones fixed, the one upon the other, the upper having a handle to turn it round, and a hole in the centre by which the corn was put in; this was very laborious work. I have seen the quern even yet at work when the quantity of corn was so small, as not to be worth while sending to the mill. It is astonishing the quickness with which a smart person could with this appliance prepare a quantity of meal. A friend of mine on one occasion had a good example of this. Visiting an old woman in the heights of Assynt, she was pressed to wait and get something to eat, whereupon the old matron went out to the barn, took in a sheaf of corn, and in a minute whipped the oats off with her hand, winnowed it with a fan at the end of the house, then placed it on the fire in a pot to dry; after that it was ready to be ground, and then, being put through a sieve, was ready to bake. The whole thing was done within an hour, from the time she took in the sheaf of corn, till the cakes were on the table, and my friend says she "never tasted better."

The diet of former days was very simple, and no doubt accounts for the immunity of our ancestors from many of the forms of sickness, with which their more degenerate posterity are troubled. They were at that time, of course, necessarily restricted to the resources of our own country, which were much better suited to build up a healthy constitution, than the foreign luxuries of the present day.

Martin, whom I have already mentioned, gives the following account of the diet of the people of Skye, about 200 years ago:—

"The diet generally used by the natives consists of fresh food, for they seldom taste anything that is salted, except butter; the generality eat but little flesh, and only persons of distinction eat it every day and make three meals. All the rest eat only two, and they eat more boiled than roasted. Their ordinary diet is butter, cheese, milk, potatoes, colworts, *brochan i.e.*, oatmeal boiled with water. The latter, taken with some bread, is the constant food of several thousands of both sexes in this and other islands during the winter and spring, yet they undergo many fatigues both by sea and land, and are very healthful. This verifies what the poet saith—*Populis sat est Lymphaque Ceresque*: Nature is satisfied with bread and water."

As far back as the year 1744, in order to discourage the use of foreign luxuries, at a meeting of the Skye Chiefs, Sir Alexander MacDonald of MacDonald, Norman MacLeod of MacLeod, John MacKinnon of MacKinnon, and Malcolm MacLeod of Raasay, held in Portree, it was agreed to discontinue and discountenance the use of brandy, tobacco, and tea.

Though they could not be said to be addicted to drink, the Highlanders of that period used a considerable quantity of liquor, but more as a daily beverage than in drams, as at the present day. Martin relates some curious drinking customs. When a party retired to any house to transact business and had a refreshment, it was usual to place a wand across the doorway, and it would be considered the utmost rudeness for anyone to intrude, while it remained there.

Ale formed a great part of the beverages of those days, and houses for the sale of ale were numerous, even in Tiree. It was not till the latter end of last century that whisky was sold in these houses.

Drinking at marriages and funerals was frequently carried to excess, particularly the latter. At marriages the dancing and other amusements helped to evaporate some of the exuberance, but at funerals, they drank to keep down their grief, and as they had often to carry the bier a long distance, they took frequent refreshments by the way, and more after the burial, with the result that very unseemly conduct often took place. The Highlanders are not more blameworthy in this respect than others, for the same was practised in all parts of Scotland at that period. These barbarous customs are happily gone, which we have no reason to regret.

The marriage feasts were great affairs. They lasted usually for four days—dancing, feasting, and singing songs, being kept up the whole time. The dancing usually took place in a barn, which in some districts, was a building of considerable dimensions, and the friends coming from a distance, for whom room could not be found in the house, were put to sleep in outhouses on shake-downs, or billeted in the neighbouring houses.

It was on the occasion of a wedding of this description, that *Rob Donn* composed the well known song, "*Briogais Mhic Ruairidh.*"

In the olden times the pipe and the song were frequently heard in every Highland clachan, and the youths of the country could enjoy themselves in a rational manner. Shinty, putting the stone, tossing the caber, and other manly exercises, were freely engaged in, the different districts and parishes vying with each other in friendly rivalry, but the Calvanistic doctrines of the Highland clergy preached all the manliness out of the people, and I don't think that even they will be bold enough to assert that they have preached anything better into them.

As Rob Donn so very graphically says of them—

> Falbh 'n an cuideachd 's 'nan còmhradh,
> Is gheibh thu mòran do 'n *phac* ud,
> 'Dheanadh ceannaiche no seòladair,
> 'Dheanadh dròbhair no factoir,
> 'Dheanadh tuathanach sunndach,
> 'Dheanadh stiubhard neo-chaithteach'
> 'S mach o 'n cheaird air 'n do mhionnaich iad
> Tha na h-uile ni gasd ac'.

> Join their clubs and society
> You'll find most of the pack of them
> Fit for pedlars and sailors,
> Fit for drovers or factors,

> Fit for active shrewd farmers,
> Fit for stewards, not wasteful,
> Their sworn calling excepted,
> Fit for everything excellent.

It is wonderful after all how tenacious our old mother tongue has been of its life. It seems the insane policy of denaturalizing the Highlanders, in order to civilize them, has not been an idea of modern years. As far back as 1795, an Act of Parliament was passed beginning thus—"Our Sovereign Lord, considering that several of the inhabitants of the Highlands are very refractory in paying to the chamberlains and factors, the rents of the Bishopric of Argyle and the Isles, which now His Majesty has been graciously pleased to bestow upon erecting of English Schools for the rooting out of the Irish Language (Gaelic) and other uses."

Strange that after two hundred years of this de-naturalizing process, the Gaelic language is spoken by more people now than it was then, and looks quite robust enough to stand two hundred years yet.

As might be expected from the rude implements of husbandry in use, the ignorance of the best modes of agriculture, as well as the want of roads and communication with the southern markets, there were occasionally seasons of severity owing to bad harvests, and in such times, the poor people were reduced to sore straits, and were it not for the kindly feeling which existed among the different classes of society, serious consequences might have happened, but in those times those that had, shared with those who had not.

In seasons of severity, many had recourse to a very barbarous means of increasing their store of provisions, by bleeding the cattle and mixing the blood with meal, which was said to make a very nourishing diet.

Besides the usual butter and cheese, they made many preparations of milk, such as "crowdy"—that is, the curdled milk well pressed, and cured with a little salt and butter. "*Onaich*," or frothed whey. This was done with a stick having a cross on the end, over which was placed a cord made of the hair of a cow's tail. This instrument was worked round in the whey swiftly between the two hands, which quickly worked it into a thick froth.

Another more simple preparation was the "*Stapag*," made of cream, with a little oatmeal stirred into it. After the introduction of the potato, there was no famine in the Highlands till the unfortunate failure of that crop in the year 1846-7, and owing to the changes which had taken place by divorcing the people from the soil; that famine is counted the severest that is known to have visited the country. Of course, it must be understood that the Highlands was not the only part of the country that had these periodic visitations of famine; such were quite common in these times in the most fertile districts of England, before the principles of agriculture were so well understood. It is, however, melancholy to reflect that while other districts of the country have been making great strides forward in social progress, and that while in every other place "two blades of grass grow where only one grew before," in the Highlands, the reverse is the case. Where corn and barley waved a hundred years ago, heather and rushes grow luxuriantly to-day —a sad comment on our civilization and progress!

For a picture of the Social State of the Country about the end of last century, the following extract from the old "Statistical Account of Scotland," 1792, referring to the parish of Assynt, by the Rev. William Mackenzie, minister of the parish, is perhaps the best estimate we could have of the condition of the Highlands at that period—"Properly speaking, though many here are poor, they cannot be represented as a burden on the parish. The natives are all connected by alliance. When any one becomes old and feeble, the nearest relations build a little comfortable house close to their own residence; and even there the distaff and spindle are well managed. These old matrons nurse the children of their relations; the songs and airs of Fingal and ancient heroes are sung in the Gaelic tongue, to which the little children dance. Old men are prudently engaged in domestic affairs, such as repairing the houses of the neighbours, &c. In short, they share with their relatives all the viands of the family. At this period the poorest stranger, even though he be unacquainted, finds charity and safe shelter; but there is a very great distance (and now no places as of old) in this wilderness betwixt this parish and the inn at Brae of Strath o' Kill. Such being the condition of the poor in Assynt Parish, there are no public funds. The little trifle of money that is collected every Sabbath day after divine worship is served, is yearly distributed amongst the most friendless and deserving poor."

SESSION, 1890-91.

[28th October, 1890.]

At the Meeting of the Society held on this date, Rev. Dr. Masson, Edinburgh, read a paper on '*Some Rare Gaelic Books.*' Dr. Masson's paper was as follows:—

SOME RARE GAELIC BOOKS.

If, forty years ago, when I was a student at the University, some friend with a competent knowledge of the subject had turned my attention to the then neglected field of Gaelic Book-hunting, what a magnificent array of Celtic trophies might to-night be at my disposal for your entertainment and instruction! But vain is the wail over lost opportunities; and 'tis idle to grasp at the vanishing rainbow-vision of joys and achievements that might have been: *cha deach Theab riamh a mharbhadh.* Let us rather be thankful that amid the general neglect, if more by chance than wise intention, yet one way or another some few copies of almost all our Gaelic printed works have somewhere been safely harboured, while one or two most precious relics have been snatched as brands from the burning. Carswell's Prayer Book has for some time been safely guarded, as one of the most precious treasures of Inveraray Castle; and now I am proud to inform you that Ford Hill's little collection of "Antient Erse Poems," mourned to the day of his death by Mr. John F. Campbell, as irretrievably lost, is safe in the hands of a countryman of my own, who knows the value of his prize, and as the guardian of so rare a treasure feels the full responsibility of his trust.

Of this rare book, till the emergence of the copy which lately passed through my hands, not one exemplar had been seen since, in 1878, it is known to have been in the possession of the late Mr. Donald C. MacPherson, of the Advocates' Library, and editor of the *Gael*. In that year Ford Hill's collection was reprinted in the *Gael*, and before the types were taken down the work was also thrown off in pamphlet form for the late firm of MacLachlan & Stewart. This little bantling —I mean the *Gael's* reprint—is certainly not much to boast of, but in its birth, it seemed as if the mother's life had been sacrificed. For the missing work Mr. John F. Campbell hunted as for lost treasure. In the British Museum and the Advocates' Library, at Trinity College, Dublin, and in the Bodleian, he searched for it in vain. Nor could the utmost efforts of experts like Stillie, and our Scottish Quarritch in George IV. Bridge, hunt up the faintest clue of the quarry. This is how Mr. Campbell writes in *Leabhar na Féinne*: "I had begun to think that the work had actually been destroyed"—presumably by the outraged partisans of MacPherson's Ossian. "I have failed to discover a copy of it in London, Edinburgh, Dublin, or Oxford." Not only had he to close his great work, so far as a too short life and the parsimony of his countrymen allowed him to close it, but he had to close his eyes in death, without ever looking on this holy grail of his quest.

That lost lamb from our little flock of rare Gaelic books has now been found, and is safely folded. Let me tell the story of its retrieval. Just a year ago I spotted the lost one in the catalogue of Mr. John Noble of Inverness. No genuine book-hunter needs here be told how my heart leaped to my mouth at the auspicious sight of this identical treasure. Yes, sure enough, there is no room for mistake: without variation of letter or point, it is the exact title of the little volume for which the editor of "*Leabhar na Feinne,*" and many another Gaelic enthusiast had long searched and sighed in vain. That important pilgrimage to the capital of the Highlands, that fevered rush from the train to the well known book store in Castle Street, need not here be described. . . . . . .

The weather, the election—for my friend was a Bailie, and in the throes and crisis of burgh electioneering—the churches, and other books in the catalogue, were all glanced at with an air of diplomacy which, I felt, was too hurried to be as natural as could be desired. "Oh, by the way, there is that little volume of Gaelic Poems reprinted from the *Gentleman's Magazine,* near the close of last century?"—"Ford Hill's, you mean?—ah, that bird is flown."—Missed by St. Patrick! Rather had I missed the fattest hind, or the noblest head of branching antlers in Coire-a-cheathaich. It was a bitter disappointment. But my luck was not so low as it looked. The prize had gone past me. But the lost was found. That was a grand point scored in the interests of the Highlands and of Highlanders in general. And the precious treasure, though lost to my collection, had passed into good hands, wherein it will have generous use and intelligent appreciation.

It had been acquired by Mr. Fraser-Mackintosh, M.P., for Inverness-shire. In a sense I was anything but unfortunate, for through the generous courtesy of the purchaser his treasure has passed through my hands. Some bibliographic notes, tenderly jotted down as I turned over the precious pages, will perhaps interest the members of your Society; while the happy owner of a treasure so eagerly sought after by brother Gaels would, I am sure, be the last man to grudge you any satisfaction in regard to it which, through his kindness, it may be in my power to give you.

It is a thin volume of only 34 pages, besides two leaves for Title and a "Notice," not paged. The size of the page is 8 by 5 inches. Two *errata* are corrected at the end of page 34; and of one of these corrections the significance, as will hereafter appear, is important. The little work seems to have been published in pamphlet form. At least one may fairly infer as much; for though this surviving copy is handsomely bound, the title stands, as is usual in pamphlets of the time, about half-way down the page. It runs thus:—

ANTIENT ERSE POEMS

COLLECTED AMONG THE

SCOTTISH HIGHLANDS

IN ORDER TO ILLUSTRATE THE

OSSIAN OF MR. MACPHERSON.

The title is printed on what would be the outside uncovered leaf of the pamphlet. On the next leaf is the following

"NOTICE:

The following Poems were first published during the year 1782 and 1783 in the *Gentleman's Magazine*; a periodical publication of considerable Note in the Annals of British Literature."

The type used is not unlike that from which the *Gentleman's Magazine* was printed in 1782-3. The ordering of the printed page appears also at first sight to be identical. For these reasons there is a prevalent belief that the separate work is not a second issue, subsequently published, but was thrown off at the time from the types with which the Magazine was printed. There is clear proof, however, that it was not so. Words and phrases have been altered. One or two short sentences have been added. The page face and its contents, and the distribution thereon of the literary matter, though at first sight appearing to be identical in the Magazine and the separate publication, are all really different.

When I come to deal with the Gaelic text of the poems collected by Ford Hill, abundant proofs of this will also occur. The discrepancies then to be pointed out will be cited for a different purpose; but their incidental bearing also on the point now in hand may here be noted. Still there is enough in the English portions of the work to shew that it was a subsequent, if not an independent, publication. On the second page of the work there is introduced a new foot-note of thirteen words. On the same page there is the misprint of "journey" for "country." On the next page I have noted the following discrepancies: a semicolon is changed into a period, followed by the opening of a new sentence; in one place two lines are omitted, and in another place no fewer than nine lines. Over the page we have this new addition to the third foot-note: "MacNab himself mentioned this to me, and seemed much pleased that his name was in print." In a foot-note on verse 36 of *Ossian agus an Clerich*, the original contribution to the *Gentleman's Magazine*, says: "This verse is not only christian, but even fanatic." For "fanatic" the separate work reads "superstitious." I have noted no fewer than twelve similar emendations—all showing the working of an educated, if also a somewhat fastidious, taste—in the purely English portions of the work. The conclusion is, therefore, inevitable that we are dealing, not with a mere transcript, so to speak, thrown off before the types of the original contributions to the *Gentleman's Magazine* were taken down, but with a separate and subsequent edition of the work.

The original letters appeared, as has been seen, in 1782-3. When were they separately published in the form now before us? The *Gael* reprint, for which the late Mr. Donald C. MacPherson is responsible, has this note within brackets: "In 1784 it was published in pamphlet form, from which this Edition is reprinted." But for the date here given I have been able to discern no authority. Neither in the Title Page, in the "Notice," nor in any part of the volume, can I find any trace of the date of publication. But Mr. Fraser-Mackintosh's unique copy bears an inscription, most probably in Mr. Ford Hill's handwriting, which shews that the date of publication cannot have been later than 1787. In a clear, well-formed, steady specimen of the literary handwriting of the time, the title page bears this inscription: "Ex dono Auctoris, Feb., 1787."

Before dealing with the Gaelic texts handed down to us by Mr. Ford Hill, it may be well to make some inquiry as to himself, and his fitness or unfitness for the work to which so patiently, and at so great an expense of time, money, and personal comfort, he felt moved to devote his energies. Save that he was a Londoner, whose home in the great city was at No. 30 Ely Place, Holborn, I know nothing of his personal history. From his book we may safely infer that he was a shrewd observer, a patient inquirer, and a cultured scholar. With bigots to right of him and bigots to left of him, and torrents of controversial objurgation seething and sweltering all round him, Mr. Ford Hill never looses his head, nor does he manifest any heat of prejudice, one way or the other, in a conflict whose passion and red hot partisanship now fills us with amazement, not unmingled with shame and comtempt. Nature very evidently had fitted him well for his self-imposed task of arbitrating in the wild Ossianic melee of his day, wherein philosophers, like Samuel Johnson, could fight like savages, and our own mild and accomplished MacNicol, clergyman as he was, could trail his coat tails, and ply the shillelah.

But well fitted as by natural temperament he thus was to moderate in the motley crew of the old Ossianic club-wielders, this good man, Thomas Ford Hill, was really the last man who should have ventured on this his self-imposed adventure. Of Gaelic he was wholly ignorant, and so little did he understand the true character of the Highland people that, in speaking of "the absurd difficulties I had to encounter in this pursuit," he thus complacently chuckles over the success, as he thought, of his little game to outwit them: "sometimes I was obliged to dissemble a knowledge of Erse, of which I scarcely understood six words; sometimes I was forced to assume the character of a profest author, zealous to defend the honour of Ossian and Mr. MacPherson." Sly diplomatist, in his own estimation! But the wool was on his own eyes, not theirs, though they were too polite to tell him so.

In setting out on his mission Mr. Hill thus formulated to himself the state of the question which he was about to investigate: "The dispute seems naturally to divide itself into three questions: (1) whether the Ossian of Mr MacPherson be really the production of a very ancient Highland bard, called by that name? (2) whether it be copied from old songs, preserved indeed in the Highlands, but written by unknown bards, and only doubtfully and traditionally ascribed to Ossian? (3) if it be wholly a forgery of Mr. MacPherson's?

That, I submit, if only the terms of the third alternative had been a little less firmly knit, is really as fair a statement of the case as your own Society could formulate for a present day paper on the Ossianic Question.

If it can justly be said that this fair-minded Englishman entered upon his inquiry with the unconscious bias of one possible prepossession, it is only that one prepossession which, in our day, fair-minded Highlanders everywhere admit, and in most cases very bitterly lament. What had Mr. MacPherson done with MSS. which admittedly had been entrusted to him? Why were these "authorities" not forthcoming, to satisfy his friends and to confound his enemies? Here, with the natural instinct of common sense, Mr. Ford Hill felt that there was something wrong. But even in the face of that too obvious "fault" in the case of Mr. MacPherson, Mr. Ford Hill is still severely impartial. The point, he admits, pierced both ways. In regard to it MacPherson's friends and his opponents were both to blame. "From such considerations I was induced to believe that the subject might be considerably elucidated by collecting these songs in their original form: and I therefore made it a part of my business, during my journey through the Highlands, to search out the traditionary preservers of them, and procure copies with as much attention and exactness as lay in the power of a foreigner, and a stranger to the language."

Mr. Ford Hill's visit to the Highlands was in the summer of 1780. His first journey was through the inland parts of the Highlands Leaving Edinburgh he visited in succession Perth, Dunkeld, Blair Athole, Taymouth, Dalmally, Glenorchy, Inveraray, Loch Lomond and Dumbarton. He then turned aside, probably on private business of his own to Glasgow, Hamilton, and Lanark. From Lanark he crossed to Stirling, and following mostly the East Coast, he visited Aberdeen, Strathspey, Elgin and Inverness. From Inverness, following the military roads, he made his way down the Lakes by Fort Augustus to Fort William, the Black Mount, Glencoe and Tyndrum, returning by Loch Earn, Dumblane, and Alloa to Edinburgh. A third tour, "in which," he says, "I was happy enough to procure for the greater number of the following songs," led him from Edinburgh to Stirling and Callander, by the head of Loch Earn to Tyndrum for the third time, or to Dalmally for the second time. From Dalmally he went to Loch Etive and Oban, where he took boat for Mull, and spent nearly a fortnight in the Western Isles, visiting Staffa and Iona, and touching also at Morven. By Loch Awe, Inveraray, Loch Lomond and Dumbarton, he returned to Glasgow.

It was at Dalmally that our author found the greater number of the old Gaelic poems which give value to his book. There he made the acquaintance of "one MacNab, a blacksmith, who lived in a cottage, near the inn and church at Dalmally, where he boasted that his ancestors had been blacksmiths for near 400 years, and where also he preserved, with much respect, the coat-armour of the blacksmiths, his ancestors."

It will be remembered that from this same *seanachie*, Dr. John Smith professes to have obtained some of the materials of his "*Sean Dàna*."

From MacNab, Mr. Hill got written copies of *Ossian agus an Clerich, Urnigh Ossian, Mar Mharbh Diarmad an Torc, Mar Mharbhadh Bran, Duan a Mhuileartich,* and *Cubha Fhinn Do Righ Lochlin*. With Mr. MacNab our author's dealings must have been comparatively easy work, for he gave him written copies of the pieces above named. With others his labours were often fruitless as they were irksome, and too often comical. From another authority, "himself a tailor, and much celebrated for his knowledge of ancient songs," Mr. Hill fared badly: "I found him in an old woman's cottage near Blair, entirely willing to gratify my curiosity, and indeed highly flattered that I paid so much attention to his songs. But he could not talk English, and I was obliged to supply myself with another cottager, to translate while he sung. The good woman assured me that if "I understood the original, it would have drawn tears from my eyes." But the translation was poor stuff indeed, if one may judge by the only specimen which has been preserved.

In telling us how he procured his copy of the "Ode of Oscar" Mr. Ford Hill unconsciously gives us a piquant picture of the comical figure which he once cut in a pretty family group: "I wrote it down immediately from the mouth of a man who was a wright at Mr. MacLeane's of Drumnan in Morven, and knew a number of these songs. Mrs. MacLeane and her son's wife, a daughter of Sir Alexander

MacLeane, were so kind as to sit by and translate for me, whilst he repeated and I wrote. In order to have some kind of check against deception, I attempted to write down the Erse, together with the translation. . . . *I shall not trouble you with the former.*" If the good man had only asked one of the ladies to write the Gaelic while he wrote the English translation, our Gaelic Poetry and the material at our disposal in the Ossianic inquiry, might have been largely the richer. But possibly he might have asked in vain. Few women at that time, even among the comfortable middle classes, could write a letter; and even if they could write in English, it is much to be feared that they could not, to save a life, write down one sentence of their native Gaelic speech.

With one word more I shall farther detain you, ere proceeding to consider, what should, indeed, be the main topic of this paper, the Gaelic texts of Mr. Ford Hill's collection.

Mr. Hill distinctly asserts that the Fingalian songs were wholly confined to Argyleshire. Every other district visited by him had its own peculiar historic songs, yet the people of one valley were scarcely acquainted with the songs current in the next, though none of the songs had any resemblance to the Ossian of MacPherson. But in Argyle these songs were distinctly Fingalian and almost everyone is acquainted with them. Yet it is remarkable that I never could meet with Mr. MacPherson's work in any part of the Highlands; and many of his defenders confessed that they had never seen it." The poems recited to him could not, therefore, have been learned from MacPherson's books.

Now to the Gaelic texts. Remember, in the outset, that our collector played at make-believe, as a scribe, able to translate and write Gaelic. Where he got written poems he took them gladly. But rarely, if at all, did he condescend to ask the donor to translate his own Gaelic into English. The pedigreed blacksmith of Dalmally is evidently not an expert with the pen. To the chance translator, who is sometimes a young family tutor, sometimes an inn keeper, sometimes a drouthy dominie fetched round to the change-house for the purpose, MacNab's handwriting is strange and uncertain. His big C and small b are undistinguishable, and his t's all uncrossed, are taken for l's. Nor is this all. The uncertain translations thus procured, along with the carelessly written Gaelic, go unrevised to a London printer, who is more familiar with Hebrew than with Gaelic. And there is no proof-reader to look after him. Need we wonder at the result? Verse 12 of *Ossian agus an Clerich* furnishes but a mild example. It runs thus:—

> Sin nuair huirt Connan aris
> Co bail leal a Ricogh bhi ann
> Cashaoleadh tu Fhinn nan Cath
> Bhiodh ann ach Flath na Riogh.

It is not the irregular spelling, alone or mainly, that at first sight makes this verse so perplexing. It is the printer's uncorrected slips that make all the difficulty. But when you change the final l of *leal* to t—when also you allow for the obvious misprint in *Ricogh*, and when you space out the knotty conglomerate which begins the third line, the meaning of the verse is plain enough.

In verse 26 we find—

    S Cinn a Dha chomhirlich dheug.

Here it is, not the printer but the translator, that misreads. He makes the line "His twelve nobles have a sweet voice"—a stupendous blunder, but one of very simple origin. Old MacNab wrote his capital C and his small b so much alike that the translator took the one for the other, reading *binn*, sweet, for *Cinn*, heads. The proper translation is "the heads of his twelve councillors." In verse 30 the translator makes a similar blunder. Taking b for C he makes the Fingalians at their midnight feasts quaff horns of *wax* instead of *beer*.

Verse 47 has—

    Triur bo mho Glonn san Fhein.

The translator here mistakes *glonn* for *clann*, and makes the three Fingalians "the fathers of most children" instead of "the three men of proudest fame." To make bad worse, Mr. Hill, with much gravity, goes on unconsciously to accentuate his translator's unhappy blunder by building upon it a showy elaborate theory of Fingalian morals!

It may be mentioned that in *Ossian agus an Clerich* alone I have counted no fewer than twelve instances of the letter *t* being misprinted as *l*. But there is another class of blunders which it is not easy, either to account for, or to understand. Here, for example, is a verse from *Urnigh Ossian*, the first word of which greatly puzzled me.

> 'Noavil ù 'm bionan e s mac Cubhall
> An Riogh sin a bha air na Fiannibh
> Dhe fheudadh fir an domhain
> Dol na Fhallamhian gun iarnidh.

But by changing '*Noavil* into '*N saoil* and the F in the last line into T, the difficulty was in large measure removed. Not unlike the difficulty of this verse, though arising in a different way, is the perplexity with which one first reads such a verse as this *(Urnigh Ossian*—verse 22.)

> Coid an tait Joghairne fein
> Aphadruig a leib has an scoil
> Nach co math 's Flathinnis De
> Ma Gheibhar ann Feigh is Coin.

But in truth this verse is very easily read. Remembering the method in madness with which you have to deal, you see your way at a glance. Change the J of the first line into I; space out the initial A of the second line from the saint's name which follows; and remember that the H of *has* has wandered away from the immediately antecedent B, and you at once have clear sense, if bad enough theology. But as regards his theology, Ossian is here "true to kind," and observes the dramatic unities. Old heathen as he is, he asks if, after all Patrick's sermonising, hell can be so bad a place after all, if deer and dogs are there. Nor is this heathen thought a new one to the part he plays in this poem. His first question to Patrick in the opening of the poem is—

>   'Bheil neamh gu harrid
>   Aig Uaisliamh na Feinne

Farther on he asks—

>   Com 'am bethinnsa ri crabha
>   Mur bheil Neamh aig Flaith no Fheinne.

"Why," he asks, "should I be religious, if heaven be not enjoyed by Fingal and his heroes?"

>   B fhear leam aon' Chath laidir
>   'Chuireadh Fiunn na Feinne
>   Na Tighearnagh achrabhidh sin
>   Is tusa Chleirich.

Of Mr. Hill's little work we have now, as it were, three editions: the first in the *Gentleman's Magazine*, the second in that separate and subsequent publication of which the sole exemplar is in the possession of Mr. Fraser-MacKintosh, and the third Mr. Donald C. MacPherson's reprint in the *Gael*. The English portion of the second issue bears, as we have seen, marks of careful and intelligent revision. But if the Gaelic of the first issue was bad, the Gaelic of the second is worse, for there was still no correction of the press, and printers' errors, like the deadly sins, if unpurged, are fatally progressive. And as might thus be expected, the third is no improvement on the second. It carefully abstains, perhaps rightly so, from correcting even the most palpable errors of its predecessors; and naturally enough it adds new misprints of its own. Thus in verse 6 (*Ossian agus an Clerich*) of Mr. D. C. MacPherson's reprint the last line stands thus "Cha dreid ficidh *d*hile do Sgeithe." The original print is "Cha d*t*eid ficidh *b*hile do Sgeithe." In verse 7 MacPherson prints "Fhallamhian" for Hill's "Thallamhain." Similarly in *Mar Mharbhadh Bran* MacPherson greatly aggravates the difficulty of dealing with an original misprint of Hill's. Hill has "An la mhaobh sinn an torc liath." But MacPherson prints this line as "An lamhaobh sinn," thus aggravating the original blunder of printing o for r. It should be "An la mharbh sinn an torc liath."

There is yet another edition of Ford Hill's collection, for the Gaelic portions of which I am myself responsible. You will find it in Mr. G. L. Gomme's *Gentleman's Magazine Library.* In that work, much to the convenience of the modern antiquary and folklorist, the promiscuous and multiform contents of good Sylvanus Urban's long series of interesting volumes are indexed and arranged in separate collections. My editing, for one of these collections, of Mr. Hill's curiously corrupt Gaelic texts had to be done without the help of his own second thoughts; for the lost edition, now belonging to Mr. Fraser-Mackintosh, had not then been recovered. I had moreover to decide whether the texts should be purged, or be sacredly preserved as an amusing literary curiosity. The more important of the texts I decided to subject to just so much correction as would make them practically available to the general Gaelic reader—no easy matter, in all the circumstances, and especially in the absence of the "copy" from which the printer worked.

This *leabhran beag* of Mr. Ford Hill has led my pen a dance, whose length I did not anticipate. When I began I fully intended speaking at some length of the Gaelic works of Alexander MacDonald, and the collection of his son, Raol Dubh, of the first edition of the Gaelic "Confession of Faith," a copy of which was sold lately in London for seven guineas, of our early Gaelic Psalters and Catechisms, and of our Gaelic version of the Book of Common Prayer. This last, like our Gaelic Bible, is mainly a revised edition of the Irish version. For many years indeed the Irish Bible and Prayer Book were the only Bible and Common Prayer Book of the Highland people. These volumes I will just shew you; and then, using this strong link between our own and the Irish sacred books as a bridge, I will pass over to those old Irish books of devotion and Christian instruction which were prepared at the Irish College respectively of Rome, Louvaine and Paris. A considerable number of such books were published on the continent for surreptitious circulation and aggressive mission work among the native Irish, in the interest of the Catholic Church, and as an antidote to Kearney's little work published as far back as 1571 to advocate the doctrines of the Church of England. The leading spirit of this Irish mission work, operating from the continental Irish College, was Bonaventura O' Hussey, a Franciscan friar, born in Ulster late in the sixteenth century. He was a voluminous writer of Irish poetry; some two thousand verses of which are said by O' Reilly to have been well known in his day. Father Bonaventura O' Hussey, or O'Hesghusa, known also as Giola Brighid, was a lecturer on Divinity in the College of St. Anthony of Padua, at Louvaine. He there published in 1608 his Irish Catechism, in prose, known as *An Teagasg Criosdaidhe*. To this he soon afterwards added a Summary of Christian Doctrine in Irish metre, extending to 240 verses.

This poem, so often quoted in Irish religious works, begins thus :—

> A taid tri doirsi air theach n De,
> Ni feidir le neach fan ngrein,
> Gan dul thriotha so fa seach,
> Rochtain a nonn do 'n Righ-theach.
>
> Na tri Subhailce diadha,
> Creidiomh, Dothchas, Gradh cialldha,
> Is iad na doirsi a deir me
> Do bheith air Righ-theach Neimhe.

I shew you the second edition of the double work, prose and verse, which was published in 1707 by the "Sacred Society for the Propagation of the Faith" at Rome. It is a rare work, and is greatly admired as one of the best specimens of old Irish typography. After the manner of the Old Irish Manuscripts, it closes with a prayer that the kind reader would remember the "poor brother," Philip Maguidhir, at whose intercession the Cardinals of the Propaganda had printed this second edition, and who also corrected the press. Bioth fhios agad (leathoir ionmuinn) gurab e an brathair bochd, dord S. Fhraonsias, Philip Maguidhir, as colaisde S. Isidor na mbrathar mionur cirionach san roime, do fuair mur athchunage o Cardinalibh an Propaganda, an obairse do chur clo, an dara huair, chionns go rachfadh ttairbhe, agus soghas spiriodalta na nanma riachd na heirinn; agus gurab e an brathair ceadna do cheartaighe an clo: do bhrighsin iaraithghe murathchune ort do bheath guidhe air.

I next shew you a work of very great rarity and interest. It also was published, as also it was written, in Rome, and from the types of the Sacred College of the Propaganda. It is the *Lucerna Fidelium* of Father Francis O' Molloy, a native of Meath, also a Franciscan friar and a lecturer on Divinity in the College of S. Isidore in Rome. It is a first edition, and was published in 1676. In the year following Father O' Molloy published at Rome his Irish-Latin Grammar, also a work of very great rarity. Some time ago there was a copy of it in the Library of Trinity College Dublin; and last week I saw another copy, the third known to me as existing, in the hands of Mr. John Noble, Bookseller in Inverness.

I will now, out of its order, shew you a book which in many respects stands out in sharp contrast to the two pious works which you have just examined. It is the "Alphabet Irlandais" of J. J. Marcel, directeur de l'imprimerie de la Republique, and is printed by him in Paris, in the fourth month *Nivose*, of the year xii, not of our Lord, nor for His glory, but of, and for the glory of, the Republic, whose delight it was to dishonour His holy name. But this book is notwithstanding very closely related to the holy *Lochran* and the *Teagasg Criosduidh*.

The work of the Infidel Republic is printed from the Irish types of the Sacred College, from which they were stolen by the first Napoleon. But Nemesis overtook this, as it did so many of his larger enterprises of unholy misappropriation. In due time, and with some impressively significant ceremonial, the stolen Irish types had to be restored to Rome,—though not till copies had been taken, which still rest in the National Press-house of France.

Returning now to the Irish mission books of the continental Irish Colleges, I shew you a specimen of the works printed at Louvaine. It is entitled—

THE ELEMENTS

OF THE

IRISH LANGUAGE

GRAMMATICALLY

EXPLAINED IN ENGLISH

BY

H. MAC CURTIN.

And it is printed at Louvaine by Martin Overbeke near the Halls, Anno 1728.

This also is a first edition and is seldom met with, though not so rare as the *Lochran* and its other Roman companion.

It is a good practical grammar, and has a useful list of Irish contractions. It contains also a valuable chapter on a subject, now again much spoken about, the old Celtic crypto-script, called Ogham. The Grammar stands first in the volume, and could easily, and openly almost, be circulated in Ireland under the very nose of the severest administrator of the penal laws. But the learned and astute MacCurtin's book was a good deal more than a Grammar. Its last 62 pages enshrine a most useful Catholic polemic. "Tea and Tracts," as a formula of mission-work, was then unknown. But "Ireland's old Faith in Ireland's old mother tongue" was then as now, a watchword to conjure with. To the Irish Catholic missionaries this little book was thus at once sword and targe. A little Irish Grammar in the English tongue—what could be more innocent? The keenest of Saxon emissaries could find lurking in it no suspicion of heresy or rebellion. But the Irish tractate, covered by the Grammar, was in its turn but the sheath of what to the Irish people was the glittering sword of power. Written in a character and in a tongue of which the Saxon could make nothing, it went right home to the Irishman's warm Celtic heart, leading him captive to a Religion which loved his speech and his people. The title of this Irish Tractate, thus circulated under cover of a Grammar, is—

> Suim bhunudhasach an
> Teaguisg chriosdaidh
> A bpros agus a ndan.

A summary of Christian Doctrine in prose and verse, the verse being that of Father O' Hussey, already mentioned.

The work I now shew you was issued from the Irish College of Paris in 1742. It is Father Andrew Donlevy's Irish-English Catechism of the Christian Doctrine, to which is again added O' Hussey's versified summary of the Christian Doctrine, and a short Irish Grammar in English. It is not so very rare a book as those above described. I know of more than one copy of the work besides my own; and it was reprinted in 1822 by the Rev. John M'Encroe, who died in Australia. The various licensures and "approbations" of the first, or Paris edition, remind us indirectly of the large number of Irishmen who in 1740 held office of one kind or another under the French Government. O' Gara, Gallaher, Macdonogh, Duany, Kelly, Corr, Mackenna, Hennesey, and Devereux, the last named being the Principal of the Irish College of Paris—these are some of the Irish names which the book brings thus officially before us. Even the Patent of "Privilege du Roy" bears the mark of the ubiquitous Irishman. It is counter-signed by "Saughran." Was he not some Irish Daniel at the French Court, on whose presence there the Irish Refugees could count as *decus et tutamen*, more valuable, according to their proverb and ours, than *crùn 'san sporran?*

The *raison d'être* of all these Catholic Catechisms was Kearnaigh's Protestant Catechism, published under the auspices of Archbishop Usher as early as 1571. This is the earliest work ever printed in the Irish character. The only existing copy of it is in the British Museum, where I had an opportunity of examining it some years ago. It is a booklet of only 55 pages. The title, which is a long one for so small a book, begins thus: *Aibidil Gaoidheilge a caiticisma a forcheadal no teagasg Criosduighe,* &c.

In its version of the ten commandments the sixth is *na dena dún mharbhadh.* It has the following *Altachadh roimh biadh*: A taid suile gach aon nach ag fechain suos, agus ag cur an dochuis annadsa a thigherna, is tu do bheir doibh biadh agus betha an ám iomchbhaidh, is tu fhosglas do lamh thoirbheartach 7 lioneas le do beanachadh gach uile chreutur beo.

This "grace before meat" is followed by a similar *Altachadh Tareis bhidh*; after which we have *Urrnuighthe oidhche annso.*

The Lord's Prayer is given thus:—

A athar ata annsna neamhaibh naomhthar hainm. Tigeadh do fhlaitheanas. Bioth do thoil mar ta ar neamh 7 ar talamh. Tabhair dhuinn aniu ar naran laetheamhail fein, 7 maith dhuinn ar bhfiacha amhuil 7 mhaithmione dar bhfiachaightthoiribh, fein, and na treoraigh do chathughadh sind, achd raor (*sic*) sind on ole. Oir is leat fein in rioghochd, an cumhachd 7 an ghloir tre bhithibh sior. Amen.

The "local colour" of sixteenth century Irish politics is significantly, if also but obliquely, reflected in twelve "articles" which are thus introduced—Airtioghuil dairighe don riaghail Chriosdaighe ata ar na geur a mach maille le hughdarras uachdaran chille 7 tuaithe na righe so na hereand is coir da gach aon nduine ata umhal do reachd Dhia 7 na bannrioghan lo ghabhail chuige 7 go sbesailte don chleir.

The twelve "articles," recited at length, are followed up by five scripture sentences, of which I give the first two—(1) Na mallaigh prionnsa do phobuil fein. (2) Mar bhuairtheadhaigh an leomhain mar sin ata fearg an righ : ante ghluaiseas he, peacaighe se anaghaidh a anma fein.

Kearney's Catechism is one of the most precious treasures of the British Museum. I do not know of as much as a fragment of the little work being any where else in existence. But I have some reason to doubt the strict accuracy of the common belief that it is the *first* thing ever printed in the Irish character. About three years ago, through the courtesy of the Rev. J. L. Lewis, M.A., the learned librarian of Corpus Christi College, Cambridge, and of Mr. T. B. Reid, the Irish Bibliographist, my attention was drawn to a most interesting Broadsheet, printed in Irish type on both sides of a single quarto sheet. This broadsheet is printed in the same type as Kearney's Catechism and bears, like it, the date of 1571. A concurrence of evidence, which cannot here be set forth, points to this broadsheet as being in strict fact the predecessor of the Catechism.

It now remains for me but to add that in quoting, whether from Kearney's Catechism or from the several editions of Ford Hill's collection, I have been careful to follow the orthography of the cited authorities.

[25TH NOVEMBER, 1890.]

At the meeting of the Society held on this date, Mr. Neil Maclean, Provost of Govan, read a paper on 'The Days of my Boyhood.'

[23RD DECEMBER, 1890.]

At the meeting of the Society held on this date, Rev. J. G. MacNeill, Cawdor, read a paper on, '*Ainmean Gàilig àitean ann an Siorramachd Narainn.*'

[27TH JANUARY, 1891.]

At the meeting of the Society held on this date, Mr. Alex. MacDonald, M.A., F.E.I.S., read a paper on '*Celticism—its influence on English Literature.*' Mr. MacDonald's paper was as follows :—

CELTICISM—ITS INFLUENCE ON ENGLISH LITERATURE.

In this paper an attempt is made to consider what influence, if any, Celticism had on English literature : to ascertain whether a Celtic element is traceable in the language and literature of our country : to find out if in any degree, and if possible to what extent, these are indebted to the Celt.

This subject, we frankly admit at the outset, is not without its difficulties, and yet it is not one which has been unattempted. Various attempts have been made to explain the origin and progress of the Celts; and various opinions have been set forth in regard to their language; some favourable, and some hostile to Celticdom. And this is just what we should expect.

A native tongue, however rude, is ever dear to those whose first thoughts are expressed in it. This pride is natural and quite legitimate, and if sometimes its merits be exaggerated, or its power or special claims be over estimated, we should be prepared to extend every indulgence—at least until we can show good grounds for withholding it. And this consideration should lead us, the descendants of this ancient race, not to over-estimate the importance of our Celtic tongue beyond what is legitimate; nor to let our strong native enthusiasm carry us beyond reasonable bounds. In so doing we expose ourselves to the attacks and ridicule of the Philistines.

But the question of determining the influence and importance of Celticism is one which is now happily beyond the sphere of passion. It has become a question of science. It has been tested by the crux of Philology and Comparative Philology. These sciences have already achieved good results, and those of us who know the language, and take an interest in its study, can very materially aid this good work. The pursuit of such a line of action does infinitely more good to the cause of Celticism than the most profuse and passionate display of mere panegyric. He who vehemently protests

that the first words spoken by Adam to Eve was
'*Ciamar'tha sibh an dingh,*' and sets forth other fanciful
claims, with far less reason than this one, is damaging
the cause of Celticism as much as the man who, with
equally fanciful and baseless speculation, and without
this native passion to excuse him, tries to bring contempt upon our people and discredit upon our language.
The former may deserve some sympathy; the latter
none.

But, whilst we should try to avoid any appearance of
Celtic extravagance, we have had reason to demur at
the manner in which everything Celtic suffered at the
hands of our fellow Saxons in the past. Historians had
not done the Celts justice. Many hard and unwarrant-
able things were said about them. A good deal of this
aversion to Celtic interests was no doubt due to the fact
that those who wrote about them knew little or nothing
of their language, poetry, and art. As a race the
Celts were apt to be misunderstood by casual observers,
however eminent, who were ignorant of their genius
and language. The popular notion that they were an
inferior race incapable of making any advance in civilization, was so implanted in the minds of Englishmen
of the past generations that we need not be surprised
to find it reflected in their histories. Hence to Englishmen of the last century the very idea of a Celtic literature was too great a shock to pass unchallenged.
Accordingly attempts were made to write down and
crush the audacious aspiration of this so-called alien
race.

But, trained up from infancy amidst such preconceived notions regarding the Celts, as many of these writers were, we should be generous enough to forgive the prejudice which animated them, though at the same time we would fail in our duty to the interests of our race did we not point out the unfitness of these critics for the task they undertook, and, as a consequence, the unreliable character of their observations. No doubt, some of these writers were great men, but they were also strongly prejudiced men. Chief among them was Dr. Johnson, whose views are too well-known to be rehearsed here. Indeed, on this side of the border, another writer, John Pinkerton, who is known as the author of an "Enquiry into the History of Scotland preceding the reign of Malcolm III., or the year 1056, including the Authentic History of that period," published in 1789, gives us little hope of making good the claims of Celticdom. We find him, for instance, declaring that "the mythology of the Celtæ resembled in all probability that of the Hottentots or others, the rudest savages, as the Celtæ anciently were, and are little better at present, being incapable of making any progress in society."

We may remark in passing that this wholesale consignment of Celticdom to savagery was no uncommon way of getting rid of the early stages of British history, as may be verified by reference to some of the ordinary text-books on English literature.

Now, however, we are in the dawn of better times. A re-action set in about sixty years ago. Learned and unbiased English writers have now not only admitted a Celtic element in our literature, but have done yeoman service in elucidating it. Every Celt and every student of Celtic literature, owe a debt of gratitude to Dr. Pritchard, Matthew Arnold, and Henry Morley, for their valuable contributions. We find Arnold, for example, declaring emphatically, "that there is a Celtic element in the English nature, as well as a Germanic element, and that this element manifests itself in our spirit and literature;" and Morley asserting "that the main current of English literature cannot be disconnected from the live Celtic wit in which it has one of its sources. The Celts do not form an utterly distinct part of our mixed population. But for early, frequent, and various contact with the race that in its half barbarous days invented Ossian's dialogues with St. Patrick, and that quickened afterwards the Northmen's blood in France, Germanic England would not have produced a Shakespeare."

In the face of these clear indications of opinion by such eminent writers we are the rather encouraged to proceed with our inquiry. But, after all, it is only natural that we should expect to find at least some traces of Celtic influence in our literature. The 'frequent and various contact' that took place between the invaders and the invaded in the early history of our country must have influenced our national character and literature. It is unnecessary for my purpose to review at length the early history of the Britons. This has been done by many able writers. Speaking generally, I am inclined to accept Morley's views as set forth in his 'English Writers.' He there quotes from the Latin writers to show that the men of South Britain were not all mere naked barbarians. According to Strabo these had knowledge to give to the youths of Gaul. These nations exported cattle, corn, ivory, bracelets, amber, vessels of glass, and small wares. Tacitus tells us that their country was cultivated, and that when Cæsar first came over he found the harvest work nearly completed. Morley makes the observation "without roads the British army could not have had, as it is said to have had, its chief strength in war-chariots. Without political organization the people could not have sent, as they did, a fleet of ships in aid of the Veneti when Cæsar made war against them."

We may, therefore, safely conclude that the Britons were not the wild uncultured race they are sometimes represented to be. And it is equally clear that they were not wholly extirpated by the Romans, for we know that some of the natives settled down under their conquerors, and enjoyed the benefits of civilization conferred by them. Too little attention has been given to this important element in the history of our race.

The Britons doubtless benefited greatly by this Roman influence, as archaeological researches now demonstrate. The Saxon invaders helped to disseminate this influence by driving many of the Romanized Celts into the Highlands already occupied by their more independent but more primitive countrymen. Nor can there be reasonable doubt that the Saxons themselves benefited by this civilization. For the Saxons were troubled in turn by the Danes who commenced a course of ravage and conquest in all parts of England which continued for several years. The new invaders destroyed part of the country by fire and sword. The Saxons fled for refuge to the hills and woods where formerly they themselves had driven the Celts. We can thus understand how in adversity these hostile races were obliged to commingle. In this way the Celtic race became intimately blended with its conquerors, and has contributed its traits to the national character.

In concluding our remarks on the historical aspect of the subject it may be interesting to give the views of Monsieur Edwards,* a great French authority on Celticism. In referring to the Celts of Britain he says: "That the Britons were destroyed or expelled from England properly so-called is, as I have said, a popular opinion in that country. It is founded on the exaggeration of the writers of history; but in these very writers, when we come to look closely at what they say, we find the confession that the remains of this people were reduced to a state of strict servitude. Attached to the soil, they will have shared in that emancipation which during the course of the middle ages gradually restored to political life the mass of the population in the countries of Western Europe; recovering by slow degrees their right without recovering their names; and rising gradually with the rise of industry, they will have got spread through all ranks of society. The gradualness of this movement, and the obscurity which enwrapped its beginnings allowed the contempt of the conqueror and the shame of the conquered to become mixed feelings; and so it turns out, that an Englishman who now thinks himself sprung from the

* Arnold's "Lectures on Celtic Literature," p.49.

Saxons or the Normans, is often in reality the descendant of the Britons."

Having thus indicated a brief historical outline of how the Celtic element has pervaded the early Saxon race we pass on to inquire whether this element is traceable in their language and literature. While we might reasonably assume from the continued mixture of these races that there is such an element, it is by a comparison of their language that its existence can be detected. Such a comparison has been successfully made with the result that not only was this Celtic element discovered, but the importance of the language of the Celt as an item indispensable to a full and intelligent system of Philology was fully established. Their language obtained an important place in the Aryan or Indo-European group.

For this service we are indebted to Continental, and especially to German scholars. The wonderful discoveries made by Grimm, and now known as Grimm's Law, revealed to linguists a fertile sphere of research. To Dr. Pritchard, who published in 1832 his 'Eastern origin of the Celtic Nation,' is due the credit of first enlisting a real interest in the Celtic language. His work attracted the attention of German Philologists, and in 1853 there appeared the greatest work on the subject. In that year I. Kaspar Zeuss after thirteen year's hard work published his *Grammatica Celtica*, which is not so well-known as it should be; but no doubt this is chiefly due to its being written in Latin. Those of us who looked over its pages must have been struck with admiration at the patience, the love of research, and the genius which pervade them. To Celts it is a work of the greatest moment. Zeuss by his unwearied investigation of their most ancient records removed all the misconceptions that arose in connection with their language—misconceptions it must be noted which entirely arose, so far as Philologists were concerned, from the want of a comprehensive historical study of their language. Such a want the *Grammatica Celtica* largely supplies.

But before beginning the comparison of Celtic and Anglo-Saxon words, it will be instructive to look for a little at the construction of British place-names. In the names of our rivers, mountains, and towns, we have clear evidence of a Celtic element. A glance at the topography of Britain will be sufficient to satisfy us on this point. For that matter we might extend our observations to the topography of Southern Europe, and there too find names which afford undoubted evidence of the early existence of a Celtic race, though with that phase of the question we are not at present specially concerned.

Confining ourselves therefore to Britain we find so many instances of the Celtic Beinn, Ben, or Pen; of Amhainn in its anglicised form Avon; of Uisg in the forms of Usk, Esk, and Ouse; of Dun or Don; of Cill or Kil; of the Welsh Aber, Caer, Caed, and Llan; of Baile or Bal; of Ach, and Ard; of Ceann or Ken or Kin; of Gleann or Glen; &c. All who care to look at a map of the British Isles can find numerous examples of these and other Celtic roots. This reference to British topography is not out of place here, for it serves to show that the Celts were not, as Pinkerton suggests, like Hottentots or other savages, but it rather indicates that their influence must have been pretty considerable amongst the Saxons. At all events the retention of so many names almost in their pristine entirety shows that there must have been a long and familiar intercourse between the races.

Morley in treating of the language and literature of the Celt says : " They not only left the names given by them attached throughout the land to lakes, rivers, and mountains, but they perhaps contributed more than is now believed to the formation of English in its earliest stage." This surmise is, I believe, a true one. It is not always possible to say with certainty that words more or less common to both languages came from the Celtic. As has already been pointed out, the Celtic language has been assigned a place in the Indo-European group, and as such is akin to the other languages of that group, which, in their turn, also influenced the English language. Consequently the manner in which words having common roots in these kindred languages found their way into English, cannot in many instances, be at once determined. When, however, we find words without an etymology in the Anglo-Saxon language, but with an etymology in the Celtic language, we feel warranted in holding that it passed from the Celts to the Saxons. Were it possible to get at the language as spoken by the early inhabitants of our country, our work of discrimination would be easier; as it is, a perusal of the words found in Anglo-Saxon dictionaries enables us to prove that there exists a stronger Celtic element in English than could have been acquired during the period of conflict between the Saxon and the Celt. I think it well to emphasise this point because some writers insist on limiting the number of words of Celtic origin to the names of certain implements, chiefly domestic ones, with which menials or servants would have most to do. And so they credit the Celts with supplying such words as pail, pan, basket, clout, &c. One writer supports this theory as follows: " probably some portion of the original inhabitants—especially British women—were preserved alive by the Saxons and kept in a menial condition." There is no doubt some reason in this theory, but it is narrow and accounts for a very limited number indeed. It entirely fails, however, to explain the stronger Celtic element indicated above.

Gaelic.	Anglo-Saxon.	English.
Asal	Assa	Ass
Balg	Baelg	Bag
Bat	Bat	Bat or Staff
Bàta	Bat	Boat
Being	Bene	Bench
Bogha	Boga	Bow
Beoir	Beor	Beer
Beirm	Beorma	Barm
Bòt	Bòt	Boot
Beir	Ber (an)	Bear

Let us now take a few words and compare their forms in Gaelic, Anglo-Saxon, and English.

Gaelic.	Anglo-Saxon.	English.
Brot	Brod	Broth
Burn	Burne	(Burn), Water
Cat	Catt	Cat
Cais	Cyse	Cheese
Carraig	Carr	Crag
Cist	Cyst or Cist	Chest or Cest
Dorch	Deorc	Dark
Dath	Deg	Dye
Lagh	Lag, Lah	Law
Maighdean	Maighmann	Maiden
Rathad	Rád	Road
Rac	Race	Rake
Reis	Raes	Race
Rop	Raep or Rap	Rope
Sac	Sacc	Sack
Sloc	Slog	Slough
Stoc	Stoc	Stock
Stiuir	Steor	Steer, (Helm)

A comparison of the foregoing words shows that the Celtic element passed into English through the Anglo-Saxon with little or no change. It is true that a few of these words (generally those of Latin origin) have their German equivalents much alike in form to those given above; as, stool (stuhl), mill (mühle), devil (teufel), circle (Zirkel), cat (katze), box (büchse), &c., but this perfectly natural cousinship in language does not interfere with our contention.

We find another class of words where this element is evident in the Anglo-Saxon language, but not in modern English.

Gaelic.	Anglo-Saxon.	English.
Achd or àithne	Ac or Acn	Act, Law
Màl	Mal	Toll
Trath	Thrag	Time
Boid	Beot	Vow
Dealaich	Delan	Divide
Locar	Locer	A plane
Lom	Lun	Bare, Poor
Tiugh	Toh	Thick
Trom	Trum	Heavy
Seal	Sael, Sel	A while
Brat	Bratt	Cloak
Ath	Ast	Kiln
Cuid	Cud	Portion
Spor	Spora	Flint
Steall	Steola	Tail, String

A further comparison of the following Gaelic words directly with their corresponding English equivalents discloses an intimate connection.

Gaelic.	English.	Gaelic.	English.
Bàrd	Bard	Beist	Beast
Ball	Ball	Beic	Beak
Bolla	Boll	Bann	Band

CELTICISM.

Gaelic.	English.	Gaelic.	English.
Bog	Soft, or bog	Leum	Leap
Bòsd	Boast	Leasg	Lazy
Breith	Birth	Luaidh	Lead
Brisg	Brisk	Plàigh	Plague
Buideal	Bottle	Poit	Pot
Bucall	Buckle	Pocaid	Pocket
Buaic	Wick	Poca	Pock
Cart	Cart	Port	Port
Carn	Cairn	Salach	Soiled, Sullied
Còrd	Cord		
Corp	Corp	Scirbhis	Service
Cosd	Cost	Seol	Sail
Creid	Creed	Seoladair	Sailor
Cleir	Clergy	Saighdear	Soldier
Carcais	Carcass	Solas	Solace
Crois	Cross	Spar	Spar
Daor	Dear	Spot	Spot
Dàil	Delay, dally	Spòrs	Sport
Deile	Deal	Stabull	Stable
Dorus	Door	Strì	Strife
Dràc	Drake	Stoirm	Storm
Druma	Drum	Suipeir	Supper
Gille	Gillie	Tom	Tomb
Lag	Weak, or lag, as in laggard and, perhaps, lack	Tuba	Tub

In the preceding list of words, taken pretty much at random, we are not to suppose that in every instance the English words were derived from the Gaelic—the Latin origin of some being obvious; where in these and other words laboured attempts are made to explain their etymology by reference to Sanskrit, Icelandic, Dutch, Old French, &c., we are entitled to submit Gaelic etymologies which appear equally—if not more reliable.

Further, we observe that there is evidence of a Latin influence in Gaelic. The English language has also been largely influenced indirectly, and to some extent directly, by the Latin. We therefore feel inclined to inquire whether any of this Latin influence passed into English through the Gaelic.

There is no doubt that a comparison of Celtic words with their Latin equivalents shows in many instances a near relationship. Indeed a close inspection almost forces one to resolve this relationship into two kinds. The first points to a time when the Celtic and Latin tongues were members of the same family, as in the following:—

Gaelic.	Latin.
Beir	Fero
Fear	Vir
Feasgar	Vesper
Fion	Vinum
Or	Aurum &c.

The second kind of relationship would seem to indicate that the Celtic language was influenced by the Latin at a time when these languages were the native tongues of distinct nations; and also that this influence was felt at two distinct periods, firstly, while the Romans were in Britain, and secondly through the influence of the church.

How much the language of the Celts was affected by the Romans during the period they lived in Britain, it would be hazardous to assert. It would, however, be foolish to maintain that it was uninfluenced by them during the centuries they occupied this country. Indeed a considerable number of loan-words from the Latin is found. Such words as, straid (stratum), priomh (primus), airgiod (argentum), ceir (cera), caisteal (castellum), arm (arma), tir (terra), mil (mel), tùr (turris), corp (corpus), seac (siccus), muir (mare), acair (anchora), litir (litera), monadh (mons), &c., belong to this class.

Regarding the words introduced at a later period through the influence of the church there is not much doubt. We have—aingeal (angelus), ministeir (minister), altar (altare), crun (corona), teampull (templum), gloir (gloria), pobull (populus), cleireach (clericus), cathair (cathedra), àirc (arca), abstol (apostolus), &c.

These examples taken from the many words which the Gaelic inherited from the Latin suggest to us that a number of them passed into English through the Gaelic.

Not only so, but many of the Latin words said to be contributed to the English through the Norman-French can be attributed with as much plausibility to a Gaelic source. The French language has, as we know, a strong Celtic basis. The common Celtic genius of French and Gaelic is seen very clearly in the manner in which each assimilates words derived from Latin, and also in their idioms. Let us compare the following:

Latin.	French.	Gaelic.	English.
Bestia	Bête	Béist	Beast
Corona	Couronne	Cruin or Coron	Crown
Curia	Cour	Cuirt	Court
Cupa	Coupe	Cup	Cup
Festia	Fête	Feisd	Feast
Floris	Fleur	Flur	Flower
Granus	Grain	Gràin	Grain
Lancea	Lance	Lann, Lannsa	Lance
Poena	Peine	Pein	Pain
Portus	Port	Port	Port
Pretium	Prix	Pris	Price
Saccus	Sac	Sac	Sack
Turris	Tour	Tùr	Tower
Truncus	Tronc	Trunc	Trunk

There can, I think, be no reasonable doubt as to the existence of a Celtic element in the class of words of which a few examples are given above. Altogether, then we have good reason to say there is a strong Celtic element in the English language.

I have confined myself, in the examples given in the preceding pages to the Gaelic dialect, because I know it best, and also because Welsh scholars have already established the claims of their dialect.

Having thus finished our consideration of the Celtic element in the English language, we pass on briefly to consider whether it is also traceable in English literature. We have to look at the matter as well as the form of the language for evidence of this Celtic element.

This part of our task is in many respects a more difficult one. It is one that demands special critical faculties. Happily for us this part of the work has been already accomplished, and by no less a person than that distinguished and lamented scholar, the late Matthew Arnold. His excellent lectures "On the study of Celtic literature" are so unique and so perfect in their way, that I shall gladly content myself by giving a summary of his researches.

In addition to the historical and philological tests which we attempted to apply above, Arnold applied another test which he styled the "literary or spiritual test," and, as the result of his investigation, he finds the influence of the Celtic genius in English poetry, art, music, style, religion, humour, and character. While he states that our country is German essentially he nevertheless finds something in us which marks us out as distinct in these vital points. This something is Celticism. He characterizes the Celtic nature as eminently sentimental, as an organization quick to feel impressions, as a lively personality keenly sensitive to joys and sorrows. Its essence is to aspire ardently after life, light, and emotion; to be expressive, adventurous and gay; to be sociable, hospitable, admired.

He points out how successful the Celt is in arts which depend chiefly on the emotional faculty; as in music and poetry. He very correctly observes that

the very soul of emotion breathes in the Celtic airs.
So, too, in poetry the Celts have shown genius. What
they lacked was the steadiness, the slow dogged per-
severance, and the creeping industry of the Saxon.
The sentimentality of their temperament was too quick,
too dashing, too impatient to achieve permanent success. It was the union of the steady-going Saxon
temperament with this sentimental Celtic temperament
that produced the qualities which so characteristically
mark the British nation. He finds in our poetry the
clearest evidence of a clashing of a Celtic dashing quickness of perception, with a Germanic plodding instinct.
He says: " It is in our poetry that the Celtic part in
us has left its trace clearest. If I were asked where
English poetry got these three things—its turn for
style, its turn for melancholy, its turn for natural
magic, for catching and rendering the charm of nature
in a wonderfully near and vivid way,—I would answer
with some doubt, that it got its turn for style from a
Celtic source ; with less doubt, that it got much of its
melancholy from a Celtic source ; with no doubt at all,
that from a Celtic source it got nearly all its natural
magic."

After pointing out how this turn for style did not
come to us from the Germans, who lack the sense for
style, he goes on to indicate a Celtic origin ; for the
Celt's quick feeling for what is noble and distinguished
gave their poetry style. He considers style the most
striking quality of Celtic poetry. There was a sort of
intoxication for style all through it. This trait was
not confined to their great poets, such as Taliesin, or

Ossian, but was in all Celtic poetry. The Celt's sensibility added another, even better gift, to his poetry—the gift of rendering with wonderful felicity the magical charms of nature. In Celtic romance, too, there are very exquisite touches which show this feeling for nature, and how deeply nature lets him come into her secrets.

Now, gentlemen, few, if any, English critics were better fitted to express an opinion on these points. Arnold's intimate knowledge of German literature, especially of German poetry, rendered him admirably qualified to act the rôle of critic, and so we may accept with confidence the results of his fine critical perception.

He sees a Celtic element clearly in Shakespeare. Keats and Wordsworth, also have this wonderful magic of nature, and Campbell has its style. And is there not in Arnold's own poetry, something of the Celtic traits which he so charmingly delineates. There is in it that intense love of nature—the magic of nature. It is true that his poetry always aims at self-culture. His songs are carefully attuned ones which disclose the polished mind. They have not the free involuntary melody of Ossian. Yet in the poetry of both the feeling for nature predominates. Take the following in which there is a decided Ossianic touch.

> But the majestic river floated on,
> Out of the mist and hum of that low land,
> Into the frosty starlight, and there moved,
> Rejoicing, through the Chorasmian waste,
> Under the solitary moon ; he flowed

> Right for the polar star, past Orgunjé,
> Brimming and bright, and large ; then sands begin
> To hem his watery marsh, and dam his streams,
> And split his currents.

Another poet who had largely come under the influence of the Celtic magic spell, was our national bard Robert Burns. His poetry almost everywhere displays characteristics which are peculiarly Celtic. Professor Kuno Meyer in a lecture on the "Genius of Celtic Poetry" delivered recently in this city, referred to the Celtic element in Burns somewhat as follows : "There was one Scottish poet on whom the genius of the Celtic muse had descended in all its characteristic beauty—Robert Burns. Burns was wholly un-English, was wholly Celtic. There was in him that Celtic fire and power of imagination, that humour—now delicate and light, now grotesque ; but, above all, that wonderful eye for nature which was peculiar to the Celtic mind."

Finally, and without entering any further into the discussion of English words affected by Celticism, it may be noted that the publication of Ossian's poems by Macpherson has been acknowledged to have influenced the poetry of Europe.

[26TH FEBRUARY, 1889.]

At the meeting of the Society held on this date, Mr. David Ross, M.A., B.Sc., L.L.D., read a paper on "*The Mythical Monsters of the Celt.*" As this paper is not available, Dr. Ross has kindly prepared a résume of the paper he read to the Society on a previous occasion (see page 88.)

THE RELATION OF CELT AND NORSEMAN IN SAGA TIMES.

The chief interest in the history of the relation of the Celts and the Norsemen is concentrated in the period of over two hundred years, from the first appearance of the hostile demonstrations of the latter on the west coast of the British Isles, A.D. 795, to the battle of Clontarf in 1014. In the Isle of Man and Scotland the relation continued to be maintained down to the battle of Largs in 1263. In the annals of Ulster under the date 795, we are informed that all the coast of Britain was ravaged by the Gáls, that is by the "foreigners." The Anglo-Saxon Chronicle notices their descent some years earlier, 787, upon the English coast at Dorset; and they plundered Lindisfarne in 793. Hence we may conclude that by 795 there was no part of the British coast unexposed to their ravages. They were heathen, bold and hardy, driven from home by the pressure of population, and by the lawlessness which resulted from the perpetual feuds between the kings or petty chiefs, then so numerous in the North. The restless spirit, thus generated, rapidly spread, till the excitement of adventure abroad, and the thirst for personal fame, made each young man anxious to go anywhere, and dare anything. Their complicated mythology and somewhat gloomy religion held out the highest awards, in a future life, to those whose prowess had been conspicuous in battle. Active and determined in executing their purposes, fierce, cruel, and careless of human life, their expeditions were everywhere the causes of alarm and horror. In Ireland they found a people among whom christianity had long been established, and where the influence of the church had softened the rigour of war; so that their cruelty caused the Norsemen to be denounced in unsparing terms.

At no period in its history does Ireland present the appearance of a peaceful happy land. Its golden age has yet to come. From the early records of the fifth century to the depredations of the Norsemen, there were constant conflicts between the various tribes of the Irish themselves. For over two hundred years conflicts of the same kind were combined with half-hearted resistance to the invaders. No sooner did the battle of Clontarf (1014) remove the yoke of the Norsemen, than the old feuds broke out with renewed vigour, both sides inviting the Norman Barons of England to their aid—until bloodshed and the weakness and disorder of both parties paved the way for the supremacy of the English under Henry II in 1172. From that date to the present time, there is little in Irish history but accounts of troubles and disturbances. But the influence of St. Patrick and his followers had modified the harshness of war, by the application of christian principles, even to the relations between avowed enemies.

The Norsemen soon found that plunder was most abundant in the religious establishments, which the zeal of the early British christians had planted in the Isles and on various points of the coasts. In many of them were the relics of the saints enshrined in silver and gold, and decked with gems, the gifts of the faithful. At Lindisfarne, St. Cuthbert's shrine is said to have been of black oak, wonderfully carved, and enclosed in another covered with hides, which again was surrounded by a third, decorated with gold and precious stones. These shrines, open to attack by sea, and defended only by unwarlike monks, fell an easy prey to the ruthless Norsemen. In 795 they attacked Iona, and burnt the religious establishment in Rechrin, that is, in Lambey, off the Dublin coast. Three years later they ravaged all the west coast, and burnt Innispatrick in the Isle of Man, probably the modern Peel. In 802, the monastery of Iona was again burnt. After this period many of the religious houses on the coast were abandoned, the inmates seeking a safer abode in the interior. Others were rebuilt of stone, and even fortified; whereas, hitherto, wood had chiefly been employed. So at the next attack, in 806, Iona made a stout resistance, but in vain, 68 of the ecclesiastics being slain. It may be well to state a typical case in detail.

In 825, on the appearance of the Norsemen off the coast, the shrine of St. Columba at Iona was hastily removed and buried in the ground. The monastery was captured, and we are told that "the heathen rushed through the houses, threatening death to those blessed men, and furious with rage, having slain the rest of the brethren, came to the Father Abbot, urging him to give up the precious metals, which enclosed the sacred bones of Columba. . . . . This booty they coveted; but the holy man stood firm with unarmed hand. He then spoke in the barbarous tongue; "I know not truly what gold ye seek, where it may be placed in the ground, and in what recesses it may be laid; but, if I knew, Christ permitting, these lips would never tell this to your ears." He was immediately slain. The relics were ultimately removed to Ireland for safety, and perhaps in part to Dunkeld. At this period only hostile relations could exist between the Celts and Norsemen. Between 807 and 830, these invaders made permanent settlements on many parts of the Western coasts, as in Sligo, and Munster. In 832, three fleets under Turgesius (Thorgil or Tryggve) subdued the greater portion of Ulster and Munster, the conqueror established himself at Armagh, and aimed at the subjugation of all Ireland. He was joined by new invaders, whom the "sea seemed to vomit forth in floods." Dublin was seized, and Norse settlers established themselves all over the east of Ireland. These last were Danes, *Danars* or black Danes; whereas the previous invaders are spoken of as white or fair men, Lochlanns, that is Norwegians. The ravages of the Danes are described as more dreadful than those committed by the others. Even allowing for some exaggeration, the language of the Irish chronicler is very striking. "And assuredly the evil which Erin had hitherto suffered was as nothing compared with the evil inflicted by them. They built Duns, and fortresses, and landing ports over all Erin, they made spoil-land, and sword-land, and conquered-land of her; they ravaged her churches and sanctuaries. This furious, ferocious, pagan, ruthless, wrathful people had no veneration, honour, mercy or protection for church, sanctuary, God or man." These Danes fought both with the Irish and with the Norwegians already settled in the land. Their superiority in armour and military skill is attested by many passages in the chronicles of the time. "There was not one of them who had not polished, strong, triple-plated, glittering armour of refined iron, or of cool, uncorroding brass, encasing his sides and body from head to foot."

By the arrival at Dublin, in 853, of Amhlaidh (Olaf the White) with an immense fleet, the Norwegian party became superior to the Danes. During the next forty years the Norsemen ravaged the Rhine valley and the Italian coast, and the Celts enjoyed a period of comparative rest. The invaders still continued in power, but they cultivated to some extent friendly relations with the Irish. Intermarriages were frequent, whence resulted a mixed race famous in northern history. About A.D. 900, the Norsemen were expelled from Dublin, many of them retiring to Iceland, bearing with them the half-breed descendants of these intermarriages. Thus we account for the pure Irish names found in the Icelandic sagas, as Cormack, and Njal (Neill).

To a smaller extent than in Ireland, Norsemen had settled in the Hebrides, and intermarried with the Celtic population. When Harald Harfagr (Fairhair) made himself supreme in Norway, about A.D. 880, many of the bolder spirits refused to submit, and took refuge with their kinsmen in the Hebrides and Ireland. Hither he followed them, breaking up their establishments, and compelling them to seek refuge in Iceland. More than half of the colonists of that island, were

Norse settlers in Britain, or their descendants. To relieve the tedium of the long winter nights in that remote region, there grew up in Iceland, the habit of recounting at the fireside, at festivals, and at the great national assemblies, the heroic deeds of old, the party fights in Norway, the expeditions to the Hebrides and Ireland, the longer voyages to and plunderings in the Baltic and the Mediterranean. Hence was developed the Saga, a species of literature peculiar to Iceland, a kind of prose epic. Often a Saga contained passages of poetry, illustrative of its theme, the work of the scalds or poets, whose duty it was to attend a chief, take note of his valiant deeds in battle, and commemorate them in martial song. Now this poetic gift was found to be best developed in the mixed Norse and Celtic race descended from the intermarriages of which we have spoken. For several centuries young scalds of this extraction set out from Iceland, Ireland and the Hebrides, entered the service of Kings and warriors all over Europe, and were in the highest esteem at every court.

In the tenth century the Norsemen in Ireland still held vast tracts of country, but they lost much of their plundering instincts and ferocious demeanour.

Of all the parties into which the unfortunate Irish were divided, the most famous had been the Dal Cais of Munster. Of this family the ablest at the time, Brian Borumha, resolved to rid Ireland of the Norsemen. With a few followers he retired to the woods and bogs, whence he fell upon his opponents killing them, as the annals state, "in twos and threes, in fives and scores, and ultimately in hundreds." At last the Irish rallied round him, and defeated the Norsemen in 968 at Sulcoit and captured Limerick. Soon after Brian became King. "He was not a stone in the place of an egg, he was not a wisp in place of a club; but he was valour after valour." Such is the historian's testimony. In 980, the Irish won the well contested battle of Tara. "It was woe to both parties, but it was worse for the foreigner." By 984, Brian was supreme, many Norsemen were enslaved, so many that it is said no Irishman needed to work at all, his slaves did everything. In 1001, Brian subdued Ulster, and in 1005 he made a royal tour of his dominions. Meantime (1000) christianity had been established in Iceland, Norway had already become christian, and in Ireland the new religion was being accepted by the conquered Norsemen. For some years peace prevailed. But a storm was brewing.

Brian had put away a somewhat shrewish wife Kormlada, whose second husband he was, and in revenge she plotted his ruin. By fair promises she obtained the aid of Sigurd, Earl of Orkney, whose collected Viking host was to assemble at Dublin on Palm Sunday 1014. The Norsemen in Ireland were expected to revolt, and aid was also obtained from other Viking leaders. The plans were well laid, and fairly well carried out. But Brian was not idle, and faced his foes at Clontarf. Of this battle very detailed accounts are given in the Saga of *Brunt Njal* and in the Irish collection known as the *Wars of the Gaedhill with the Gaill.* Both parties regarded the approaching battle as certain to mark an era in Irish history, as determining not merely race supremacy in Ireland, but as in some way or other deciding the superiority of the christian or pagan faith. For in the hour of danger, not a few of the Norsemen exhibited a hankering after the rites and ceremonies of that heathen worship, which had so long animated their fathers, and had enabled them to pass from victory to victory. So at least they thought. Deep anxiety oppressed the combatants. In the battle as had been predicted, the Irish were victorious, but at its close Brian was seen and killed by a reckless foe, who was at once cut down. Henceforth the Norsemen in Ireland, either gradually emigrated to join their countrymen in Scotland, Norway, or Iceland, or ceased their opposition to Irish rule, and became absorbed in the general population.

For two centuries later the Kings of Norway, claimed and often exercised authority over Man and the Hebrides. This claim led to considerable trouble, when the Scottish Kings established their authority over all the mainland. An arrangement was come to that King Magnus, (A.D. 1098), should keep all the islands between which and the mainland he could steer his vessel. By drawing his ship over the isthmus of Tarbert, while he sat and held the helm, Magnus claimed Kintyre, as well as all the Western Isles. But the last trace of the Norse power was removed in 1263, by the battle of Largs, which effected for Scotland what that of Clontarf had done for Ireland, two and a half centuries earlier.

[31st March, 1891.]

At the meeting of the Society held on this date, Mr. John MacPhail, M.A., read a paper on "Celtic Mythology." Mr. John Mackay, Kingston, read a paper on "The Celtic Muse in Lowland Garb." Mr. Mackay's paper was as follows :—

THE CELTIC MUSE IN LOWLAND GARB.

A great deal has been written and spoken within the last few years about the Highlands and Highlanders. We are living in the midst of a Celtic *renaissance*, when, after many years of misfortune and misrepresentation, the Highlander has risen superior to his difficulties, and reasserted his right to meet his southern rival on equal terms in every sphere of life. It is indeed the case that the Celt is quite able to occupy the highest position wherever a fair field is given to the best talent, whether it be in the learned professions, commerce, art, or literature. It is now fashionable to be "Highland,"—to be able to boast of some distant relative who was a Macdonald, a Cameron, or a Mackay, and so claim a connection with the "land of bens, and glens, and heroes," a relationship which I daresay a few years ago was considered unworthy of mention. This past year has witnessed another "rising of the clans," another "awakening of the Gael," which, we are fain to hope, will prove a more successful, and less hazardous enterprise than the ill-fated rising of the '45. I am sure we all wish prosperity to this new movement ; it has done much to arouse an interest in Celtic matters,— in the history, language, literature, and antiquities of the Highlands. May it help to make Highlanders more worthy of the names they bear, and of the mountain land which gave them birth!

One of the most interesting results of this awakening of Celtic feeling is the prominence which is now given to the literature connected with the Highlands, and vast numbers of the descendants of Highlanders born in the south are now taking a sincere interest in the literature and music of the land of their forefathers. All kinds of books dealing with such subjects are in great demand, but as the best of these works are scarce, it is not easy for the average reader to consult many of them. But still more unfortunate is the position of the student who, desirous of making himself acquainted with the literature of the Highlands, and not possessing a knowledge of the Gaelic language, finds himself unable to do more than merely reach the borders of this promised land, where he knows that "gems" (literary gems) of the greatest value are to be found abundantly. Our friend, Mr. Duncan Reid, the able teacher of the Gaelic class, may offer to help us to overcome that difficulty; but then, if every student had to acquire the language of any nation before he could command a knowledge of its literature, his opportunities for possessing a general knowledge of European and classical literature would be scanty indeed. However, this difficulty has, happily, been removed, and by means of excellent translations, we may read the choicest works of almost any nation in the English language. Of course, in the process of translation much that gives power and grace to the original is lost, but then, the *substance*, which is, after all, the most essential element, may be had correctly and fully. It is certainly a pity that those qualities which help so much to make a great work interesting—such as grace of language, impassioned rhetoric and poetic genius—are either lost or only faintly reproduced, yet our desire is more to know the author's opinions on the subject of his book, or poem, rather than to learn his manner of expression.

This leads me now to speak specially of the literature of our own mountain land, which, more than that of almost any other country, has been wrapped up in a language which comparatively few students of other nationalities have taken the trouble to acquire. There certainly were translations published many years ago, but no representative collection was published until of recent years, so that the literature was but imperfectly understood by the general reading public. Macpherson's "Ossian" certainly gave some insight into the beauty of Gaelic literature, and attracted attention all over the world, but as the Ossianic period was only dealt with in his translations,—or, if you will, "adaptations"—it left untouched that wealth of Gaelic poetry which has been bequeathed to us by the bards of a thousand years. However, recently some most valuable work has been done by patriotic Highlanders in translating these Gaelic poems into English verse, and placing them within the reach of those desirous of possessing some knowledge of the literature of the Highlands.

It is my intention to-night to deal briefly with this literature of translation, in the hope that my experience may prove of service to those of our number who may have had the misfortune to be born in the south, and whose opportunities of learning the language of our fathers and mothers may not have been as favourable as we might have wished. To those of you who speak and read the "language of Eden," I cannot hope to teach anything, but I trust that I shall amuse, if not interest you, by introducing to your notice some old favourite songs transformed into English verse.

The translations are scattered through scores, nay hundreds of books, magazines, and papers, and the number that have passed through my hands during the past two or three years would astonish many who are unaware of the extent of this literature. It is not my intention to criticise the merits of these translations, or of the different renderings of the same poems, but merely to accept them as giving some estimate, however inadequate, of the extent and value of the literature of the Gael. And before entering into the subject in detail, I should just like to express my indebtedness to several distingushed members of this Society, the value of whose contributions to this literature cannot be overestimated. No one has done more in this direction than our much respected chairman, Mr. Henry Whyte, perhaps known to Highlanders generally by his *nom-deplume* of "Fionn"; Mr. Malcolm Macfarlane's translations are always sweet and graceful, Professor Mackinnon, of the Celtic chair, Professor J. S. Blackie, Sheriff Nicolson, Rev. Dr. Stewart, ("Nether Lochaber"), Mr. Alex. Carmichael, of Edinburgh; Mr. John Mackay, Hereford, and several others have added more or less to this literature, while we should not forget there are several Gaelic bards on our roll whose compositions have been deemed worthy of translation; and we have among us two publishers who have given to the world collections of these interesting and valuable English renderings. With these introductory remarks I shall now deal as briefly as possible with the rather wide subject which I have chosen for this paper.

When one has made himself thoroughly acquainted with the songs of the Gael, he will notice that many of the best of them are the compositions of two or three bards whose works give them the right to the first place in the literature of their country. The most popular of these are Duncan Ban Macintyre, Alexander Macdonald, Rob Donn Mackay, William Ross and Dugald Buchanan. Several of these were, in a special sense, district as well as national bards, and a good many of their poems describe the beauty of the land of their birth, and extol the virtues and warlike prowess of the respective clans to which they belonged. Thus we find Duncan Ban never tired of praising the majestic grandeur of Ben Dorain; Alexander Macdonald is equally enthusiastic in his praise of the Western Isles and the territory of his race; and Rob Donn is never in a happier mood than when he eulogises Ben Hope and Strathnaver, and the places renowned in the history of his clan. Although in every sense true national bards, they had that special warm love for their native place which is to be found in the hearts of all Highlanders, and which in no respect detracts from their national patriotism.

We further find that in one particular way the songs of the Highlands resemble those of the Lowlands. Many of the most beautiful of these compositions were the only literary productions of their several authors. Inspired by some overpowering feeling, whether of joy or sorrow, these Gaelic minstrels sung one song, breathing in fervent language the innermost feelings of the heart, and having given expression to their sentiments the poetic inspiration left them, perhaps never to return. As might be expected the greater part of these songs relate to the affections. The occasion of the poem may have been the death of some one near and dear to the bard, or it may have been the expression of some dreaded or real disappointment, or, perchance, the song may have been the marriage psalm of some happy lad or lass whose heart was too full of gladness to descend to the common-place of prose, but must be sung in the language of Parnassus. While this peculiarity is true of the songs of almost all nations, it is especially true of the Scottish people, of whom it may be said that all possess the poetic spirit, and while some can express it in song, the greater part live with the music in their hearts.

As the time at my disposal is so brief I must leave a general dissertation on the peculiar characteristics of these songs to some future time. Meanwhile, I shall arrange these translations into their respective classes, and illustrate each with an example to show in what respects they differ. As the "Love songs" far outnumber every other kind of Gaelic poetry, I cannot do better than begin with them. Most of these songs are of a mournful character; others again have a hearty ring, while not a few are witty enough to provoke a merry laugh. Of the pathetic songs the one I like most is that beautiful lyric popularly known as "The Boatman." The air to which it is sung is really delightful and seems wedded to the words. Like many other Gaelic songs, it expresses the feelings of a maiden whose lover is a "boatman," and has been absent. I have before me as I write several translations of this poem, but the following verses from Mr. Lachlan Macbean's excellent rendering will give some idea of its pathos:—

> Broken-hearted I droop and languish,
> And frequent tears show my bosom's anguish;
> Shall I expect thee to-night to cheer me?
> Or close the door, sighing sad and weary?
>
> My heart is weary with ceaseless wailing,
> Like wounded swan when her strength is failing;
> Her notes of anguish the lake awaken,
> By all her comrades at last forsaken.

This reference to the wounded swan deserted by its comrades is a touch of nature, and appeals to our feelings. In another well known song, "*Och, och, mar tha mi*" (Och! how lonely) the same simile is used:

> I'm like the swan that drops wounded—dying;
> My love exhausts me with bitter grieving.

Some lyrics, quite as pathetic, were composed by lovers lamenting the death of their fair ones. Of these

I daresay the finest example is a song sung to a most charming air "My dear little May" *(Mo Mhali bheag og)* which will be known to the most of my hearers. Another very pretty song might be quoted *(Oran mulaid)* from the excellent collection made by our President, Mr. Henry Whyte:—

>Life's bright star she shone,
>   Shone to cheer and guide me;
>I must drift alone—
>   Now death's shadows hide me.
>   Sick and sad am I.
>
>Nought can ease my pain,
>   Now she is departed;
>Why should I remain,
>   Sick and broken hearted?
>   Sick and sad am I.

Quite a number of other beautiful songs of a similar character suggest themselves to my mind, but we must pass on to the love songs breathing a happier atmosphere. Of these there is no end, and yet it is strange that even in the most joyous of them there is a suspicion of doubt or foreboding. It is, however, a reflex of the true character of the Gael, who somehow always takes a peep into the shadowy side of life.

Perhaps the most popular Gaelic song of the present day is "My brown-haired Maiden" *(Mo nighean donn bhoidheach)*. Its sentiment is light hearted, and the melody has a merry ring about it. Almost every worker in the field of translation has given us a rendering of this beautiful lyric. Mr. Malcolm Macfarlane, one of our most enthusiastic members, has given us one of the best of these that I have yet seen. The following verse will give the key note to the spirit of the song:—

> Thine eye with love is gleaming,
> Thy face with beauty beaming,
> When waking, or when dreaming,
> My thoughts dwell on thee.

Even in this joyous song there is a little "sighing and glooming"—

> I often sit and sigh love,
> And wish that you were nigh, love,
> To bring joy to me.

Many of the love songs partake largely of a full and particular description of the manifold charms of these bewitching Highland maidens. The poet goes direct to nature to find a suitable counterpart to their loveliness—he finds nothing so fascinating but he can trace some feature in his lady's form more excelling in its beauty. The prettiest flower finds its reflection in the colour of this maiden's eyes; the glistening rowans dripping with the morning dew, serve only to remind him of her rosy lips; the white-breasted sea-gull, the froth-crested billows, and the purest moorland *canach* are not more-dazzling than the whiteness of her breast; while her voice is like music in the night, or as the melody of birds rejoicing in the sunshine. These are all very instructive, but occasionally the bard is enticed into giving expression to some pretty conceits. Ewan Maclachlan is responsible for the following:—

> The mavis and lark at the breaking of dawn,
> Make a chorus of joy to resound through the lawn;
> But the mavis is tuneless, the lark strives in vain,
> When my beautiful charmer renews her sweet strain.

One philosophical poet, however, is a little sarcastic about the outward beauty of women. Beneath all these attractions he fears a hidden danger, and thus warns us that—

> Pink cheeks of fair fashion
>   And blue dazzling eyes,
> Though they rouse a short passion
>   Their glory soon dies;
> Red lips may do duty
>   To hide a sharp tongue,
> If their virtue is beauty,
>   It cannot last long.

There are two pleasing features about these love songs that are worth noticing. It is their unaffectedness and their purity. They are quite free from those grosser forms of ridicule and repulsive satire that we find so characteristic of many of the English satirists. The Gaelic Bards may be at times boisterously humorous, but we seldom find anything that we would wish had never been written.

Before passing from this branch of my subject, a brief reference might be made to the humorous love songs. There is always the amusing side to love-making, and the Highland poets were not slow in depicting in ridiculous terms the humours of courtship. One tell us that he went to the valley to woo Mallie, and fared rather badly—

>Wi' bosom high-swellin' I cam' to her dwellin',
> I kent she was willin' to list to my tale;
>I startit a-showin' my love overflowin'.
> She stopped me by throwin' about me the pail.

Some of these Highland lassies had a pretty perfect ideal of what they would like in the way of a husband—

>God save me from a heartless man,
> A mite that folk despise,
>Both mean and keen my acts to scan
> With sharp and watchful eyes;
>Who has with other men no weight,
> No kindness in his face,
>Who has no humour in his pate,
> Nor any other grace.
>
>But oh! a handsome stalwart youth,
> Not haughty in his mind,
>Who could be resolute for truth,
> But could also be kind;
>Who is not spoiled by worldly pelf,
> Nor one that want pursues—
>If I might choose my man myself,
> This is the chiel I'd choose.

By way of contrast I might allow the Highland lad to describe his fanciful choice. He is certainly not so difficult to please—

>Oh, I could love a pretty maid,
> Good, beautiful, and meek

> What matter though she had no cash
> When 'tis herself I seek.
>
> But, if she happens to have both,
> High praise and well filled purse,
> (And she were wise and sensible)
> She would be none the worse.

And now we come to what is known in Gaelic poetry as the "feeling for nature," a quality which more than any other is characteristic of the songs of the Gael. There was a period in the history of English literature when the poets went direct to Nature to find a fit subject for their rhymes. This feeling was quite a recent one in English poetry; it was the inauguration of a new era, and its birth and growth was the subject of much self congratulation. And what of the feeling for nature in Gaelic poetry? Was it a new experience for the Highland bard to sing of the beauty of his native land, of its glorious mountains, its echoing caverns, and rushing cataracts, its picturesque valleys, with smiling pasture fields and lowing kine? Did not "Ossian," the noblest of all our poets, away back in the misty ages of Highland history, sing in sublime language of the "land of hills, glens, and heroes"—of the romantic straths of Skye, and the mist-covered hills of Morven; of the night wind moaning its sad story among the dark pines; of the moon, and the sun, and the stars beaming on the sons of men through the ages of man's being; of the excitement of the chase, and the love which Highlanders cherish to be buried beside the graves of their forefathers? Yes, these poor Highlanders, the subjects of Dr. Johnson's pious attentions and "Highland Tours," wrote and sung of nature long before the English poets realised that the morning hymn of the lark had a spiritual lesson, or that there were in good truth "tongues in trees, sermons in stones, books in the running brooks, and good in everything." When one recollects the general tone of scorn, contempt, and even pity, with which English literary men of last century, and part of this, spoke and wrote of Highlanders and Highland matters, it is hard to restrain one's self from speaking quite as bitterly of them. In poetry, as in many other things, the supercilious Saxon, with his superfine airs and impudent assurance, has been taught by the Gael, and it is not unlikely that the Highlander will continue to educate his southern neighbour in many other matters in regard to which his education has been neglected.

There is nothing in the poetry of any nation that can surpass the grandeur of Ossian's "Address to the Sun." It has been translated by many able writers, but I choose Mr. Lachlan Macbean's rendering, as it happens to be in verse.

> Oh, thou that movest through the sky,
>   Like shield of warrior round and bright,
> Whence is thy glorious gleaming high,
>   And whence, O sun, thy lasting light?
> In peerless beauty thou dost rise,
>   And all the stars before thee flee;
> The pallid moon forsakes the skies
>   To hide beneath the western sea.
>
> Thou movest in thy course alone,
>   And who so bold as wander near?

> The mountain oak shall yet fall prone,
> The hills with age shall disappear,
> The changing main shall ebb and flow,
> The waning moon be lost in night,
> Thou only shalt victorious go,
> For ever joying in thy light.

Almost all the bards described the beauties of nature, but perhaps none excelled more in this respect than Duncan Ban Macintyre and Rob Donn Mackay. The following on the simplest of subjects, "A Sprig of Heather," is a perfect gem of word painting.

> The bonnie, clinging, clustering,
> Green heather, growing slenderly,
> With snowy honey lustering,
> And tassels hanging tenderly.
>
> In pink and brownish proud array,
> With springy flexibility,
> Its scented wig all powdery,
> To keep up its gentility.

Rob Donn's "Song of Winter" is really one of the most realistic descriptions of nature to be found in the whole range of Gaelic poetry. Anyone who visited "Bonnie Strathmore," in the Reay country, where the scene is laid, with Ben Hope rising sheer up from the edge of the valley, and a thousand silvery rivulets rushing down its hoary sides, will understand the wonderful descriptive power of the poet. The appearance of this secluded strath in winter is very desolate. I have often passed the place where the sweetest songster of the Mackay country, Rob Donn, composed the following poem—

> At waking so early
>   Was snow on the ben,
> And, the glen of the hill in,
> The storm drifts so chilling,
> The linnet was stilling
>   That couch'd in its den ;
> And poor robin was shrilling
>   In sorrow its strain.
>
> 'Tis the season of leanness,
>   Unkindness, and chill ;
> Its whistle is ringing,
> An iciness bringing,
> Where the brown leaves are clinging
>   In helplessness, still,
> And the snow rush is delving
>   With furrows the hill.
>
> How mournful in winter
>   The lowing of kine,
> How lean-backed they shiver,
> How draggled they cower,
> How their nostrils run ower
>   With drippings of brine,
> So scraggy and crining
>   In the cold frost they pine.
>
> Such songs that are saddest
>   And dreariest of all ;
> I ever am eerie,
> In the morning to hear ye
> When foddering to cheer the
>   Poor herd in the stall—
> While each creature is moaning
>   And sickening in thrall.

The above translation was by Dr. Angus Mackay, a son of the late piper to the Queen. Rob Donn's Strathmore song leads me to speak of another group of Gaelic songs which are well worthy of our attention, namely, those dealing with the Highland clearances and emigration. Perhaps there are no songs which appeal to the best feelings of a Highlander more than the pathetic wails which were wrung from the hearts of those who were driven from their native land to seek a new home over the seas. Strathmore, in Rob Donn's day, was the happy home of a splendid race of men—a nursery of military and commercial enterprise. The young men from this and other northern straths went out into the world, and made their names famous in every country and in every sphere of life. Six months ago I walked down Strathmore, and only saw two shepherd's houses. The beautiful strath was a veritable desolation—the heaps of stones which marked the sites of former happy dwellings, and the lonely graveyard, being all that remained to show that it was once inhabited by a numerous population. When speaking of these dark deeds it is difficult to restrain one's self from saying bitter things. I venture to think that the Duke or Sir who would to-day attempt to revive these gloomy memories would soon find the Highlands too small to hold him. Our poets have sung sweetly and sadly of these days of depopulation and broken hearts.

> The ancient customs and clans are vanished,
> No more are songs on the breezes swelling,
> Our Highland nobles, alas! are banished,
> And worthless upstarts are in their dwelling.

The poet-laureate of Gaeldom, Neil Macleod, the Skye bard, in several of his songs refers to the desolation of the Highlands—

> The homes of our fathers are bleak and decayed,
> And cold is the hearth where in childhood we played;
> Where the hungry were fed and the weary found rest,
> The fox has his lair, and the owl has her nest.
> - - - - - - - -
> The lads once so buoyant in innocent mirth,
> Oppression has reft from the land of their birth.

"Fionn's" beautiful song, "The dispersion of the Highlanders," is an eloquent commentary on the policy of expelling the native inhabitants and putting sheep in their place.

> To make room for the sportsman their lands were all taken,
> And they had to seek out new homes over the wave.

We look back with fond regret to the life which our forefathers lived in the fertile straths of the Highlands — they had few wants which they could not supply, and as they had no desire for luxuries such as we enjoy, they never felt the want of them. In the good old days which the poet sings of, "when all the birds in Gaelic sang,"

> Love, pity, and good will were spread,
> Among the people everywhere,
> From where the morning rises red
> To where the evening shineth fair,—
> When all the birds in Gaelic sang.

Amongst a maritime population, such as we find in the Western Highlands and Islands, we might expect to find many songs connected with the sea. Indeed, some of the most popular of the Highland melodies are wedded to "boat songs," which are usually sung to keep time to the swing of the oars. A beautiful air to which I have already alluded, "The Boatman," is a special favourite, its measure being well suited to keep time to the oars of a heavy boat crossing a Highland loch. I remember two summers ago a party of Mackays rowing across Loch Eriboll, a wide estuary on the north coast of Sutherland, and this song was sung in unison with the sweep of the oars, the chorus being heartily joined in by the large company in the boat. William Black, in his Highland novels, frequently introduces these boat songs with much effect. The following example is from "Altavona," one of Professor Blackie's most delightful Highland books—

> What though a lowly dwelling
>   On barren shore I own,
> My kingdom is the blue wave,
>   My boatie is my throne!
> I'll never want a dainty dish
>   To breakfast or to dine,
> While men may man my boatie,
>   And fish swim in Loch Fyne.

Generally these boat songs are wedded to spirited music so as to inspire the rowers with energy in their labours. The words are appropriate to the character of the melody.

> To Mull we go, to Mull we go,
>   That island worth adoring,

> To Mull we go, though winds may blow,
>   And billows fierce be roaring;
> Mid flying foam, I feel at home,
>   At sea I'm in my glory,
> Our crew and boat, the best afloat,—
>   Their fame shall live in story!

In the olden times, and the practice is still to some extent continued, when the chief or some important member of a clan died, it was the custom for the pipers to play at his funeral the Lament of his clan. Each clan possessed one or more of these beautiful and mournful airs, which were originally composed in honour of chiefs of the clan who had by their valour or other commendable qualities endeared themselves to their clansmen. Nothing could be more impressive than to see a Highland funeral, the coffin borne shoulder high, and pipers in front playing an air, such as "Lochaber no more," or "MacCrimmon's Lament." It gives the ceremony an air of unutterable sadness. Everyone knows the peculiar circumstances under which "MacCrimmon's Lament" was composed by the piper's sister. He took part in the illfated rising of 1745, and never returned—

> O'er Coolin's face the night is creeping,
> The banshee's wail is round us sweeping,
> Blue eyes in Dun are sadly weeping,
>   Since thou art gone and ne'er returnest.
>
> We'll see no more MacCrimmon's returning,
> Nor in peace or in war is he returning,
> Till dawns the great day of woe and burning
>   For him, for him, there's no returning.

The "MacIntosh's Lament," and "Lord Lovat's Lament" are both very beautiful melodies. Rob Donn wrote several exquisite laments, and set them to music of his own composition. The one on "Hugh Mackay" is worth quoting.

> Oh sad this voice of woe we hear,
> And gone our cheer and pleasantry,
> One common grief, without relief,
> Has seized on chief and peasantry;
> In hut or hall or merchant's stall,
> There's none at all speaks cheerfully;
> Since that sad day he went away,
> Naught can we say, but tearfully.
>
> * * * * * * * *
>
> Oh, many a man was filled with gloom
> That round thy tomb stood silently;
> Hearts that were buoyed with hopes—now void,
> By death destroyed so violently.
> By clansmen prized and idolised,
> His worth disguised humanity,
> But this fell blow, alas! will show
> There's nought below but vanity.

Others of Rob Donn's elegies are in quite a different strain. With a Highlander's love of generosity and hospitality, he hated every form of meanness and greed, and liked nothing better than to expose to the ridicule of his countrymen those who evaded the sacred duties of hospitality. His elegies on the "Rispond Family," and Grey, the tacksman of Rogart, are excellent examples of humorous satire.

I can only refer here briefly to the Sacred Songs of the Gael. Naturally of a religious and solemn disposition, occasioned perhaps by the grand, and at times awful, nature of the scenery by which he is surrounded, and various other circumstances, the Highlander gives much thought to the termination of his earthly life, and the brighter and happier world beyond the grave. Such subjects as Death, the Last Day, the Resurrection, and the great day of Judgment, were favourite sources of poetic inspiration to the Gaelic bards. The greatest of our sacred songsters was Dugald Buchanan, while many others such as Grant, Maclean, Rob Donn Mackay, and MacGregor contributed to this literature. Buchanan's description of the "Day of Judgment" is not only circumstantial, but graphic in its conception—

> On fiery chariot Christ shall ride
> With thunders rolling round His path,
> To bear His voice through heaven wide
> And rend the clouds with storm and wrath.
> Out from His chariot wheels shall go
> The fiery torrents of his ire,
> The flaming floods shall downward flow,
> And set the world around on fire.

Mr. Malcolm Macfarlane, an honoured member of our own Society, has contributed two very pretty hymns to Mr. Lachlan Macbean's collection. In "Beckoning," he teaches the wisdom of avoiding evil and seeking all that is good and true.

> Beckoning, beckoning,
> Wealth and fame are beckoning;

> May our youthful hearts abide
> Untouched by discontent or pride.
>
> Beckoning, beckoning,
> Grace and love are beckoning,
> Teach us, Lord, and let us be
> From ignorance and folly free.

A word of reference might be here made to the beautiful "Uist Old Hymns," which our esteemed friend Mr. Alex. Carmichael, has collected among the pious Catholics of the Island of Uist. As Mr. Carmichael purposes giving these most valuable examples of sacred song to the public in a permanent form, and as reference to them has been made, very appropriately, in these Transactions, I need not do more at present than emphasise the great literary value which should be attached to these stray fragments of Gaelic song, which have been orally handed down to us from our early forefathers.

Among the most spirited of the Highland melodies are the "Marching songs." Every clan had its own marches, and several are of much historic interest. That well-known tune "We will take the Highway," the air of which cannot fail to remind us of earlier years, has quite an atmosphere of romance attached to it. Its inspiring notes led the Highland clans into the battles of Prestonpans, Falkirk, and numerous other conflicts, and it is still very popular wherever Highlanders meet. The sentiments expressed in the first verse have given our critics in the South a foothold to argue that it was not pure "patriotism" that prompted the clans to rise in the '15 and '45, but the cheering prospect of plundering the fat herds, and rich stores, of the Sassenach.

> We will take the good old way,
> We will take the good old way,
> We will take the good old way,
>   The way that lies before us.
> Climbing stiff the heathery ben,
> Winding swiftly down the glen;
> Should we meet with stragglers then,
>   *Their gear will serve to store us.*

Of course, we stoutly repudiate any such insinuation. In those days it was counted gentlemanly to—shall I say visit the Lowlands in the pale moonlight?—and in all gentlemanly pursuits each clan did its best to specially excel. My own clan seems in this respect, to have been perfect gentlemen, for a Gaelic proverb speaks of them as "The Mackays of the Spoils."

It has been often asserted that Highlanders are totally devoid of the sense of Humour. The statement is so absurd that I fancy no one will expect me to seriously attempt to prove its untruth. No one who knows anything of Gaelic poetry will deny that it is rich in the quality of humour, and that often of the keenest and most subtle kind. At other times it is boisterously humorous, provoking the reader to immediate laughter. I have not time at my disposal to do more than quote one short example of this kind of Gaelic poetry, culled from Mr. Pattison's splendid collection, a new edition of which has just been published by our friend and fellow member, Mr. Archibald Sinclair—

> I went away with Breigein Binneach
> And MacGregor Clairy,
> He told me of his splendid house,
> His kitchen and his dairy.
> But not a house or hall saw I,
> Save, on the hillside airy,
> A little bothy where he lived
> With his sister Mary.
> He has got but one dun cow
> Though he bragged so rarely,—
> It hardly gives enough of milk
> For himself and Mary :
>
> In my father's barn at home
> I could lie as fairly,
> As in this bothy by the hill
> Which is so damp and airy.
> I would leave it fast enough,
> If my sire forgave me ;
> I would werk and work enough—
> Do anything to save me
> From the Breigein Binneach's tongue
> And his sister Mary's,
> I'd thrash, or plough, or keep the cows,
> Or cart or keep the dairy.

Several of what are known as the "Drinking songs" are very amusing. There are quite a number of these, which go to show that from "waulking cloth" to "drinking whisky," the Highlander had songs appropriate for the occasion. Sheriff Nicolson is responsible for the following translation of Duncan Ban's well-known song—

> He that has gold will
> Get what he wishes for,
> He that is prudent
> Need not come here ;
> He that is niggardly
> Ne'er can we suffer him,
> But the true gentleman,
> Let him draw near.
>
> He that is pithless,
> This will inspirit him,
> He that is weary,
> 'Twill cheer his soul ;
> The sick it will raise,
> And make him merry.
> The cure for all ills
> Is the well filled bowl.

Another very interesting class of songs are those concerning the Fairies and the Nursery. Indeed among these will be found some of the most beautiful of the Gaelic melodies. Sir Walter Scott's "Lullaby of an infant Chief," is very pretty.

> O, hush thee, my babie, thy sire was a knight,
> Thy mother a lady, both lovely and bright ;
> The woods and the glens, from the towers which we see,
> They all are belonging, dear babie, to thee.
>
> > O ho ro, I ri ri, cadul gu lo,
> > O ho ro, i ri ri

I fear that I have exhausted your patience, although I have not by any means exhausted the subject which I have chosen for this paper. I feel that I have so far only touched upon the fringe of this interesting and profitable study, and that a large sized volume, instead of a short essay such as this, would be required to do it full justice. There are several important phases of this subject which have been left almost untouched, such as, for instance, the "Patriotic songs," of which we have capital examples in "Mary Macleod's Ditty," Neil Macleod's eulogy on his "Native Highland Glen," and J. MacCuaraig's song on "The Happy Age" of long ago, when

> No tax or tribute used to fall
> On honest men, nor any rent ;
> To hunt and fish was free to all,
> And timber without price or stent
>   When all the birds in Gaelic sang."

It will be also observed that the songs of the "Domestic Circle" have been unnoticed, and, as everyone knows, the joy and happiness of home have been sung in as sweet a measure as in any of the other songs to which I have referred at greater length. Duncan Ban's "*Mairi bhan og*" (Fair young Mary), is a perfect picture of domestic bliss, and John Campbell, of Ledaig, expresses the sentiments of us all when he sings—

> Gie me my ain fireside, my friens
> Gie me my ain fireside,
> The cosiest place in a' the warl',
> Is just my ain fireside.

And then, what of the martial songs of the Gael? What of the poetry of the clans, for each clan had its deeds of honour immortalized by its bards? Did not the chivilrous rising of the '45 inspire the poets to sing of "Morag" of the Flowing Locks, and the Highland rush of tartans and claymores at Falkirk and Prestonpans, not to speak of the mournful laments to which bloody Culloden gave birth. Then there are the military songs of the past hundred and forty years, since the time when the Black Watch of glorious renown stemmed the torrent of Irish and French victory at Fontenoy, and later on, lay in heaps outside the impregnable walls of Ticonderago, till the Highland lads swept over the ramparts at Tel-el-Kebir, and showed that Highlanders could yet do and dare. These deeds of valour have been immortalized in spirited verse; and in our own generation Sheriff Nicolson, in his popular "Highland Marching Song," has given us a musical index to Highland feats of arms during the past eighteen hundred years—

> Now we're ready for the march,
> Slope your arms and step together.
>
> Agus O, Mhòrag,
> Horo, march together,
> Agus O, Mhòrag.
>
> Think of them who went before us,
> Winning glory for the tartan!
>
> Vainly did the mighty Roman,
> Check the Caledonian valour.

R

In the ranks of great Gustavus
With the bravest they were reckoned.

As it was in days of yore,
So the story shall be ever.

Where the doughtiest deeds are dared,
Shall the Gael be forward pressing.

Where the Highland broadsword waves,
There shall graves be found the thickest.

Think then of the name ye bear,
Ye that wear the Highland tartan !

Jealous of its old renown.
Hand it down without a blemish.

Agus O, Mhòrag.
Horo, march together,
Agus O, Mhòrag.

And now I must conclude this rather lengthy paper. If there is one thing that has been left unsaid, and which deserves mention, it is that the Music of the Highlands is in every respect worthy of its poetic literature. When we remember that the air "O' a' the Airts," and many other of Burns' most beautiful songs, were old Gaelic melodies, we need no further proof of this statement. Many of the most popular, and most delightful of those songs which we usually consider truly Lowland, are set to Gaelic airs, thus showing that in this, as in many other respects, the Highlander has been wealthy enough to lend to the Lowlander. I cannot say that the loan has been repaid. To my mind the lending has very largely come from the one side.

[28th April, 1891.]

At the annual meeting of the Society held on this date, office-bearers for the succeeding session were elected. Mr. Hugh Macleod, Writer, read a paper on "*Ancient Celtic Laws.*" Mr. Macleod's paper was as follows:—

ANCIENT CELTIC LAWS.

In choosing Ancient Celtic Laws as the subject of my address, I did not count upon the difficulty and labour attending its treatment in a manner worthy of this Society and satisfactory to myself. The most careless thinker, and the most casual and superficial reader of history cannot fail to realise how very difficult it is to speculate with any degree of certainty upon any event, even in modern times, far less to tear asunder the veil of haze and obscurity that surrounds early institutions. To penetrate beyond the age of writing and printing, and deduce with a sure degree of satisfaction any authentic account of men and events is well nigh impossible. But unfortunately, the task is rendered almost insuperably hard with reference to the early history of the Celts in Britain, owing to their hatred of anything foreign and to the backward state of their civilization. We must candidly admit that as far as the Celts in Britain are concerned, we are absolutely without any *reliable* information. However partial or one sided a nation's history may be when written or narrated by the prejudiced native, it is upon the whole more to be relied upon than that which is furnished by the foreigner who knows neither the language nor the customs of the people of whom he is writing. So it is with us. We have only a few hoary traditions of military prowess, of feud and faction, of blood and battle, of love and enmity. For an account of the early inhabitants and institutions of Britain, we have to rely upon Roman historians, whose works, in my estimation, are, for the most part, the coloured, exaggerated and prejudiced reports of the early traveller into a strange land. The still more unfortunate fact is that our own early writers differ so materially on so many events relating to the conditions of the people, and important events relating to our history, that one is left to grope amidst a chaotic mass of myth, mystery, fable and fact, and each for himself conclude and deduct according to the bent of his mind, or the object he has in view. As the Duke of Argyle puts it in that remarkable work of his "Scotland as it Was and Is," which all of you should read, however much you may differ from his conclusions—"The Celtic period of Scottish History has been peculiarly the field of a fabulous narrative of no ordinary perplexity due to the rivalries and ambitions of ecclesiastical establishments and church parties." We are therefore groping in the dark for any authentic account of the jurisprudence—if we may at this stage use that term—of our ancestors. All Law was no doubt traditionary, originating in the authority of the father as head of his family, and as the early unit of society in Roman and Greek communities, but, with us, I rather think in the customs of the family, so that in Celtic communities law would be peculiarly traditionary, there having been such a strong prejudice, in fact, discouragement of written precepts. We must therefore look to local customs and usages, and unrecorded practices, where we can find these generally observed, for the Laws of Scotland, down, at all events, until the Kingdom of Scotland was consolidated in the 12th century. Now can we with any degree of truth assert what the early institutions of Caledonia were, say, up to the 12th century? I trow not. I fear the reason is obvious and that on two grounds. First we have no written account of any system of jurisprudence: all we have is legendary. Secondly, I fear none such existed as a completed system. It would seem rather that each social unit, be it the family, or the "fine," sept, or *tuath*, or clan, formulated and enforced its own private behests; and in general *might* prevailed. The rude comprehension of justice and right gave way before lawless ambition and selfish proclivities. Certainly by the aid of modern Philology we can trace back the meaning of certain words and phrases, and, applying these to certain customs, we can form a more or less hazy idea of what were the more general prevailing customs in our Celtic communities in Scotland. Our difficulty therefore is to predicate with certainty that general customs prevailed to such an extent as to warrant us in applying to them the term Law. Generally speaking we must assume there were; for without some defined checks upon waywardness and rapacity, which would be common to all, there could be no cohesion. But when and whence did these early customs spring? It is impossible to say. It is obvious that many customs which existed, and now exist among tribal communities of the Aryan stock, may have existed among their remote ancestors prior to their dispersion. But as I have said, some general principles did exist which regulated certain relations of life and which had the sanction of the greater part of the community, and were accordingly observed whether they could at all times be enforced or not, we may safely conclude. As Chalmers says, *Caledonia*, Vol. I.—"We need not however go back for those to Teutonic tribes of Germany, for the inhabitants of North Britain were Celtic and their jurisprudence was analogous to the nature of a Gaelic people. Nor need we trace their principles back to feudal principle." And as Argyll says, "These were at best modern introductions to North Britian, were long opposed and were antagonistic to the genius of the Celtic people and a Celtic race".—*Scotland as it Was and Is.* Now we have traces of customs from an early age, which regulated the succession to crowns, to land and title, to chiefship, to church patrimony at a later stage, and to marriage; and it will be my object for a few minutes to examine a few of these and pass on to the consideration of a Celtic system of jurisprudence as beautiful and as mathematically precise, and withal, as authentic as the legal maxims of Solon or the minute compendium of the Twelve Tables. I refer to the early Laws of Ireland—the *Seanachus Mór*. Before doing so, however, let me here state that the earliest codification we have of what is termed Scotch Law, is that contained in the work called "*Regiam Majestatem*, (first published in 1609), so called from the first two words in the compilation. The title of this work which has caused so much bitter discussion, is so quaint that it is worth quoting.

REGIAM MAJESTATEM.

THE

Auld Laws and Constitutions of Scotland.

Faithfullie collected fruth of the Register and other Auld Authentic Bukes fra the Dayes of Good King Malcolm the Second, until the time of King James I. of Gude memorie, and trewlie corrected in sundrie faults and errors committed, Be ignorant writers, and translated out of Latin in Scottish Language, to the use and knowledge of all the subjects within this Realme, with ane large Table of the contents thereof

BE

Sir John Skene, of Curriehill, Clerk of oure Sovereign Lord's Register, Counsell and Rollis, Edinburgh.

Printed by John Wood and sold by him.
J. Bell and C. Elliot.
1774.

This work is of very doubtful origin. Craig and Stair, two of our greatest feudal Lawyers and Jurists, contend that it is not a Book of Scottish Law at all. It has been ascribed to Malcolm II. as *Leges Macolmi Secundus* and to David I., but from internal evidence this could not be so. It contains, however, as Scotch Law many Celtic customs. Perhaps the surest and safest theory to adopt concerning it is that of Chalmers, viz:—that it is a compilation of English Law, Scotch and Celtic customs, and ecclesiastical canons handed down as a Scotch Code. Poor old Sir John Skene, however, stoutly maintains its authenticity against the more formidable opinion of Stair and Craig.

Let us then examine a few of the Celtic customs which we may regard, perhaps with hesitation, as worthy of the name of Law in the sense of the term as understood by us. Take for example what is known as *Byr* Law. That is short Law or summary Law. This system of jurisprudence was determined by consent of neighbours who were elected in Byr Law Councils. It was in fact a Law of arbitration. The system was analogous to our present system of appointing two neighbours to fix any damage to land or property. (See O'Brien and Shaw's Dictionary.)

In this relation mention may be made of Calp Law, or the right of the chief to an ox, cow, mare or horse on the death of his clansman. This can best be described in the words of the Statute abolishing it in the year 1617. "His Majesty's Lieges have sustained great hurt and skayth these many years bygone by the chiefs of Clans within the Highlands and Isles of his Kingdom, by the unlawful taking from them their children and executors after their decease, under the name of Caulpes of their best Aucht, whether it be ane mare or horse, or cow, alleging their predecessors to have been in possession thereof for maintaining and defending of them against their enemies and evil willars of old. Therefore it is ordained, &c." (Acts of Parl, vol. IV. p. 548.)

EARLY CELTIC CHURCH.

With regard to the early church law of Scotland, we are on safer ground; for from the time of the introduction of christianity by St. Columba, we have a comparatively authentic account of ecclestiastical matters. Due allowance, however, must be made to the natural inclination or bias of early clerical writers to make their own and their church's doings appear glorified in the early pages of history. The early religion, if we may so use the term, was Pagan—a species of Fetichism peopling all the objects of nature with evil Beings. These evil spirits were the cause of all the peculiar changes and phenomena existing in nature. In other words nature was personified, and the mysterious Beings composing it, who were required to be appeased or dreaded, lived in the Heavens, or in the Earth, or the Sea. The priests of this order were called "Druidh." They exercised great authority among the people, and were supposed to be able to work great wonders. Mr. Skene deals with this subject very elaborately and points out that the popular conception of the Druids, with their stone, circles, and cromlechs, said to represent temples and altars, human sacrifices, and worship of Baal—is quite wrong. As we know the first christian church was founded in Iona in 492 by St. Columba. Some centuries later the chief seat was removed to Dunkeld. It was, of course, a branch of the Irish church and was, accordingly, governed by the same laws; the Abbot being the chief ruler, had under him Bishops who were under the Monastic rule and who celebrated the Eucharist. St. Columba was of the Hy Neill tribe of Ireland who were patron Saints of many ecclesiastical establishments; therefore on his death, according to the Celtic Law, his successor as Abbot, who required to be of the tribe of the patron Saint, was found in the person of Baithene, a cousin of St. Columba, and superior of the monastery of Tiree, and, of course, of the Hy. Neill. Skene tells us that prior to 1139, celibacy was enforced upon Monks. It seems not to have been unlawful before then, and, as a consequence, a direct descent from the ecclesiastical persons themselves came in place of the older system, and church offices thus became hereditary. As Abbots and Superiors did not frequently take orders, laymen were appointed to perform many ecclesiastical functions, such as a "Sagart." These laymen soon came to secure all the privileges and emoluments of the Abbacy.—Skene vol. II. p. 341. In the early church Saturday was by law a day of rest, and on the Sabbath was celebrated the resurrection. It is stated that Margaret, wife of Canmore, urgently pleaded for this at a Council at which her husband acted as interpreter.

The early influence of ecclesiastics in the formation of laws we shall see when dealing with the *Seanachus Mòr*, but it may be here pointed out also. Thus Adamnan,* who wrote the life of St. Columba, went in

* What appears very strange, Adamnan in his Life of St. Columba chronicles the most minute details about the life and work of St. Columba and his Monks; but not a word as to the character and social condition of the people among whom those laboured.

697 to Ireland, accompanied by Bruide, son of Deird, King of the Picts, to attend a synod of 39 ecclesiastics and 47 chiefs, presided over by the King of Armagh, and passed a law exempting women from what was called "Fecht" or "Sluagad"—the duty of attending Hostages or Expeditions—this was afterwards appropriately termed "*lex innocentium*." Again, the church synod of Cashel decided in 1172 that all church lands shall be free from all exactions on the part of secular persons, Mormaors, or Tosseachs, &c. We thus see that Law and Religion were closely related, and, while the Abbot acted as Priest and legislator, the Druid, earlier still, very often did the same, and decreed according to traditional maxims. They sometimes shared their powers with the chiefs and heads of tribes and were termed Fear gu-breath, of whom more anon under the name of Brehon or Breathibh.

Adamnan tells us of the Island of Council where a council of 12 sat daily for the administration of Justice; and I suppose you all have heard of the Statutes of Iona. In the time of James VI., Commissioners and chiefs and clergy met in Iona and decreed—

I.—That Inns be provided at certain places.

II.—That chiefs be compelled to find their own supporters.

III.—That Sorners be punished, &c.

IV.—That Bards, &c. be punished in stocks, and by banishment.

LAW OF CORONATION.

An early custom was that of crowning the Kings

on a coronation stone, and proclaiming them from the coronation chair on the stone which was placed on an eminence;* this was a necessary legal ceremony. Thus we are told that Kenneth McAlpine, 850, Mal. II. 1006 and Robert Bruce, 1306, sat "Super montem de Scone." In Scone the hill was called the Mute-hill, Quothgran Law in Lanark, and Tynwald in Man. In like manner the inauguration of a chief was celebrated.

The next custom which is is worthy of the name of law is

GAVEL.

The succession to the land was called Gavel; although on the establishment of the Feudal system the latter may fairly be said to have regulated both the succession to the chiefship and, undoubtedly, the land. According to the law of Gavel, brothers succeeded before sons: the brother being considered one step nearer the common ancestor than the son. The chief characteristic of this system was that females were entirely excluded, the land of the clan being divided in certain proportions amongst the male branches of the family. A great portion of the land however remained with the chief, as well as the principal residence or seat, and, by this distribution, the chief surrounded himself by members of the clan who had been freed from selfish ambition, and whose interest it was to support the head of the family. This principle was

---

*The office of placing the king on the coronation stone was the hereditary right of the Earls of Fife.

evidently the outcome of military instinct, as it tended very much to strengthen the power of the chief, extend his connections, and secure the obedience and co-operation of the more powerful branches of the clan.

It would appear that this system differed from the Gavel Kind of the English, and also the Brehon Law, for, under the latter, the system was pretty much the same as that which prevailed in Scotch Law, whereby the widow and children succeed to the deceased's moveable estate.

Here is an instance of the form of charter given by the Lords of the Isles to some of their followers. You will notice it is in rhyme.

> "Tha mise Domhnul nan Domhnuill
> Am shuidhe air Dun Domhnuill
> Toirt coir do Mhac Aoidh air Kilmaluaig
> On diugh gus am màireach
> 'S gu la bhrath mar sin."

The chief then knelt on the Black Stone and confirmed the grant.

LAND AND ITS BURDENS.

Going back to a very early period of our history we find, according to Skene, that the members of the Tribe were divided into *Saor*—free, and *Daor*—unfree. But there was another distinction of rank depending upon the wealth or possession of the individual. Such as the "Fer Midba" or inferior man, the "Bo-aire" or cow lord. Owing to the superior wealth in cattle of the Bo-aire, he at a remote period got beyond the family unit and became entitled to the possession of a household for himself. Of the Bo-aire class there were six grades, the Og-aire, the Aitchech ar Athreba, Bo-aire febhsa, Bruighfer, Fer fothla, and Aire Coisring.

With regard to the burdens on land they were "Cain" and "Conveth." These were fixed payments in kind by way of rent, generally the produce of the land. "Cain" originally meant "Law." *Conveth* or *cean mhath* was a payment of first fruits. In its early form it resembles "Maills and Duties" of Scotch Charters, or the "Coinmhedha" or Coigny of the Irish—a night's meal or refection, which latterly became a fixed amount of produce when the tribe land became crown land or feudal land. In the Western Isles it took the name of "Cuidiche" or "Cuid oidhche" a night's portion. This was continued as a burden on land in Athol as recently as 1720.*

Another burden was "Feacht," a service in war on behalf of the chiefs to which the possessor of land was subject. "Feacht" and "Sluagad" are the "*Expeditis* or *exercitus* of the Feudal charters, and we find them awanting in Ecclesiastical charters.

Then there was what is called "Coin and Livery." This consisted in what we now term military requisitions. The chiefs perpetually quartered themselves and their retainers upon their tenants. Another

---

* See Skene's "Celtic Scotland," Vol. III.
  Scotland as it Was and Is—Vol. I.
  O'Brien and Shaw's Dictionary.

name for this was "Bonacht," or a right of living at free quarters upon the tenants.

"Coshering" was another burden on land. It means the visitations and progresses made by the Lord of the land and his followers among the tenants. Then there were Sessings of the Kerne, or support for Lords, horses and attendants, and so forth. Similar burdens were Tallages and Spendings.

LAND TENURE.

With regard to land tenure it cannot be disputed that the chief had in modern times no better title to the land, than that his ancestors possessed it from time immemorial. The pen that wrote his charter was the sword, and the ink was the blood of his clansmen. Many chiefs were greatly alarmed when Bruce required them to exhibit their charters. Thus Macdonald of Keppoch, 1678, disdained to hold by a sheepskin parchment the lands of Glenroy. The Mackintosh had a crown charter for these lands and claimed them, but Keppoch and his clansmen fought and thrashed the Mackintosh, who thereupon renounced his claim. It is also well known that the ancestors of Lord Reay had no charter for their Lands until 1499. Among the Gaelic race, the social unit was the "family" or "Tuath," and not, as now, the individual. This word "Tuath" was latterly applied to a community and to the territory occupied by it. So that the land at a very early stage was vested in the community. The clan lived in patriarchal fashion, at all events down to the 15th century; but from that date the practice of giving charters to individuals became common, and had the effect of not only depriving the general body of the clan of any right to clan territory, but also divested a portion of the clan, who held indefeasible rights to particular lands, of all claims upon these lands. It is unnecessary here to go into the question of the position or jurisdiction of the *Maormor*, whether he preceded the chief, had a clan right or a crown right to lands, or whether he was merely a Lord High Steward appointed by the King. But whatever power or position he held, that power was broken up in the 16th century, and many clans sprang prominently into existence, choosing for leaders very often Saxon nobles, who at once obtained charters and became Feudal landlords; and, thus forever, ended the ancient form of succession to land in the Highlands.*

The next custom of importance in the early, middle, and later period of the purely Celtic dominance, and which is worthy of the name of Law, is that of Tanistry.

TANISTRY.

The law of Tanistry not only decided chiefship, but, until 1056, it determined the succession of the Kings of Scotland during the Celtic dynasty. During his life a chief often appointed his successor from the members of his family. Hence the name.

The word *Tanistear* is derived from *Tanaiste*, signifying equal, and *fear*—a man. *Tanistear* is therefore one equal to, or parallel with the chief.

* Skene, "Celtic Scotland," Vol. III.

Generally the duty of the Tanister was to lead in battle. The descent by Tanistry was to the oldest and most worthy of blood and name, but the consent of the clan was absolutely necessary. The Tanister required to give proof of his military abilities; a male although illegitimate being preferred to a female. Indeed it is asserted that women were excluded in general by the Tanist Law; but cases occur where they held the sovereignty of the clan by hereditary right. Age and experience, and power to lead and command, were the great considerations. Logan maintains that he was equal to being Captain of the clan, or Toshich; while Dr. Macpherson thinks they are quite distinct; and "Nether Lochaber" holds that *Tanistear* is the origin of Thane. The Tanister maintained himself out of lands set apart for that purpose out of tributary possessions. In some of the Western Isles it went the length of a third of the estate during the lifetime of the chief. If Tanister and Toshich be synonymous, we have the origin of the MacDuffs. Malcolm Canmore gave Macduff, Thane of Fife, a grant to him and his heirs to lead the van of the Royal Army as Toshich—hence Mac in Toshich, the Macintoshes. The same system prevailed in Ireland, and in the Saxon Heptarchy. *Vide* Sir James Ware's Antiq. Hist. of Ireland, Cap. 8. "The Tanistear was the third in dignity. The Rhi being first and Tierna or Tigherna Ti—one; and fearann—land, being the second."

HANDFASTING.

A most remarkable custom prevalent in early Celtic

Scotland was "Handfasting." To us moderns it may appear surpassing strange, but on reflection we may readily conclude with what purpose it prevailed so generally in an early social community; and it is on account of its generality of observance that I venture to introduce it here as an early Celtic Law. The law of "Handfasting" consisted of a contract between an intended husband and wife, whereby they cohabited as husband and wife for the period of one year and a day. If at the lapse of that period there were no issue, each was at liberty to return to his or her own domicile. Of course the contract was between the parents; but if there were issue from the lady the marriage was *ipso facto* good, and no formal or religious ceremony was required to validate the marriage. The marriage was good in law. The object seemed to be to secure the lineal succession to the chief. This custom or law prevailed until well on in the 16th century, for we find then that the issue of a Handfast marriage claimed the Earldom of Sutherland. The feudal law however had by this time engrafted itself so strongly on Highland Law, and *prevailed* in Scotch Law that his claim was not admitted; that Law, in contradistinction to the Highland Law, regarding the issue of such marriages as a bastard.

Now side by side with this early marriage law, there was what is termed in the Latin tongue the *Jus primae noctis*, or *Merchetae Mulierum*; the ancient equivalent of what is known in Feudal Law as the casualty of marriage. Some historians assert that such a barbarous law never prevailed in the Highlands, but we have good authority for holding that the Cummings were expelled from their lands in Lochaber for a more than harsh exaction of this right. (Logan's Scottish Gael, Volume I., page 219.) In comparatively modern times it was termed *merchet* or maiden fee. This fee was paid to the Superior on the marriage of a daughter of a dependant. It ranged from one calf in the case of a poor man, to that of twelve cows and more in the case of the daughter of an Earl. (See Acts of Parliament, Vol. I., p. 640.)

FOSTERAGE.

Then there was the Law of Fosterage, which in unbroken observance has been handed down to us, at all events to the memory of living man, as rigid and inexorable in its principles as the Laws of the Medes and Persians. It however corresponds so exactly with the same system which prevailed in Ireland, that the very limited treatment which it can receive at my hands, may be left over until we come to deal with the *Seanachus Mòr*, which contains most unique details concerning it.

PRESCRIPTION OF CRIME.

I am not aware that it has ever been contended that the crime of murder could be expiated by self banishment for a time, but I have noticed one case in which it would appear that at least in one portion of the Highlands, a certain law of prescription of this nature held good. I refer to the case of one Farquhar MacRae, from Kintail, who had committed murder. He voluntarily banished himself from his country and kindred for a period of 7 years, and on his return he was held to have expiated the crime. No proceedings were taken against him.

CREACHS.

The rule of law applicable to cattle lifting were inexorably enforced and accordingly observed. These creachs were only made on hostile tribes, not on friends. The chief through whose lands the foray passed was entitled to a certain contribution. If none such were paid, the clan set out in pursuit, and on recovery of the spoil, the chief got two thirds, and the captors one third. In 1341, Munro of Foulis refused to pay this contribution to the laird of Mackintosh through whose lands he passed. He was pursued and his party soundly thrashed and deprived of the spoil. When the track of the cattle was lost, the person on whose property it might happen became liable either to recover the trace or make restitution of the amount lost.

Tasgal money was a reward offered for the recovery of stolen cattle.

BREHON.

While such was the state of indefiniteness regarding laws properly so called in the Highlands in early Celtic Scotland, it is pleasing to turn aside to the consideration of the early Celtic Laws of Ireland, concerning which there can be no manner of doubt. These are embodied in what are called the Brehon Laws or Brehon Tracts, a most unique and interesting collection of laws embracing almost every conceivable relation and form of sociology, in many respects corresponding to many of our own Gaelic customs— "The natives of the North part of Scotland being a colony of the Irish used the like customary Laws" says Usher, see discourse, Vol. I. p. 95. The Laws are, according to Argyll, (Scotland as it Was and Is, vol. I) "traces and relics of times when Celtic usages and ideas were the same as those of all their Aryan brethren, and which led to the glorious history of the "Twelve Tables." In Gaelic the Brehon Laws are known as the *Seanachus Mòr*—a term for which, in the Glossary of the first volume, different derivations are given.

Whatever be the meaning of the word, the Brehon it may be premised had a clerk or *Clerach* who registered his proceedings, or his *dicta*. The office was hereditary in certain families, but the Brehon had no *exclusive* jurisdiction in any particular district nor any fixed salary for his services. He was indeed a consulting lawyer with a knowledge of precedents. He sat on a hillock and sometimes on the middle or key stone of a bridge. Logan thinks this a relic of Druidism. David I. sat at his Palace gate deciding questions arising among the poor. Again circular stone enclosures—*cearcail* or *circus* were used, and latterly the church or chapel, but this was found to conflict with the original dignity of such a building and the practice was discontinued. Thus we can trace the courts of justice of the early Greeks who also at first held their courts in the open air, and at quite a modern date, the same prevailed in the Isle of Man, (Logan vol. p. 212). Does it not also remind us of the glorious days of the early Greek Philosophers, when Plato and Socrates, lectured on abstruse problems of Philosophy in their Academic Groves. The *Seanachus Mòr*, or Brehon Laws, retained their authority in parts of Ireland until the beginning of the 17th century—a period of 1200 years—until the power of the Irish chieftains was finally broken in the reign of Queen Elizabeth—of course, English Law prevailed there from the time of Henry II. in the 12th century, but only within what was termed the English *pale*.

The origin of the *Seanachus Mòr* is ascribed to the decisions of Brehons who were Judges and Law Givers, to Kings and to Poet Judges—the first of whom was *Amergin Ghungel*. The *Seanachus Mòr* was composed in the time of Laighair, son of Niall of the nine Hostages, King of Erin, about 432—between six and nine years after St. Patrick's arrival in Ireland, or according to the authority of the Four Masters 438 to 441 A.D. The supposition is that St. Patrick who was himself the son of a Roman Magistrate, and a true christian, having seen in Ireland the barbarous pagan customs which regulated the so-called jurisprudence of the country, introduced so much of the Theodosian Code (438) as was christian and conformable to the Civil Law of Rome, and grafted it on to such of the Irish customs as were humane and reasonable in his evangelic light. He himself assisted in writing it along with eight others.

It was composed at *Temhair* or Tara celebrated in History and Poetry, and at Rath-gathair, 16 miles from Tara. The former was, as the Glossary states, a Royal Residence, and more pleasant in Summer and Autumn, and the latter more agreeable in Winter and Spring.

The MSS. of the *Seanachus Mòr* are four in number in Irish Black Letter. Three of these are in Trinity College, Dublin, and one in the Harleian Library, Brit. Museum. This latter is very complete and is dated 1578. The Translators were two of the foremost Celtic scholars living, Dr. O'Donovan and Professor O'Curry.

The text and the Glossary differ very much, and from the number of obsolete words appearing in it, the work of translation was so very difficult that the learned authors had to leave untranslated several words.

The first vol. of the *Seanachus Mòr* deals with what was called *athgabhail*—a law of distress. It will be interesting for a moment or two to consider a few examples of this law, and the different ways in which it was maintained. The *athgabhail* or law of distress, was the universal remedy by which rights were vindicated and wrongs redressed.

The Plaintiff in court having first given the proper notice, proceeded in the case of his debtor—not a chief—to distrain. If a chief, he was bound to give notice, and also "to fast upon him." This fasting consisted in going to his residence, and waiting there for a certain time without food.

If he did not within a certain time, receive satisfaction for his claim, or a pledge, therefor, he forthwith accompanied by a law agent, witnesses and others, seized distress and his debtor's cattle.

Distress when seized, was in certain cases liable to a "stay." (*Anadh* which was a period varying according to fixed rules during which the debtor received back the distress—the creditor having a lien on it. "Athgabhail air fut" was "a distress with time," and an "immediate distress" was *(tul athgabhail)*—the peculiarity of the latter was that during the fixed period of the "stay," the distress was not allowed to remain in the debtor's possession, but in that of the creditor, or in one of the recognised Greens or Pounds. If the debt were not paid at the end of the stay, the creditor took away the distress and put it in pound. He then served a notice letting his debtor know where the cattle were impounded. The distress lay in the pound a certain period termed "dithnin," and expenses thereby occasioned ran against the distress. At the end of the delay in pound, the forfeiting time "lobadh" ran during which the distress became forfeited at the rate of three Seds per day. If the entire value of the distress thus forfeited was equal to original debt and the subsequent expenses, the debt was liquidated, if less, a second distress was taken, and if more—surplus was returned. All this was managed by the party himself, or his law agent with witnesses and other necessary parties.

Debtor could give a pledge or "Gell" e.g. his son, or an article of value, that he would within a certain time try the right to the distress by law, and the creditor was bound to receive such pledge. If he didn't go to law, the pledge became forfeited for original debt. At any time up to end of "dithuin," the debtor could recover his cattle by paying the debt and such expenses as had been occasioned, but if he neglected to redeem until the "dithuin" had expired, then he could only redeem such of them as were unforfeited. It may here be mentioned that this Law of distress has a parallel in Hindoo Law.

Then we have innumerable cases in which distress could be levied. Thus the distress of one day for weapons for the battle, for withholding food tribute for the King, for taking care of a son from the breast, or a son of a mad, a diseased, deaf, blind, &c., woman. Two days for one woman speaking evil of another, three days for hosting, for the crime of a son using a neighbour's horse, or boat, stripping the dead &c. Five days for satirising a woman after her death, for a nick-name, for the right of a poet crossing a territory &c. Ten days for robbing a hunter's tent, or digging a churchyard &c.

The 2nd vol. of *Seanachus Mór*, completes the treatise in the Law of distress, and deals with

(1) The Law of Services and Hostage Sureties,
(2) The Law of Fosterage,
(3) The two Laws of Tenure, &c.,
(4) The Law of Social connexions.

As to the treatment of distress when taken, it was prescribed that it was to be brought into a strong place for secure keeping, and protection. The mode in which distress is to be carried into effect, differs in the case of different animals, and in relation to persons of different tribes, occupations or professions, all indicating that the chief wealth of the country consisted then as now in cattle, sheep and pigs. The most notable peculiarity, however, points to the great estimation in which bees were held; indeed, there is in the Brehon Laws a short code on the subject. No doubt honey would be in great demand, there being no such thing as sugar, which was used in Europe only as a medicine until 1466, and as giving us an indirect proof of the date of the MSS., we have no mention of potato as an article of rent payment, although as we know the excellent weed was introduced into Ireland by Sir Walter Raleigh in 1610. As regards persons, Kings, Bishops, and Chief Poets were freed from distraint, but their Officers or Steward Bailiffs were called in their place, a custom handed down to the present day in the case of Royalty, when the Lord Advocate or the Attorney General sues or is sued in place of the Queen.

As to the limitations of distress, a rule existed something similar to that which existed with ourselves, until recently in the form of the landlord's hypothec in agricultural lands

As to the exemptions certain cattle were exempt, if other less valuable cattle were present sufficient to satisfy the claim.

In the case of fools, madmen, idiots, and dumb people, their persons were exempt from distress, but their guardians could be distrained. Women and boys were liable for their own debts only.

Distress could be kept in two kinds of Forts. "Lis"

and "Dun" of which there are many in Ireland.

With regards to the Law of Hostage Sureties, this branch arose from the division of authority owing to Ireland being composed of different Provincial Kingdoms, and sub-kingdoms, corresponding to the modern Baronies.

The "Giall" or hostage surety of the defendant was one whom a plaintiff might sue if the defendant absconded, and from whom a plaintiff was bound to accept pledges or securities. Hostage surety of either party on payment, was entitled to indemnification.

Fosterage, or "Cain Iarrath"—or the Cain Law of fosterage. "Cain" meaning Law—as a law applying to all Ireland. A Law which prevailed in Wales, (See Ancient Laws of Wales folio vol. 1841 p. 393) among the Anglo-Saxons and the Scandinavian nations. There were two kinds in Ireland as in Scotland. Fosterage for affection in which case there was no remuneration, and fosterage for payment, the terms of which were regulated by the rank of the parties. The most ancient scale given in the *Seanachus Mòr* is three "Seds" for the son of an og-aire chief; five for the son of a Bo-aire-chief; ten in the case of an Aire-desa-chief, and of an Aire-tuise-chief, and 30 for the son of a King. There were seven grades of poets, and in their case the price of fosterage varied according to the grade. There are various regulations as to the dress and food to be given to the foster sons. There are most interesting provisions as to the instruction to be given to foster children, from herding in the case of boys, and grinding corn in the case of girls in the humbler ranks, to horsemanship, shooting, chess-playing, and swimming, in the case of boys &c., sewing and embroidering, in the case of girls, of the higher ranks. While among other privileges the son of a King was to have a horse in the time of races.

There are very intricate, minute, and precise rules regulating when and why a foster father might return the foster child, and when the child could be taken from the foster father; and the fee varied accordingly. In any case fosterage terminated at the age of selection—14 years in the case of girls, and 17 in the case of boys. There were mutual obligations on the part of the foster father and the foster son, and when the foster father restored the child, he gave a parting gift called the "Seds of lawful maintenance."

Probably the most important, and to us the most interesting of the early Celtic Laws, is that regulating the tenure of land, and while this subject is most exhaustively treated in the *Seanachus Mòr* we can only in the space of this lecture, deal with the main characteristics. The principal heading under which Land tenure is dealt with are *Cain Saerrath* and *Cain Aigillne*, words of a technical meaning. *Cain-Saerrath* meaning the Cain-Law of *Saer* stock tenure, and *Cain Aigillne*, the Cain-law of *Daer*—stock tenure. Generally speaking the early Land system of Ireland resembled that which subsisted in the Roman Colonies —indeed to the present, I think, in the north of Italy—viz. *Metayer* tenure, by which the chief supplied the stock and the occupier the labour. It would thus appear that the chief's claim for *rent* depended on his supplying stock, which he might do in *Saerrath* or *Daerrath*—interpreted by the learned translators of the *Seanachus Mòr* to mean *free* and *base* tenancy. Dr. O'Donovan, however, objected to this meaning pointing out that *Saer tuatha* and *daer tuatha*, do not mean " Noble " tribes and "Unfree" tribes. Be that as it may in *Saer* stock tenure it seems the chief gave the stock without requiring any security from the tenant, the return being manual labour, attendance at military expeditions, &c. By means of this class of grants a chief could soon raise a formidable army around him. The tenant however might come to terms with the chief whereby he could take the stock with security—on *Daer* stock tenure. An almost perfect illustration of this early land tenure we have in our own country to the present day in the shape of Steel-bow; and in the South country is the very common practice of farmers letting out cows on hire to what are termed Bowers—the custom is termed Bowing.*

That most generally used was the *Daer* stock system, and from its optional nature the lawyers called it *Cain Aigillne*—the security being termed "*Giallna*"—security. This contract could not be broken at will by either party, and there were very stringent rules regarding its observance, and penalties enforced in the event of either party putting an end to it in an arbitrary manner. The stock supplied under this system was termed *Scoit turchuithe*, viz.—horses and oxen and "turcrec" a certain number of cattle. Each occupier of land must

* *Seanachus Mòr* and "Scotland as it Was and Is."

belong to a certain tribe, and be liable for tribal obligations, such as the support of old members of the tribe who had no children and liable in all contracts entered into by others of the tribe, if made with the consent of the tribe. At this stage, and when land was tribal, no occupier of a part of it could dispose of it in any way, the tribe being able to protect itself by proclamation. The chieftainship of the tribe, the learned translators clearly show, was an office which was held at the will of the tribe, and not as a matter of right. Thus the law prescribed.

"Every head defends its members, if it be a goodly head, of good deeds, of good morals, exempt, affable, and capable. The body of every head is his tribe, for there is no body without a head. The head of every tribe should be the man of the tribe who is most experienced, the most noble, the most wealthy, the wisest, the most learned, the most truly popular, the most powerful to oppose, the most steadfast to sue for profits, and to be sued for losses."

Here we have every characteristic detailed which our own Highland ancestors required in their rulers or chiefs. In short the whole of the provisions of the early system of Irish land tenure, go to show that both chief and tenant entered into their so-called contracts on equal terms; the rights and obligations of each being equally recognised. So true is this that we find this semi-social relationship treated of in the *Seanachus Mór* under the title "Cain Lanamhna," or the law of "Social Connections." Thus we find that in return for "offering *requiem* for souls," and the receiving of a son for instruction, &c., the tenants in this case termed *Saer Manaich* and *Daer Manaiche* gave tithes, first fruits and alms, and full "honour price" when strong and in health, and one third "honour price" at the time of death. The Law of Social Connections or Family Law is exhaustively dealt with in Vol. II. Here are a few illustrations. Where a father was under obligation to foster his daughter and pay the price of her fosterage, he receiving the whole of her first "*Coibche*," or wedding gift and certain portions of the other gifts down to the twenty-first. The brother who succeeded to the father as heir was under the same obligations and entitled to the same rights as the father in respect of his sister; a custom which it is said resembles the Hindoo Law. The mother's obligation was to foster her son. He was to aid his mother in poverty, and support her in old age, as well also as his foster mother. Similar obligations subsisted between the foster-tutor or literary foster-father, and his pupil. Under this division it is stated that the wife was equal to the husband, where each had equal property. Except in very few cases it was unlawful to make contracts without the consent of each— a condition of relationship which even we of the present day with our modern enlightenment have scarcely yet attained. Although it is only fair here to state that in England the Law is more favourable to woman in respect to her separate property, but possibly in that respect alone, than it is with us in Scotland.

This part of the *Seanachus Mòr* deals further with such subjects as Separation, Adultery, Abductions,

Violence, Deceit, Lunacy, Irregular Connections, &c.

Among the Celts almost every crime was expiated by a payment made over to the party injured, or his representatives in the event of death, and sometimes to the chief. It was called "*eric*"—a reparation. It differed in amount according to the *status* of the individual; and a great deal depended on whether the culprit was Bond or Free; which by the way, was also the case with regard to dues on marriage.* The principle of *Eric* was not peculiar to the ancient Laws of Ireland, or to the Highland customs. The same thing practically subsisted in the English Law in the form of appeal to combat, which according to Messrs. Hancock & O'Mahoney had its origin in those times when a pecuniary satisfaction called "Weregeld" was paid to the relations of the injured party. It is sometimes called *Cro*, with us, and "assythment" in Scotch Law. The Germans had the same law, and the Swedes under the name "Kimbote."† The Salic, Frank, and Greek Law contained the same principle. The standard of value put upon the crime and rank was termed "Honour Price" or Enechlann. The *Cro*, which may mean cows or death, and *Cru* blood—of the King of Scotland was 1000 Kye, or 3000 ounces of gold, and his "Kelchyn" was 100 Kye. *Kelchyn* is "giall," a pledge; and *Cine*, kindred. This was a fine on confession of guilt. The *Cro* differing with rank, points clearly to there having been some classes of these early communities treated as *free*, and others as *servile*.

* Skene's "Celtic Scotland," Vol. III., Cap. 6.
† Neilson's, "*Trial by Combat.*" Skene, Vol. III., 110.

The third volume of the *Seanachus Mòr* contains what has been termed the "Corus besena," or customary Law of Ireland, as well as the Book of Aicill, which gives valuable information regarding the life and condition of the people. It deals chiefly however, with wrongs or crimes, or in English phraseology *Torts*, going into minute details of the *Eric* or *Cro*. In this connection it may be pointed out, that in all early communities crime was not crime in the sense we understand the term. Crime partook more of the nature of a wrong which could be palliated or attoned for by a payment in money or otherwise. Hence the *Eric* or *Cru* just referred to. Crime in early times was not looked upon as we now do as an offence against the State. Crimes were simply offences against the particular individual, and the State put in motion civil machinery something like that for trial of a civil cause and it was not until after a great advance in civilization had taken place that crimes were looked upon and punished as breaches of good order and government. But time will not permit of our pursuing this subject further. Any one with leisure and inclination can find much that is interesting in the study of the customs of our country; while it is matter for special congratulation that our Irish brethren at a time when the most of Europe was groping in darkness, possessed a Code of Laws, civil and moral, of which nations of this enlightened age might well be proud.

Of course there have been many Highland Customs to which I have not even referred. These could by no means be dignified by the name of Law, therefore they lay beyond my province; and in any event my friend, Mr. Whyte, has dealt with these in his address in a manner more attractive than I could.

Archibald Sinclair, Printer & Publisher 10 Bothwell Street.

www.ingramcontent.com/pod-product-compliance
Lightning Source LLC
Chambersburg PA
CBHW030757230426
43667CB00007B/999